REGIS COLLEGE LIBRARY
100 Wellesley St
Toronto, On
Canada M5S 2Z5

WITHDRAWN

SO-AJF-797

"In this warm, practical, and challenging book Gaventa opens up the area of spirituality and disability in a way that not only increases our knowledge, but also challenges us in deep ways to change our practices. *Disability and Spirituality* presents a wonderfully clear overview of the historical and contemporary developments within the area of spirituality and disability and lays down a firm foundation for future conversations. Gaventa fills a space that has been empty for far too long."

—JOHN SWINTON, *Professor in Practical Theology and Pastoral Care, University of* ABERDEEN

"With this book Bill Gaventa has added an intellectual masterpiece to his already astonishing practical work in the field of disability and religion. The main idea of his book—that disability and spirituality are mutually connected both in reflection and experience—is both a conclusion from a lifelong commitment to people with disabilities and their families and an opening of new avenues for enriching professional supports to improve their lives."

—HANS S. REINDERS, *Professor of Ethics and Bernard Lievegoed Professor of Ethics in Long-term Care, VU University Amsterdam*

"Through the prism of disability Bill Gaventa, in his inimitable style and informed by his wealth of lived experiences, has illuminated the essential meaning of spirituality. His thesis, eloquently explored in this volume, is that spirituality and disability can be a two-way process. Spirituality can lead us to a deeper understanding of disability, but the reverse is also true. I know of no other book which has so effectively combined the wealth of experiences of the writer with his deep insights into the essential humanity of all people, but especially those with lifelong disabilities. *Disability and Spirituality* will be an invaluable reference for people with disabilities, families, support staff, and anyone who has the privilege of walking beside people who are so often marginalized in our society."

—TREVOR R. PARMENTER, *Professor Emeritus, Sydney Medical School, University of Sydney*

SRTD
STUDIES IN RELIGION, THEOLOGY, AND DISABILITY

SERIES EDITORS

Sarah J. Melcher
Xavier University, Cincinnati, Ohio

and

Amos Yong
Fuller Theological Seminary, Pasadena, California

This book is dedicated to three of the first people I supported in my ministry: Raymond, Donna, and Dennis. No longer "residents" or "clients" but friends.

Series Introduction

Studies in Religion, Theology, and Disability brings newly established and emerging scholars together to explore issues at the intersection of religion, theology, and disability. The series editors encourage theoretical engagement with secular disability studies while supporting the reexamination of established religious doctrine and practice. The series fosters research that takes account of the voices of people with disabilities and the voices of their family and friends.

The volumes in the series address issues and concerns of the global religious studies / theological studies academy. Authors come from a variety of religious traditions with diverse perspectives to reflect on the intersection of the study of religion/theology and the human experience of disability. This series is intentional about seeking out and publishing books that engage with disability in dialogue with Jewish, Christian, Buddhist, or other religious and philosophical perspectives.

Themes explored include religious life, ethics, doctrine, proclamation, liturgical practices, physical space, spirituality, and the interpretation of sacred texts through the lens of disability. Authors in the series are aware of conversation in the field of disability studies and bring that discussion to bear methodologically and theoretically in their analyses at the intersection of religion and disability.

Studies in Religion, Theology, and Disability reflects the following developments in the field: First, the emergence of disability studies as an interdisciplinary endeavor that has had an impact on theological studies, broadly defined. More and more scholars are deploying disability perspectives in their work, and this applies also to those working in the theological academy. Second, there is a growing need for critical reflection on disability in world religions. While books from a Christian standpoint have dominated the discussion at the interface of religion and disability so far, Jewish, Muslim, Buddhist, and Hindu scholars, among those from other religious traditions, have begun to resource their own religious traditions to rethink disability in the twenty-first century. Third, passage of the Americans with Disabilities Act in the United States has raised the consciousness of the general public about the importance of critical reflection on disability in religious communities. General and intelligent lay readers are looking for scholarly discussions of religion and disability as these bring together and address two of the most important existential aspects of human lives. Fourth, the work of activists in the disability rights movement has mandated fresh critical reflection by religious practitioners and theologians. Persons with disabilities remain the most disaffected group from religious organizations. Fifth, government representatives in several countries have prioritized the greater social inclusion of persons with disabilities. Disability policy often proceeds from core cultural and worldview assumptions that are religiously informed. Work at the interface of religion and disability thus could have much broader purchase in social, economic, political, and legal domains.

Under the general topic of thoughtful reflection on the religious understanding of disability, Studies in Religion, Theology, and Disability includes shorter, crisply argued volumes that articulate a bold vision within a field; longer scholarly monographs, more fully developed and meticulously documented, with the same goal of engaging wider conversations; textbooks that provide a state of the discussion at this intersection and chart constructive ways forward; and select edited volumes that achieve one or more of the preceding goals.

Contents

Acknowledgments

My work at the intersections of faith and disability began in the early 1970s. So many people have been guides and companions on that journey, and thus they have contributed to this book. Sometimes the experience at the intersections of faith and disability was more like a collision than it was a collaboration, but I learned from those as well.

You will meet a few of these people through some of the stories in this book. I think of the parents who first opened their stories and homes to me as a very young chaplain in North Carolina and of Dr. Harrie Chamberlain, the director of the Division for Disorders of Development and Learning, who, along with other staff, welcomed me to that strange new clinical pastoral education (CPE) assignment, and later championed my work and supported my role for another year and a half. We moved to Rochester, New York, where people like Dennis Benton, Donna Smith, Ray Swartz, Sally Nesselson, Harry Brown, Helen Scavuzzo, Michael Giumento, and multiple others at Newark and Monroe Developmental Centers helped teach me about different faith traditions and ways of expressing one's spirituality and its importance to them. I think of families who supported every new initiative toward more inclusive faith supports. Wonderful colleagues in the community—Roman Catholic, Protestant, and Jewish—also caught the vision. We helped baptisms and bar/bat mitzvahs to happen in community rather than institutional settings, memberships to begin, and new forms of programming and connections that brought people together. Those eight years at Monroe Developmental Center are the times and places I return to in my dreams.

Ann Davis at the Jewish Community Center in Rochester was the chair of my advisory board. The JCC and the board sponsored a conference called "Merging Two Worlds" in 1986, a conference where I first met Parker Palmer, whose thinking and writing about spirituality, community, and disability has guided portions of my work. Little did I realize then that his openness about his own experience with depression would become a lifeline for me years later in New Jersey when I had my own dive into the depths of that world. The staff and colleagues at the Elizabeth M. Boggs Center on Developmental Disabilities, particularly the director, Deborah Spitalnik, and associate director, Michael Knox, not only welcomed me back out of that pit but continued to welcome and support my role at the Boggs Center for more than twenty years. They exhibited that same kind of hospitality, along with a willingness to go down paths that were new to all of us, when I first knocked on the doors of their first offices in old trailers at Robert Wood Johnson Medical School some years before.

Along the way, CPE supervisors were the ones who first sent me into what I thought was a new world of intellectual and developmental disabilities, but the CPE process helped me remember multiple other experiences with disability in my life. Claude Deal, Bob Morgan, Ed Dobihal, Maxine Glaz, Stuart Plummer, Cindy Strickland, Jap Keith, and Dwain Parker were both supervisors and colleagues who guided my journey toward certification as a supervisor, enabling me to run programs with seminarians and clergy at both Monroe Developmental Center and the Boggs Center. Students went on to become colleagues and friends. Rabbi Evan Jaffe became a champion of the Boggs Center program. He said I was his "rebbe," and I, in turn, considered him "minister" but, more importantly, deep friend. We loved doing inter-faith worship services together with CPE students and people with intellectual and developmental disabilities, especially his using his background as a dancer to join in a movement version of the Lord's Prayer. The American Baptist Churches USA endorsed my role as a chaplain and provided a denominational home in ways that reflect their commitment to ecumenism.

Then there have been colleagues in the American Association on Intellectual and Developmental Disabilities who first welcomed me and then became mentors and friends: Wolf Wolfensberger, Bob Perske, Rud and Ann Turnbull, and countless others. The AAIDD and the Association for Clinical Pastoral Education have been my professional association homes. Those national connections grew through the Association of University Centers of Disabilities, where I first met people like Erik Carter, Amy Hewitt, Steve Eidelman, Liz Weintraub, and Ginny Thornburgh. Ginny got me invited to the signing of the ADA on the White House lawn, where another mentor, Harold Wilke, started the ceremony with his marvelous invocation and the famous use of his toes to accept a pen from the first President Bush. There was as wide and diverse a group of people on the White House lawn that day as I have ever seen, a life-affirming day of the power of democracy and the rights of *all* people.

Then, in the past fifteen years, my friendships with scholars and leaders like Hans Reinders, John Swinton, Tom Reynolds, Debbie Creamer, Amos Yong, Jeremy Schipper, Julia Watts Belser, Darla Schumm, and Erik Carter became partnerships as they have all contributed time and talent, as we Baptists love to say, to the beginning and sustaining of the Summer Institute on Theology and Disability. Each of those institutes became its own community, with "aha" moments unique to each, a whole always greater than the sum of its parts. The members moving in and out of that community have also helped us all learn what community can be, where diverse identities and stories can help us clarify our own while celebrating all.

I know I am leaving people out. Forgive me. You know who you are. You all share one common trait: gift to me and many others. But I cannot leave out my own brother, John, who has taken our history as missionary kids into a very different kind of human and social development in work around the globe and who has been friend as we lost both of our parents. Then my seminary brother, Jim Gertmenian, and his poet spouse, Susan King, whom we have known and with whom we have sat, most often on the shores of Maine, for the past forty-eight years. Forty-six of those have been as married couples, forty-six with my amazing spouse and love, Beverly, with whom I have journeyed from place to place in our respective careers and who literally carried me and kept me alive during my two descents into the hell of depression. She's a better and more prolific writer than I, yet our son Matthew may be even better than the two of us. It was Matthew first, and now his wife, Sarah, and our grandson, Charlie, who have also helped keep my feet on loving and level ground. All of them have helped me learn that an old dog can learn some new tricks, and that "take care" means of yourself as well as others.

Finally, speaking of old dogs, Carey Newman has indeed taught me to be a better writer. This book is what it is partly because of his guidance, and the excellent copyediting done by Carrie Watterson. Thank you!

Preface

Any conversation about vocation or call involves the paradox of whether we find our vocation or it finds us. Both feel true for me. Thinking I was headed toward parish ministry or hospital chaplaincy, one of my first assignments as a clinical pastoral education (CPE) intern was to spend a tenth of my time as a trainee in an interdisciplinary diagnostic, evaluation, and training center in the arena of what was then called "mental retardation." At first I was lost, for there was no defined role for chaplain or pastoral care in that highly structured, interdisciplinary, medical model of intellectual and developmental disabilities.

So I just listened to families talking and sharing their stories and we sat together watching various kinds of assessment processes. I began to hear about their faith journeys as well. Most of those journeys at that point in the 1970s did not involve helpful, inclusive supports from their congregations or clergy. My call was born. I now know there were many dimensions to those empowering moments, but it set me on a journey that I sometimes call the journey of a "deinstitutionalized chaplain." I extended my stay at that center for another year and a half and then became Protestant chaplain at Newark Developmental Center thirty miles outside of Rochester in upstate New York. Newark was one of the old warehouse institutions that began to empty out in the 1970s. I moved from a pastoral role within an enclosed world to a role at a smaller center in Rochester where we reframed the chaplain as a bridge between institutional services and community congregations as people with intellectual and developmental disabilities moved into community settings.

Thus, my job began as a connector between two worlds, the institution and the community, with the hope of building effective congregational hospitality and welcome as people moving out of Monroe Developmental Center sought to find a sense of home in the communities where they lived. It changed again with moving into statewide services and supports for families working from the organizational base of the Georgia Council on Developmental Disabilities. Then, in New Jersey, I moved back into the kind of center where I first started, now called a University Center of Excellence in Developmental Disabilities, where I had roles and responsibilities in both disability services and spiritual supports, with the third task of continuing to foster collaboration and partnerships between the two.

The bridges between the gaps have kept changing, from institution to community to bridging the world of secular services and supports with spiritual communities of all kinds. There were bridges between the secular projects that I helped develop with others in my portfolio addressing faith communities. There were interfaith, multifaith, and cross-cultural bridges to build, especially in New Jersey. There were also bridges between professionals in disability services and supports, community members, people with disabilities, and families. In the professional literature I read and the conferences I attended, there was little attention to spirituality in either the scientific or advocacy discourses about disability. Likewise, in pastoral care and theology, there was little attention to either the scientific discourse about disability or to disability itself. The task of bridging between individuals with disabilities and faith communities has involved helping clergy and faith communities understand that implicit attitudes and practices that have caused individuals and families to leave their church, synagogue, or mosque. Even worse was the lack of any response at all, or explicit requests to individuals and families for them to leave. When working with secular providers of services and supports, and with the theories that guided policy and practice, the task has been to help professionals within the disciplines of scientific human services to pay attention to spirituality and religion by translating spiritual and religious questions, needs, and supports into terms and policies they can both understand

and use, while also urging them to continue to see clergy and faith communities as important sources of support and community.

The lives of people with disabilities and their families were in the center of all that work. They were individual, whole people and families, but they were diagnosed and divided up into different worlds of understanding and supports. The primary question for me has been helping the secular, scientific world of disability to understand its spiritual dimensions, and vice versa. As both worlds evolved over the past forty years, this book is a result of lessons learned in keeping my feet planted in each while trying to help them come together in support of individuals, families, and those whose who provide care.

Suffice it to say, people with disabilities and their families have been my best teachers along the way. I have also learned from colleagues in ministry, professionals from many disciplines in human services, direct care staff, policy makers, and advocates from many of those backgrounds. From whatever background we come, all of us who work to support people with disabilities and their families need to remember that the questions, strengths, needs, and gifts of people with disabilities and their families are what called us in the first place. We have the honor of being invited into their lives even if many of them would probably say they have sometimes desperately sought for our support, or any support at all. Everyone I know who works in this arena has had transforming moments in relationships with people with disabilities and their families that have touched the very core of their spirits and souls. They have been our teachers and guides.

There is also a danger in that statement and recognition. When "we" say that we have learned so much from people with disabilities and their families about ourselves and core dimensions of being human, "we" are assuming a difference between "us." Disability advocates might remind us that we should not have to "use" people with disabilities to discover those questions and work them out, especially if we define their purpose as teaching others. Some people with disabilities are comfortable with that unrequested, and probably unavoidable, role. None of us can keep another from projecting questions and feelings onto us. But other individuals and family members quickly get tired of it, wishing "we," the so-called normal or temporarily able-bodied people, would get our own act together and interact with them simply as human beings, friends, coworkers, and companions, working out, together, our individual and communal identities and values, connections, and sense of purpose and calling. Individuals with disabilities, family members, and caregivers often get put in the roles of being "special" bearers of truth and enlightenment. What would be truly special is a community where individuals can form and work out their own sense of identity based on a common understanding that limitation and vulnerability is the foundation on which life is built. To do that well, we need diverse input and perspectives as well as a new understanding of the wholeness in which we all live, breathe, and have our being.

There are far too many individuals, families, colleagues, writers, and leaders who have impacted my thinking and work for me to name them all. This book is dedicated to three people I first met as young adults in the wards and "cottages" of Newark Developmental Center, three who moved out in community lives and roles, and three who have called me friend, and I them. As my work broadened from "Protestant chaplain," I have found hospitality and revelation in multiple faith traditions other than the one in which I grew up, as well as in the lives of people who have not identified themselves with any faith tradition. No matter how interfaith and multifaith I will try to be in this book, it will be clear that I come out of a Christian background, I hope that the readers can translate what I am trying to say into their own experience and tradition. There are universal human themes in spirituality and faith, but we are called out of, and back into, specific traditions and communities. Similarly, inclusion would not mean a lot unless it was in the lives of specific people in their own specific congregations, communities, cultures, and societies.

I have had friendships and working relationships with people with a wide variety of disabilities—cognitive, sensory, motor, and psychiatric. Most of my experience has been in the world of intellectual and developmental disability. The perspective of this book might be different if my primary background was in other arenas, like acquired disabilities, deafness, blindness, or psychiatric services. However, I believe my foundation in intellectual and developmental disabilities helps this discussion on the ubiquitous inclusiveness of spirituality because I have tried for a long time to understand spirituality as lived by and experienced in the lives of people who are assumed to have little reason or intellect. Some of the most loving, hopeful, and, indeed, faithful people I have known are people with intellectual and developmental disabilities. We might easily say that hope and love do not depend on intellectual ability, but we do not often say the same thing about faith. Why? The key reason is that spirituality and faith are too often equated with, or defined as, cognitive belief. One result is that the secular world of disability wonders how spirituality can apply to people with limited intellect, and, likewise, the worlds of spirituality and faith wonder how individuals can really understand the complexity of religious dogmas and creeds. That is why the definition of spirituality that I will use in this book is one that is formed on the importance of identity and meaning, connection and relationship, and motivation/purpose/calling. Intellectual ability and capacity can deepen understandings of all those areas, but they can also impede understandings of spirituality as lived experience by individual people in their own life's story.

Thus, this book tries to bridge and bring together my understanding of my story with multiple other stories. As a missionary kid who grew up in two worlds, I have learned that I have been bridging worlds all my life, trying to bring them together and help others and myself to find the meaning of home, a deep experience of community undergirding great and magnificent diversity. The questions raised about life, faith, hope, and love by people with disabilities are ultimately not questions about disability but about all of us. That is the whole of it.

BILL GAVENTA

Introduction

Larry used to come see me frequently in my chaplain's office in the old Newark State School, then Newark Developmental Center, or what had been once the Newark State Custodial Asylum for Feeble-Minded Women. He knew there was something wrong with him, or he thought so. Why else would I be here? Why am I different? And he had a self-diagnosis. He was, in his words, "too short." He wanted one of two things: new technology—a device that could stretch him and make him taller, and the prayers of a chaplain that could do the same. Perhaps because of his sense of shame, of just being wrong, he also thought he had a great sin. One day I encouraged him to pray, in his words, not mine. It was one of the most profound I have heard. "O Lorda Goda, please take-a away the sin in my heart. Please take it away . . . [a short pause] . . . it's gone! It's gone. Thank you, Lorda Goda, for my prayer."

————

Larry thought he needed to be fixed or repaired. There were two ways he thought that could happen, the first being some form of new treatment, machine, or technology, and the second being the power of prayer to bring about a miracle. Despite my enthusiasm for my new role, both were well beyond my powers. Yet both were perfectly "normal" expressions of two contrasting yet similar views of disability in the past two centuries in the Western world.

First, disability has often been addressed with the implicit (though often explicit) and pervasive belief that the worlds of science and

1

medicine offer a possible fix. Find the right treatment, the right gene, the right treatment plan, the right kind of medicine (or avoid the wrong kind), or the right therapy, and a fix or cure might soon follow, or at the least, a prevention. But, when those strategies fail, the same kinds of knowledge and technological prowess can and have been used to fix the disability by eliminating the people with disabilities.

Second, pervasive belief in a fix has also been a central part of many religious understandings of disability and the responses proclaimed as treatments. Having a disability has often been interpreted as the result of a sinful act by individuals, their parents, or both. Far too many people with disabilities and their families still encounter the question that asks for a guilty plea: "What did you do that you, or your child, got this disability?" The treatment plan followed: "Confess that sin honestly. Then pray, have faith, and if you pray the right way or have enough faith, healing will follow." If it does not, then that must be because you do not have enough faith or because you have already been condemned. (Which means we are justified in excluding you.)

Those two interpretations and belief systems are vastly different, yet Larry held them both. In more subtle ways, the two worlds of medicine and science, on the one hand, and spirituality and religion, on the other, have operated in separate realms of influence and opinion. As the field of medicine and science grew after the Enlightenment, they became the primary cultural interpreters of disability, first as an abnormality and disease, then as a chronic health condition. The World Health Organization and others, like the American Association on Intellectual and Developmental Disabilities, are the primary holders of the scientific definitions of disability and intellectual disabilities, respectively. As other human services and social sciences rose in prominence, they too became part of the scientific discourses about disability, many of these leading to impressive results and improvements in forms of treatment.

The social model of disability began to arise on the heels of legal initiatives in the rights of persons with disabilities and their families and soon became what it is today, a model that includes the voices of many disciplines in the humanities as well as some of the social sciences. That movement and model has focused on disability as an outcome of disabling environments, attitudes, values, and cultural prejudice rather than as a medical condition. Again, these voices have led to huge improvements in our understandings of disability and to a recognition that disability, as but one aspect of a person's life, can be interpreted through multiple lenses.

Both the medical and social models were and remain leery of religious and spiritual interpretations of disability, in large part, I believe, because of the experiences of judgment and exclusion that many people with disabilities and their families faced in their churches, synagogues, and mosques and other places in which the religious attitudes about cause and treatment impacted cultural beliefs and traditions. But that wariness is also a result of the uneasiness between religion and science in general as different realms and methodologies of understanding life and interpreting truth.

However, religion and spirituality have also impacted the lives of people with disabilities and their families in a multitude of positive ways. Many of the early services and supports were begun by people motivated by their faith and sense of calling, as they still are today. For example, some of the initial call for reform of psychiatric hospitals came from conscientious objectors who worked in those hospitals during World War II. As national networks of families and people with disabilities began to grow in the 1960s, faith communities began to respond in ways that both supported those organizations (e.g., special education classes or programs starting off in church basements) and moved toward inclusion in the life of faith communities themselves. Special religious education programs and special ministries began in ways that mirrored special education. As the focus has shifted away from "special" toward inclusion in the past thirty years, there has been a rapid growth in theological interpretations of disability, new historical explorations and discovering of the multiple ways disability has been interpreted in scriptures and histories of major faith traditions, and increasingly creative, diverse forms of inclusive spiritual supports and ministries by clergy and faith communities.[1]

In the middle between science and religion, so to speak, understandings of spirituality and its relationship to health began to grow as an arena of interdisciplinary discourse and research. Some of that started in reexamining spirituality in the world of psychiatry, which had for a couple of decades all but decided that religious beliefs were a symptom of disease rather than a support. Spirituality has grown as a form of integrating medical and religious perspectives in multiple areas of health and illness with one lagging exception—the arena of disability, and particularly that of intellectual and developmental disability. Part of the reason, I think, are still the assumptions made by both the world of science and the world of religion that equate faith with the capacity for reason.

But Larry was one person, one whole person. A family with a member with a disability is one family, one whole family. The human family includes all kinds of diverse people, including people with disabilities, but we are still humankind. Why have those two worlds of disability and spirituality been so separate and seen as having little to do with one another? Understandings of disability, the language used to describe it, and the worlds of services and supports rarely talk about or explore the ways that spirituality is a central dimension of human experience and thus a potential well of support. Both the world of science and that of spiritual communities and religious traditions have often (but not always) struggled to believe and to recognize that the core spiritual questions and needs in the lives of people with disabilities and their caregivers are the same questions and needs that everyone has.

In terms of wholeness, then, separating people into two worlds, whether "normal" or "disabled" or "secular/scientific" and "spiritual," is a disservice to the people who need support as well as, ultimately, an illusion that these are separate worlds. The common shared experience of disability, which most of us will face at one time or another, is how people live their lives. In 1987 Lou Heifitz, then at Syracuse University, wrote a perspective piece for the journal *Mental Retardation* comparing the two worlds to two children playing in the same sandbox but not with each other—parallel play.[2] Said another way, it is time for the researchers, educators, and practitioners in both arenas to "get it together" by remembering we are seeking to support the same whole people and families in ways that enable them to deal with the barriers of attitudes and participation that so frequently separate the experience of people with disabilities from true membership in communities of all kinds. Nobody can do it alone.

The problem of helping those two metaphorical children learn how to both work and play together is the issue this book addresses. How do we understand disability? How do we understand spirituality? How are those understandings shaped by the partially true caricatures that each has of the other? What if spirituality permeated the multiple ways in which disability is understood and supported in ways that are hidden in plain sight? What causes those limitations in our experience and the resulting frames of reference that keep us from seeing? Is it possible to bring those two spotlights to focus, together, on ways to deepen our understanding and capacity to support people with disabilities and their families as they seek to live lives full of quality and meaning?

There is a Hebrew phrase, *tikkum olam*, meaning, "repairing the world" (or "healing the world"), which suggests humanity's shared responsibility to heal, repair, and transform the world. It also sometimes means repairing the breach between God and humankind. *Tikkum olam* is a call, vocation, and mission statement. Bridging the gap between spirituality and disability, as they are commonly understood, is the purpose of this book, hopefully with the result that people with disabilities, their families, and those who support them can do so in ways that do more collaborating than separating on the journey to inclusive, holistic lives and communities. It will be up to you and your experience, as you read this, to determine whether we reach that end.

I

DISABILITY AND SPIRITUALITY
Each Leads to the Other

1

Naming and Defining Disability
A Brief History

I never expected to be a minister working with people with intellectual and developmental disabilities and their families. Soon after seminary, I did a year of clinical pastoral education at North Carolina Memorial Hospital in Chapel Hill. My interest in pediatrics led to an involuntary assignment of 10 percent of my time for the year to a new interdisciplinary center for families with children with intellectual disabilities connected to the medical center called the Center for Disorders of Development and Learning. My first question to my supervisor's directive was, "What does that mean?" In the language of the time, its mission was to serve as an evaluation and diagnostic center for families whose children would often end up with the label of "mental retardation." Not long thereafter, I was hooked.[1]

When my wife and I moved to Rochester, New York, in 1975, I began my first "real" job as the Protestant chaplain at Newark State School, one of the large, old state institutions that had been built a century earlier as the "progressive" way to help individuals and families. Early in my tenure there, one of the "higher-functioning" residents named Mike came up to me and asked, without any sense of irony, "Hey, chaplain, you want to hear some moron jokes?" Several decades earlier, "moron" would have been the state-of-the-art scientific label, the very one he would have received as his diagnosis.

As I got to know the hundreds of "mentally retarded residents" of that center by name as individuals, I decided to conduct what now might be called a simple experiment in qualitative research. I started asking a number of my "Protestant flock," "What does it mean to be a person?" I should have written down and kept all the answers, but the two I remember were:

> "I don't know, but I know it is the best thing you can be."

> "I don't know, but God knows, and he likes it."

As a seminary student, I heard nothing about disability. As a very part-time trainee in that North Carolina center, one of the early University Affiliated Facilities inspired and initiated by the Kennedy administration, I was suddenly in a world where spirituality was suspect or nonexistent, or so it appeared. The major focus was to help families receive a comprehensive, scientific, interdisciplinary evaluation and correct diagnosis, with little attention to what happened next. In the social and historical context of the 1970s, the ways of understanding, diagnosing, and serving people with disabilities were in the early stages of a major revolution led by families, individuals with disabilities, and leaders in public policy, as well as human service professionals.

Spirituality and religion took a back seat, if any at all. Scientific assumptions about ways of knowing had often been seen as antithetical to spirituality and religion. The negative personal experiences of many individuals with disabilities and their families in faith communities obscured the positive roles that religion and spirituality played in many other people's lives. Not only had the scientific community struggled to recognize the power of those religious experiences, but faith communities were also doing little to include children who were by and large hidden in institutions or special schools and programs. Religious leadership was largely absent from the new civil and human rights initiatives focused on people with disabilities, culminating with the fact that the faith community excused itself from the policy table in key provisions of the Americans with Disabilities Act (ADA) in 1990.

In those decades and since, the debate about what diagnostic labels to use grew and, essentially, sped up. So did the awareness that any new way of naming difference or disability could morph into a slur or pejorative. Dig deeper, however, and this is more than a scientific and civil rights story. On the one hand, there is a fundamental spiritual foundation in the act of naming. Mention the sitcom *Cheers*, and most anyone can tell you the appeal about being able to go somewhere "where everybody knows your name." On the other hand, adjectives about one aspect of a person have the tendency to become labels and then nouns, overwhelming the multiple dimensions of a person's life and character. Thus, the power of finding a name or diagnosis can be used for good or for bad. It can provide understanding and hope or be interpreted as a tragedy or death sentence because of public stereotypes and value judgments about the meaning of disability. A Down syndrome awareness poster in the 1980s used the phrase, "Sticks and stones may break my bones, but names can really hurt me." The profound paradox is that the history of disability comes back full circle to recognizing that the spiritual ways by which we determine meaning, community, and purpose are pivotal in the evolution of more humane supports and a more inclusive society.

THE IMPORTANCE OF NAMING FOR DISABILITY

How we name a personal characteristic, whether a strength or weakness, can then shape what it means to be a person. A family could find their child labeled with "mental retardation," or now an "intellectual or developmental disability" such as autism, and suddenly hear their child described as one of "the disabled," rather than as a "disabled child" or a "person with a disability." We are pushed to ask what "disability" really means. Disability is often seen as an objective, or "substantial," reality—a noun—but by others it is seen as simply an adjective describing particular personal attributes. Disability can also become a verb, as in a malfunction that "disables" a car by the side of the road or "handicapping" a horse race or golf score. A label or classification can thus serve a function; that is, it is a tool or construct, but, like any tool, it can be used in helpful or destructive ways. The act of naming and labeling can thus have great power, a power heightened by the question of who gets to bestow that label and why.

The names of personal characteristics or conditions related to disability are thus just that: names, words that are created (or constructed) and used to order, organize, and share information about something or someone. In the Judeo-Christian tradition, the act of naming starts in the story of creation as God creates, separates, names, and blesses the earth, sky, and all that has life, and then invites man and woman to help in the act of naming.[2] Naming thus brings something into existence by recognizing it. From the perspective of major religions and spiritual traditions, naming is a spiritual act, a bestowing of identity, meaning, connection, power, authority, and purpose. A name could signify worth, reputation, function, transformation, and ownership. Knowing some-one's or something's name was partially a way of obtaining power over that person, creature, or experience.[3] The power to name is then passed on to humans, or developed by them, with its most personal use in the historical rituals of the naming of a child. Communally, naming that which was experienced to be holy, sacred, or beyond understanding made names sacred, hence for many the importance of the name of a place or anniversary related to that experience. Names and languages multiply as different cultures grow and organize systems of communi-cation that separate what is known and understood from the unknown, good from bad, right from wrong, and humans from other creatures and from one another.

At least two constants remain: the act of naming is a way to orga-nize and communicate knowledge, and naming is an act of power. As such, names can then be both blessing and curse. The current "powers that be" are usually the ones that get to do the naming, a fact recognized by the critique of "ableism" and an ableist perspectives in the current disciplines of disability studies.[4]

Similar to many of the assumptions underlying the medical model of disability (i.e., disability is an aberration), the ableist societal world-view is that the able bodied are the norm in society and the ones with the authority to name difference. People who have disabilities must either strive to become that norm or should keep their distance from able-bodied people. A disability is thus a "bad" thing that must be over-come. The ableist worldview holds that disability is an error, a mistake, or a failing, rather than a simple consequence of human diversity, akin to race, ethnicity, sexual orientation, or gender.

There are multitudes of examples. Ask any person with a disabil-ity about his or her experience with disability labels. Take a look at Kathy Snow's "Disability Is Natural" website.[5] The current political battle in North America to "Eliminate the R Word" has become vocal and successful, at least from its impact on legislation. One only has to recall the recent professional and public battles in the latest revision of the *Diagnostic and Statistical Manual of Mental Disorders* (*DSM-V*) over who and what was covered by classification of "autism."[6] It was a theoretical issue, but it was also fueled by who was doing the naming and the fear about potential loss of supports and services if the label no longer applied to people previously considered to be on the "spectrum."

The history of naming disability is never static. Words for sensory and motor impairments have been around for a long time: blind, lame, deaf, mute, and so on. Words used to describe what we now call psychiatric and intellectual disabilities have been in constant evolution, especially since the rise of medical and scientific knowledge after the Enlightenment.[7] Names and labels once considered helpful and scientific became culturally pejorative, as my friend wanting to tell me "moron" jokes demonstrated. The interactions between science and historical/cultural context have led to periods of great advancement, for example, in the early educational institutions in the nineteenth century and in the past fifty years of recognizing the rights and humanity of people with disabilities. But at the end of the nineteenth century, those interactions also led to horrors in the age of eugenics and, in more modern times, strategies of treatment and therapy that promise far too much and too often harm, like patterning, aversive conditioning, and any number of "cures" for autism.

One of the most recent poignant examples of the ambivalent power of naming and classification for me has come from conversations with parents of relatively young children with one form of disability or another. On the one hand, finding a name or diagnosis is a relief in the face of the unknown, for with the name comes an assumed plan for amelioration or cure. On the other, one of the paradigmatic lenses for exploring disability is from a person-centered, strengths and gifts approach, rather than a more traditional medical, deficit-based perspective, as illustrated in the relatively new field of positive psychology.[8] Parents have told me that their own journey of coping and adjustment has led them, in fact, to be able to celebrate the strengths and gifts of their child as well as the limitations.[9] However, they are often forced to work with the health, human service, and educational systems of diagnosis and classification to assess a child's disabilities in ways that maximize the deficits and needs of their child. Otherwise, he or she might not be eligible for the desired services. The "gatekeepers" to eligibility have the power, which, it turns out, has long been the case. Some parents have called it "crazy making" for them, an emotional and spiritual roller coaster with whiplash effects.

DEFINITIONS OF DISABILITY: AN EVOLUTION

Over time, understandings and definitions of disability have radically changed. It is not easy to describe overarching trends or models because historical materials have been difficult to find. Most accounts have been written primarily by those who controlled the delivery of services rather than by those with disabilities or their families. It is also extremely hard to generalize across all types of mental, physical, and sensory disabilities.[10]

In biblical times, for example, there were ways of naming disability that were simply a description of particular physical or sensory limitations, for example, the "blind," the "lame," and the "deaf." Before the advent of medical care and services, people with disabilities were simply part of the community or on the fringes thereof like many others marginalized by poverty, class, or condition: "Disability in the ancient world was treated as a family and civic condition, rather than a medical one, in which what was conceived as 'problem' was inherent in the individual."[11]

Disability was also seen as inherent in the family and thus the family's responsibility, an understanding of disability that is still prevalent today in many parts of the world without access to medical services and where a family's social status can be radically impacted by a family member with a disability. The cause of a disability or, indeed, any abnormal health condition, often had to do either with the issue of sin by the person or the parents,[12] demonic control, (especially in the case of what we would now call psychiatric disabilities), or the dominant "humoral" theory of medicine, which attributed disability to the bad fluids and forces within one's body.[13]

The gatekeeping function of naming disability began a long time ago as a way for charities and states to determine eligibility for military pensions based on the origin of disability, or, in other words, a way of determining the level of societal supports. The same is true with current diagnoses serving as gateways to eligibility for public services. Disability was thus a social and political construct to help administer benefits, with medical and other health services gradually emerging as part of that benefit package.[14]

The nineteenth and twentieth centuries saw a rapid rise in medical and scientific understandings of disability along with diseases and other health conditions. The "moral model" in the 1800s believed strongly that "idiocy," a "sign of man's departure from the natural laws of God," could be significantly transformed by good, scientifically based education and treatment in protected settings, a methodology around which some form of "cure" was even thought possible.[15] That enthusiasm led to disillusionment, and a cultural shift in the latter part of that century and the early twentieth century. In the face of hundreds of thousands of new immigrants coming to America, the key value became the protection of American society from "impurity" through the rise of eugenics and one of its consequences, the institutionalization and sterilization of young women with very loosely defined forms of disability. (Such was the origin of the Newark State School, originally called the Newark State Custodial Asylum for Feeble-Minded Women.) Scientific theory in eugenics then became cultural doctrine that was used in its most radical form in Nazi Germany, where institutionalized people with disabilities became the first victims of the Holocaust.

Even with the rise of institutionalization, most people with disabilities still lived in communities. Common cultural images other than the eugenic, medical model included "beggar," "freak," "charity," and "citizen" along with new public images of disability in photographs, advertising, movies, and art.[16]

After World War II, three social movements motivated change. One, as in centuries before, was the societal task of assisting veterans impaired by war. The second was the birth of a parent movement that rebelled against the professional and cultural creed that they should institutionalize their disabled child. Third, the experiences of many conscientious objectors as caregivers in institutions during the war led to the exposure of awful conditions and demands for change, especially in psychiatric facilities. The expansion of rehabilitation, technology, special education, and community-based services changed understandings of "mental deficiency" to "mental retardation" and then to "developmental disabilities." The Kennedy presidency helped bless and fuel a new moral imperative in scientific, public policy, and cultural circles to treat people with what we now call intellectual and developmental disabilities in humane and "normal" ways. Parents and families advocated along with social scientists and educators like Wolf Wolfensberger, whose construct of "normalization" was that all people should be treated in typical, normal ways, whether or not they could become "normal."[17]

Disability rights initiatives, born with the leadership of veterans, grew and broadened to include people with many forms of disability and gave birth to the self-advocacy movement in the lives of people with intellectual and developmental disabilities.[18] Disability studies began as an interdisciplinary academic exploration of the understandings and meanings of disability and a new focus on a "social" rather than "medical" model of disability. The Individuals with Disabilities Education Act (IDEA; 1975) and the ADA (1990) codified the new focus on rights and participation into law, along with international initiatives like the 1980 Year of the Handicapped and the current UN Convention on the Rights of Persons with Disabilities (CRPD). Autism began its rise as a newly named classification with a very active advocacy community, bringing with it an increasing focus on neurological and genetic research into the causes of developmental disabilities. The rise in the diagnosis of autism has also increased attention to the interaction of people and their social environment as well as to the understanding of disability as another form of diversity.

"Disability" is thus a name and construct that has personal, scientific, social, cultural, philosophical, and, indeed, spiritual dimensions. The models, or lenses, through which one explores understandings of disability each has its own epistemology and values, its ways of understanding and response.[19] The history is fascinating and complex, with new research uncovering multiple forms of writing that embodied changing cultural attitudes and understandings.[20] The evolution of best practices in definition and classification from the perspective of medicine, social sciences, and public policy has been the way of codifying new understandings of disability that were then used to provide supports in line with new visions and values.[21]

CURRENT DEFINITIONS: RECOGNIZING CONTEXT
AND COMPLEXITY

Over the past fifty years, the medical and social sciences developed new definitions of disability that moved the focus from a personal defect and an "individual" issue to understandings of disability as a level of functioning resulting from the interaction of impairments, abilities, and the environment. Three of them deserve more specific attention.

The International Classification of Impairments, Disabilities and Handicaps (ICIDH) of the World Health Organization, 1980

When I was the young chaplaincy trainee at the University Affiliated Facility in North Carolina (the former name for what are now called University Centers of Excellence in Developmental Disabilities), the program was organized around two- to three-day multidisciplinary evaluations of a child in search of a diagnosis and support plan. There was great professional attention to the interdisciplinary team that would gather to decide upon a diagnosis and plan of treatment, followed by the "interpretive conference," when parents would be told what the team had found and decided. Those meetings could be, as you might imagine, charged with emotions on both the part of the parents and the professionals involved, the kinds of events Robert Schalock and Ruth Luckasson, two key leaders in evolving definitions, call "high-stakes" clinical encounters.[22]

Then I went to the Newark State School where I read multiple charts of the residents in order to get some insight into their personal histories, often seeing a box that said "etiology unknown." Too often I saw other medical notes that read, "Will not progress beyond a vegetative state," one of them talking about a young man who was one of the liveliest, friendliest, and most engaging people at that institution. It did not take me long at that institution to realize that the biggest tragedy there was not the disability of its residents but the loneliness, lack of connection, and lack of affirmation embedded in its very structure. About five years earlier, while I was still in New York City, Geraldo Rivera had blown open the doors of Willowbrook State School on Staten Island with his famous exposé of its living conditions and herd-like treatment of its residents.

Those memories and stories come from a time of swirling narratives, changes in classifications, and directions in services. The World

Health Organization stepped into the picture with a new conceptual framework for understanding disability in 1980, known as the International Classification of Impairments, Disabilities and Handicaps (ICIDH), outlined in the diagram below.

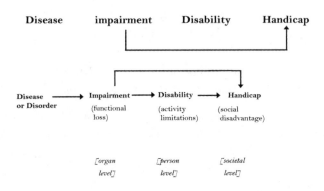

FIGURE 1-1. *ICIDH Model (WHO 1980)*

That model made immediate sense to me by distinguishing between genetic and health conditions, the impairments ("any loss or abnormality of psychological, physiological, or anatomical structure or function") that led to "disability" ("any restriction or lack, resulting from an impairment, of ability to perform an activity in the manner or within the range considered normal for a human being") and then "handicaps" ("a disadvantage for a given individual, resulting from an impairment or a disability, that limits or prevents the fulfillment of a role that is normal [depending on age, sex, and social and cultural factors] for that individual").[23]

At Newark State School, like other institutional settings, those "social and cultural factors" were disadvantages built out of traditions and attitudes that led to deliberate exclusion, lack of awareness, lack of relationships, and often, simply, ignorance and fear. The definition was extremely useful in working with community and religious groups to help unpack their expectations, projections, and fears as well as to realize and empower their sense of capacity to help, especially by confronting the attitudes that came with the label of "handicap."

*International Classification of Functioning, Disabilities, and
Health (ICF), World Health Organization, 2001*

Critique of that 1980 model began immediately, centered on what
seemed to be the linear causation rather than dynamic interplay of the
factors in the diagram and conceptual model. People with disabilities
had also not been involved in its development. Self-advocacy organizations, first in the United Kingdom and other European countries
but then in others, along with social scientists, wanted a model that
reflected a better balance between the individual (medical model) and
the social environmental factors hinted at in the understanding of handicap. Disability as a "social construct" began to be explored and defined,
starting first in the United Kingdom. The critique of the WHO was
that it still seemed to assume "normality" and to "blame the victim."[24]

In response, the WHO released a new version in 2001 that was
soon named the International Classification of Functioning, Disabilities,
and Health (ICF) and is now used around the world.[25]

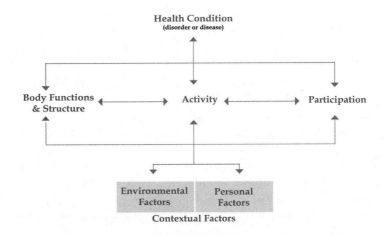

FIGURE 1-2. *ICF Model (WHO 2001)*

The *International Encyclopedia of Rehabilitation* explains it this way:

> To analyze health conditions and health-related states, the model
> refers to two far-embracing terms: disablement and function-
> ing. Disablement is the interaction between the individual, with

his/her health conditions, and the environment (in its negative aspects), while functioning is the same interaction but in positive terms. . . . Body functions are defined as "the physiological functions of body systems (including psychological functions)" (WHO 2001). Body structures are "anatomical parts of the body such as organs, limbs and their components" (WHO 2001). Alterations in body structures and functions are called impairments. . . . Activity is defined as "the execution of a task or action by an individual" (WHO 2001). And participation is "involvement in a life situation" (WHO 2001). . . . The ICF model also analyzes the relationship between the individual and the environment, describing contextual factors, which are divided into personal and environmental ones. They represent all that surrounds a person and that may have some influence on the functioning of the individual and, therefore, on his/her body structures and functions, on his/her capabilities (as an individual or as a member of a social group). These influences can be either positive or negative, depending on whether these factors operate as facilitators or as barriers.[26]

Notably, this model is applicable for everyone with some kind of health condition impacting ability and participation, not just people with some form of impairment. The either/or distinctions between medical models and social models (or constructs) of disability became more of both/and.

The AAIDD (American Association on Intellectual and Developmental Disabilities)

The American Association on Mental Retardation, now AAIDD, had already developed its *Ninth Manual on Classification* in 1992 that adopted a "socio-ecological" model of disability, one that described and classified strengths as well as weaknesses and limitations, and one that shifted the focus from the individual to the determination of needed environmental supports.[27]

That model was further developed in the Tenth and Eleventh Editions, in 2002 and 2010 respectively, now called *Intellectual Disability: Definition, Classification, and Systems of Supports* (11th ed.). The new definition starts from the concept of "human functioning" to identify strengths and weaknesses in key areas of functioning, but, more importantly, it focuses on assessing the types and levels of support needed to address those areas.

> "People with intellectual disability (ID)" refers to those with "significant limitations both in intellectual functioning and in adaptive behavior as expressed in conceptual, social, and practical adaptive skills. This disability originates before age 18," as defined by the American Association on Intellectual and Developmental Disabilities (AAIDD) in its manual, *Intellectual Disability: Definition, Classification, and Systems of Supports* (Schalock et al., 2010), and the *Diagnostic and Statistical Manual of Mental Disorders, 5th Edition (DSM-5)*, published by the American Psychiatric Association (APA, 2013). "People with developmental disabilities (DD)" refers to those with "a severe, chronic disability of an individual that (i) is attributable to a mental or physical impairment or combination of mental and physical impairments; (ii) is manifested before the individual attains age 22; (iii) is likely to continue indefinitely; (iv) results in substantial functional limitations in 3 or more of the following areas of major life activity: (I) Self-care, (II) Receptive and expressive language, (III) Learning, (IV) Mobility, (V) Self-direction, (VI) Capacity for independent living, (VII) Economic self-sufficiency; and (v) reflects the individual's need for a combination and sequence of special, interdisciplinary, or generic services, individualized supports, or other forms of assistance that are of lifelong or extended duration and are individually planned and coordinated," as defined by the Developmental Disabilities Assistance and Bill of Rights Act 2000. In everyday language people with ID and/or DD are frequently referred to as people with cognitive, intellectual and/or developmental disabilities.[28]

The assessment instrument is called the *Supports Intensity Scales*, replacing prior understandings of levels of mental retardation in a person (mild, moderate, severe, and profound) with levels of services and supports needed in someone's environment.[29]

Note, then, that classification and assessment is now back to assessing levels of support coming from outside the individual. That takes assessment or planning teams, along with varying degrees of involvement by individuals and their families, to name what they think is important for someone. That process thus involves, as the first WHO definition describes it, social attitudes toward disability. The second

WHO definition gets more explicit about both the personal and social constructs about disability—what the individual and community think about disability, its implications, and meaning. A tension then emerges between an objective, measureable definition from the realm of the sciences with the subjective areas of personal and cultural attitudes and values.

Wil Buntinx, a social scientist from the Netherlands, makes an important distinction in his description of both the ICF and the AAIDD frameworks:

> These frameworks do not take subjective experiences and personal life goals into consideration, and people seldom express the goals and ambition of life in terms of the ICF. So, the notion of supports calls for an orientation or perspective that goes beyond disability. . . . Two developments at the end of the 20th Century answered this problem. One was the introduction of the concept of quality of life and the other is the human rights approach to disability.[30]

Quality of life frameworks, he notes, allow for the assessment of both subjective and objective criteria. "Objective norms can be found in legal and professional standards. Subjective norms can be obtained by simply asking the person about his or her life experiences and by using satisfaction inventory methods."[31]

CONCLUSION: NAMING DISABILITY

The names and words we use depend greatly on the perspective and historical time of the one doing the naming. Names have been primarily assigned by public systems of care and treatment, not from perspectives from the world of arts, theology, or literature, much less by people with disabilities themselves. One might also define disability simply as diversity, one of the logical directions in which it has been moving with the understandings of disability as a social construct.

The importance for summarizing the relatively recent models of classification is first of all to note the common move toward, or balance with, what is called a socio-ecological model of disability. They all end up with wide open questions about "personal and environmental contextual factors" that impact someone's weaknesses and their strengths. They point toward the importance of disability rights based on universal moral standards and on quality of life perspectives, each of which embodies both individual and cultural perspectives. Definitions thus can describe the kinds of personal and environmental supports and changes that are needed to build upon a person's strengths as well as to mitigate the negative impact of traditions, cultural norms, beliefs, stereotypes, and prejudices that get embedded (and sometimes enshrined) deeply in the public norms. Rights, quality of life, and person-centered approaches to supports, as contrasted to what one might call "professional or system-centered supports," must have allies in laws, value-based policies, and more compassionate cultural norms in the wider public. That discussion leads to experiences, concepts, questions, and forms of language and discourse that are fundamentally spiritual.

2

Disability
From Definition, Diagnosis, and Assessment to Meaning

As models of disability have evolved, there is no nondebated, static, universal, or objective definition of disability. The current definitions do not depend solely on physical impairments or measures of intelligence. Efforts to understand and name disability depend significantly on the context in which disability is understood, defined, and described. That context includes the perspectives and values of the people doing the defining.

The omnipresent medical model of disability has evolved in the wider context of how we understand health. Is health the *absence of* illness or the *presence of* certain qualities in human lives? Defining, or naming, health also turns out to be an evolving, changing construct. Health, like disability, does not have a static, completely objective understanding or definition.[1]

A holistic understanding of health and disability takes into account personal, communal, and cultural constructs that shape what it means to be well or sick, nondisabled or disabled. Religious and spiritual beliefs and practices have long played a major role in shaping how people interpreted both health and disability. The rise of science first challenged the ancient, traditional understandings of the direct connections between spirituality and health that were often expressed in superstitions and unhealthy practices. However, there has been growing research into the connections between spirituality and health in the past fifty years,[2] research that has included relationships among physical and mental health, spirituality, recovery, and healing. The rising tide of spirituality and health research has taken place in almost every discipline of the health and human sciences, including medicine, psychology, psychiatry, social work, occupational therapy, and the like.

The arena of disability, other than in mental health, has been by and large left out of this growing movement in research. The sciences of disability have avoided explicit exploration of religion and disability for the most part. Why? One key reason is the negative experiences of many people with disabilities, their families, and professionals with religious attitudes and practices around the naming and meaning of disability, its origin, and understandings of healing.[3] Researchers and professionals have heard those stories. Ironically, those wounding and negative experiences are a backhanded statement about the power of the linkage between individual and cultural spirituality and the personal and social constructs of disability.

While the explicit linkages have received little attention, four other dimensions in the scientific and social models of disability lead to implicit, though usually unacknowledged, spiritual dimensions: (1) the socio-ecological understanding of disability, (2) rights, (3) quality of life, and (4) the core public policy values of independence, productivity, inclusion, and self-determination.

DISABILITY AS A SOCIAL CONSTRUCT AND THE
IMPORTANCE OF ENVIRONMENT

In the 1980 WHO definition, the concept of handicap—issues coming from the individual's interaction with his or her environment—raises the spiritual questions of the accessibility, attitudes, hospitality, and welcome of that environment. The subsequent 2002 ICF definition, with its focus on *personal* and *environmental* contexts and the capacity *to participate* in typical life activities, makes those questions even stronger. Are public spaces conceived and built in ways that see people with disabilities as a natural part of that community with whom others will interact as they do with anyone else? Are they seen as citizens and members or as strangers, known by their labels more than by their names? Have we moved past the two dominant attitudes in the past that Timothy Shriver names as "purge or pity"?[4]

A common refrain in the disability movement is that attitudes are more difficult to change than architecture.[5] Anyone familiar with the "worlds" of disability knows the stories, studies, and writings that reveal the fears, anxieties, uncertainties, ignorance, lack of experience, and projections that shape stereotypes, build prejudice, and get solidified in discriminatory practices. Building communities that value and welcome individuals with disabilities and their families requires a transformation of feelings, understanding, and values; an openness to relationships; and a compassionate willingness to listen. Advocacy movements rely on those traits , as well as shared commitment, purpose, and vision in each of their members. Advocacy movements, by virtue of their being a community of support, reflection, and action, have often served as a parallel or primary spiritual community for individuals and families when their experience in faith communities has been negative or wounding. The negative attitudes and practices in communities and congregations can and are being countered by more positive spiritual beliefs, norms, and practices embodied in the members of faith communities and other organizations. Spirituality is about personal identity, meaning, values, life-giving relationships, and purpose, all of which shape individuals and their environments.

Attitudes about disability can change. In the 1970s Fr. John Aurelio, a chaplaincy colleague in upstate New York, and I were talking about initiatives at the institutions we served, which were trying to bring large numbers of volunteers into the facility for a day of fun and friendship. He noted that people not familiar with people with disabilities usually go from fear/hate to pity to anger to love. (The anger comes when you begin to know someone's story and almost universal experience of barriers or injustices faced because of disability. Love is the arrival at a sense of mutuality, shared gifts, and contributions.) That discussion became a framework that I have developed to outline the "stages" of attitudinal change and spiritual growth in people without disabilities. After a young woman with cerebral palsy heard me use that paradigm in a workshop in Richmond, she commented, "That's exactly what I have gone through. I hated myself because of my disability, then felt sorry for myself, then began to get angry, and now have a new self-image, based in my faith, in which I can say I love myself."

The model is also a framework for talking about the transitions that a congregation can undergo as it seeks to welcome and include people with disabilities. Fear and exclusion meant that many faith communities did not welcome people with disabilities. They were "apart from" both congregation and community, sometimes at the exhortation of clergy and faith communities.[6] New programs for "special children" beginning after World War II were based on pity, copied by congregations as "special" supports or ministries *for* or *to* children and adults with disabilities. Many congregations have evolved to ministries *with* people with disabilities and their families and, finally, to ministries *by* people with disabilities, recognizing the gifts that individuals and families bring to others. In very broad strokes, the progression also summarizes stages in the history of services in the past hundred-plus years: fear or exclusion of disability moving to "special" services (a charity and pity model) to advocacy and rights and, finally, to experiences of shared contributions, belonging, and community membership. Those words (fear, hate, pity, anger, and love) are one simple way of talking about the "spirit" of that movement and history as well as both personal and communal transformations. Spirituality and religion thus has great power to shape both personal and social constructs of disability and experiences related to it.

RIGHTS: THEIR FOUNDATIONS AND LIMITS

If attitudes are the spirit of individual and social changes, then laws are the legal embodiment. The positive changes in laws have come from recognizing that the rights of people with disabilities are no different from anyone else's rights. Human rights have deep spiritual and religious roots.

The importance of recognizing and honoring the rights of people with disabilities in the past fifty-plus years cannot be overestimated. To cite just a few, the establishment of rights in law and policy is exemplified in laws in the United States such as the Rehabilitation Act of 1973, the Individuals with Disabilities Education Act in 1975, and the Americans with Disabilities Act of 1990. Similar legal and policy actions occurred in other countries, and, more recently, internationally, in the form of the UN Convention on the Rights of Persons with Disabilities.[7] Laws and policies have also been worked out in the United States

through significant court cases decided by the Supreme Court, such
as the *Pennhurst* decision of 1984, which led to the first closure of an
institution, the *Cleburne* decision of 1985, which established the rights
of people with intellectual disabilities to live in a group home in a
neighborhood, and the *Olmstead* decision of 1999, which established the
rights of individuals with disabilities living in institutional settings to
live in the community. People with disabilities, families, professionals,
veterans, and others have fought tirelessly for these changes through
organizations like the independent living movement, ADAPT,[8] and
multiple parent organizations.

The *Cleburne* decision fought the cultural and political wars over
the "not in my backyard" (NIMBY) protests in many communities as
people moved from institutions back into community settings. The
Olmstead decision cemented the right of choice by people in institutional
settings to move into the community. In the mid-1970s, I had a conversation with a young woman named Donna Smith, institutionalized at
Newark State School because of her cerebral palsy. We were talking
about one of the first NIMBY battles raging over a proposal to move
a few people into a group home in the town of Newark, down the hill
from the institutional grounds named for the town. She asked, "When
will normal people learn to accept handicapped people the same way
that handicapped people have to learn how to accept normal people?"

Her question was, in essence, the Golden Rule, expressed in one
way or another by all of the major religious and faith traditions in the
world[9] and a code based on a belief that all are equal in God's eyes,
however one defines God. The moral foundations on which human
rights have been based come out of religious and spiritual traditions
as well as philosophical or political histories. Understandings of freedom, dignity, individual rights, equality, responsibility, the treatment of
others, and obligation all have their foundations in the Judeo-Christian
tradition and parallels in other traditions.

Rabbi Julia Watts Belser names four primary themes in Jewish
tradition and texts that undergird the rights of persons with disabilities. First is *b'tselem Elohim*, the equality and infinite value of the
individual coming from God's creation of humankind "in his own
image." Second is *areyvut*, the belief in communal responsibility for
one another and inclusiveness. Third, the principle of *kavod*: freedom

means the respect of the agency and dignity of every person. Fourth is the Jewish commitment to social justice, based on the principles of *tsedek* (righteousness and justice) and *tikkum olam*, the obligation to work for repair of the world.[10]

Rabbi Jonathan Sacks, the 2016 recipient of the Templeton Prize in Religion, writes in his book *The Great Partnership: Science, Religion, and the Search for Meaning*:

> (God) is the author of nature which he created by a free act of will. By conferring his image on humankind, God gives us freedom of the will. This generates the entire moral world of the Bible with its vision of the human person as a responsible, choosing moral agent. . . . The great religions are the most effective moral tutors the world has ever known. They begin by turning our gaze outwards, to the human other who is a reflection of the divine Other. They give us habits of virtue by getting us to do ethically demanding things . . . and they are done in the context of community.[11]

Sacks allows that there are other sources of morality, including philosophical perspectives from both before and after the Enlightenment that argue that human beings must create their own moral code. He readily admits that spiritual faith does not always lead to moral action, even the exact opposite at times. Citing Darwin, he notes the research on the ways that communities of living beings exhibit altruism. But he also notes that philosophers and atheists like John Stuart Mill and Bertrand Russell have examined how religion serves as a force of social cohesion. The religious origin of both rights and responsibilities, Sacks asserts, is unmistakable.

There is, however, a profound paradox in the relationship between rights and inclusion of people with disabilities, as well as other marginalized or stigmatized persons. Rights give all people equal protections, due process, access to public spaces, and inclusion in the public services and supports accorded to all citizens when they are observed and enforced. Rights create space for people in community life and the opportunity for social connections. However, rights do not guarantee relationships, friendships, and other spiritual needs such as a positive sense of identity, belonging, and purpose.

Being part of a spiritual community can illustrate the paradox. One of the infamous limits of the ADA is that it exempts religious organizations on the basis of hiring issues. In spite of that, many advocates from faith traditions have argued that faith communities have the moral responsibility to include and welcome people with disabilities on the basis of the faith foundations of rights, justice, and hospitality. After all, most of the signs out in front of congregations say "Everyone's welcome!" In addition, a person with a disability has the moral and spiritual right to access and inclusion in a building, worship service, and other activities. But that does not mean that they will be welcomed, valued, or able to move toward true membership and belonging.

Dutch ethicist and theologian Hans Reinders notes that, in a liberal society, with its core values of freedom, choice, and equality, no matter what that society says about the dignity of every person, people with disabilities (most notably people with intellectual and developmental disabilities) will end up as second-class citizens because of the assumptions (i.e., constructs) made about their capacity for reason—their intellectual ability to choose.[12] Rights are too often impacted by the beliefs and perceptions of the people doing the defining or granting of the rights themselves. In the United States, for example, it has taken most of this country's history to expand the constitutional understandings of rights to people who were not originally seen as "men"—for example, women, African Americans, and sometimes other minorities.

That second-class citizenship for people with intellectual and developmental disabilities has sometimes been expressed in the legal battles over competence and guardianship. A relatively new perspective called "supported decision making" is countering the removal of rights to decide with the affirmation that all people have the right to have their choices, preferences, or decisions honored. It is up to society (and those around a person with a significant disability) to figure out what these choices, preferences, and decisions are, rather than assuming that there is a point beyond which their rights to choose do not apply.[13]

The oldest way of stating that every person should be respected is the Judeo-Christian religious understanding that each person is created "in the image of God," thereby endowed with value and the right, or the divine imperative, to be treated equally as our neighbor and fellow citizen. Life is a gift from God, coming with the human freedom and responsibility to treat others knowing that they are created in the image of God as well. A Jewish saying originating in the Middle Ages succinctly states, "In front of every person there is a host of angels saying, 'Make way for the image of God.'" That affirmation of the divine spark in every person is broader than interpreting that "image" as the capacity for reason and will. It is about gift, creation, and relationship.[14] Disability has been explained theologically by some as evidence of the "broken" world, the rift caused by the actions of Adam and Eve. But the book of Genesis speaks first about the "goodness" of all creation. The Gospel of John notes in its beginning that, in God, all things were "good." Thus one might argue that disability makes no difference to God and that people with disabilities were and are simply part of the created world. In other words, they belong by virtue of their creation. They are already included, and others need to recognize that. Exclusion from society and the equal rights due to every person requires justification, not inclusion.[15] The Bible, in many places, goes on to judge the righteousness of a society by the way it treats those on the margins.

QUALITY OF LIFE

Quality of life (QOL) is one of the major constructs in health care and disabilities that impacts the goals and vision of care and supports. Ironically, the construct, like spirituality, can be used to help and to harm.

On a more positive and helpful side, QOL is used in the world of intellectual and developmental disabilities, in particular, to help assess what is most important to people with disabilities and whether those core life values are being met. In the legal world, value and respect are measured by the full and free exercise of one's rights. QOL, on the contrary, attempts to assess the experience of disability by the importance of subjective life experiences and personal life goals. The World Health Organization's definition of the "quality of life" is summarized by Wil Buntinx as

> an individual's perception of their position in life in the context of the culture and value systems in which they live and in relation to their goals, expectations, standards and concerns. It is a broad ranging concept affected in a complex way by the person's physical health, psychological state, personal beliefs, social relationships,

and their relationship to salient features of their environment (WHO 1997, p. 1). . . . An essential feature of the construct of Quality of Life is the acknowledgment of both subjective and objective criteria for evaluation. . . . Objective norms can be found in legal and professional standards. Subjective norms can be obtained by simply asking the person about his or life experiences or by using satisfaction inventory methods.[16]

The important and pioneering work done in developing the QOL construct and its application has been extended to people with disabilities, their families, and, really, to everyone.[17] But it has also been used to deny care to people with disabilities. The assumptions that are made in bioethics and health-care practice about the QOL of people with disabilities too frequently reflect more of the assumptions and prejudices of nondisabled caregivers than they do the actual opinions of people with disabilities and those who are close to them. Those assumptions impact prenatal and neonatal care, resource allocation, and issues around end of life care, including withdrawal of treatment and assisted dying.[18]

That impact is familiar to many family members and caregivers who have stood with people with severe or multiple disabilities in many standard acute care medical facilities. They have heard or seen treatment predicated on the assumptions about QOL made by health-care professionals. QOL thus often depends on the context of those doing the judging (e.g., the general public, standard medical care providers, disability services professionals, individuals with disabilities, or their families). Attitudes about disability are different, as are the amount of personal experience with disability and, above all, personal relationships. All beg for and frequently involve an awareness of the spiritual and religious perspectives that different players bring to those ethical roundtables and caregiving relationships.

Two of the three major theoretical models for QOL do in fact cite spirituality as one of the major dimensions in QOL. Those models are summarized and compared in a table by Wil Buntinx entitled "Domains of Quality of Life According to Three Major Authors: Schalock et al. (2007), the World Health Organization (WHO 1997) and the Quality of Life (QOL) Research Unit, Toronto."[19]

World Health Organization	QOL Research Unit, University of Toronto	Robert Schalock et al. in definitions used by the AAIDD
1. Physical health	1. Physical being	1. Personal development
2. Psychological	2. Psychological being	2. Self-determination
3. Level of independence	3. Spiritual being	3. Interpersonal relations
4. Social relations	4. Physical belonging	4. Social inclusion
5. Environment	5. Social belonging	5. Rights
6. Spirituality/religion/ personal beliefs	6. Community belonging	6. Emotional well-being
	7. Practical becoming	7. Physical well-being
	8. Leisure becoming	8. Material well-being
	9. Growth becoming	

First, the WHO model above was developed with "understandings of health" as the overarching concept. The explicit domain of "spirituality/religion/personal beliefs" is defined as the following:

> This domain/facet examines the person's beliefs, and how these impact quality of life. This might be by helping a person cope with difficulties in his/her life, giving structure to experience, ascribing meaning to spiritual and personal questions, and more generally providing the person with a sense of well-being. This facet addresses people with differing religious beliefs (including Buddhists, Christians, Hindus, Muslims, etc.) as well as other people with differing beliefs that do not fit within a specific religious tradition.
>
> For many people, personal beliefs and spirituality are a source of comfort, well-being, security, meaning, sense of belonging, purpose, and strength. However, some people feel that religiousness has a negative impact on their lives. Questions are framed to allow this aspect of the facet to emerge.[20]

The major focus of the questions in the WHO spiritual assessment model and tool is on the importance of "personal beliefs" and their impact on personal capacity.

In contrast, second, note that the University of Toronto Research Unit defines QOL as "the degree to which a person enjoys the important possibilities of his or her life." Their website notes, "The Centre for Health Promotion conceptual model is seen as applicable to all persons, with or without developmental disabilities. It was developed on the basis of an analysis of the literature on quality of life and qualitative data we collected in the context of focus groups and in-depth interviews with persons with and without developmental disabilities."[21] It was further refined in work with adolescents and older adults.

Their visual model is:

FIGURE 2-1. *QOL Model (University of Toronto, 2003)*

Their domain of spirituality is under the sphere of "being," and it includes personal values, personal standards of conduct, and spiritual beliefs. The striking feature of this definition, especially for someone familiar with the languages of spirituality, is that the model as a whole includes what could be called the spiritual dimensions of life: being, belonging, becoming.[22] Included in "being" is self-concept, or what I will call "identity." "Belonging" includes personal, social, and community belonging. "Becoming" includes concepts and descriptions of connections in which experiences of growth, purpose, and development as a human being take place.

The third QOL model, developed by Robert Schalock and colleagues in North America and Europe, also came out of the commitment to find a QOL model that can be effectively used in working specifically with people with intellectual and developmental disabilities, one that includes both objective and subjective domains. Objective domains can be legal ones, such as whether one's rights are observed or measuring whether professional standards of care are met. Subjective norms are measured by asking people about their life experiences and using the equivalent of "patient satisfaction surveys" in acute care medical services. The consequence of not making spirituality explicit in this model is that spirituality could be seen, and argued, as an overarching construct that impacts all its eight domains. Thus, the model either appears to leave spirituality out of consideration or to relegate and confine it to a subcategory of one dimension. Spirituality is a domain that definitely has both objective and subjective components.[23]

A second problem with the model is asking people about their subjective experiences of QOL or using satisfaction inventory scales in an attempt to get answers that qualify as scientific. The QOL construct is partly determined by the context in which it was developed; what one asks; and the way one describes, measures, or analyzes the results. If you use inventory methods that conform to observable and measurable experience—scientific methods—what you get is very different that when you ask people to answer questions about QOL domains. There, you will get narrative and story as well as beliefs and practices. One may try to measure those by qualitative research methodology, but *story*, even more so than *belief* (as highlighted in the WHO definition), is the major way of describing personal spiritual experience.

The impact of spirituality and religion on both physical and psychological health, as well as what one might call the qualitative research domains, has a rich and ever-growing body of research and literature, but not so much in the area of disability, and especially so in intellectual and developmental disability. Thankfully, new researchers such as Erik Carter, Belva Collins, Melinda Ault, and their colleagues are asking people with intellectual and developmental disabilities, and their families, about their understanding of spirituality, its importance in their lives, and whether that part of their lives is respected and supported by both secular and religious care providers.[24]

Why do two of the models explicitly include spirituality while the Schalock and colleagues and AAIDD models do not? The answer may simply depend on the context and framework from which the three models are operating, or, in other words, the culture and its accepted modes of discourse. The Schalock and colleagues model has decidedly come out of the scientific and policy frameworks of the AAIDD definition and classification system of intellectual and developmental disabilities. It has been further developed in collaboration with colleagues through the International Association for the Scientific Study of Intellectual Disability. In their book for professionals on clinical judgment, Schalock and Luckasson also note that the foundation for any clinical interaction needs to be *respect of individuals with disabilities and families*. Respect includes "explaining the relevance of information and how that information will assist them in making personal decisions that are consistent with their values and beliefs."[25] The questions that remain are: (1) Whether and how does the model adequately try to assess those values and beliefs? (2) How do underlying dimensions of the constructs of "science" and "professional" influence the minimal attention to the constructs of spirituality and faith as they impact understandings of disability and the QOL domains? (3) How are they included, if they are not assessed, in supports planning?

The WHO model is also meant to be a scientific model that can be applied worldwide. Its limits are that it focuses primarily on beliefs, rather than being more inclusive of practice and experience. One question for its scientific model is why it does not try to figure out ways to take into account the impact of spirituality and religion on areas of health because they shape so many cultural and personal understandings, habits, and responses to issues of physical and psychological health.

The University of Toronto Quality of Life Research Unit is attractive from a holistic and spiritual perspective because (1) spirituality is included explicitly and (2) the model as a whole is more dynamic and open to story and meaning. In addition to its description of the development of its model, it is perhaps telling that the research unit (while very interdisciplinary in focus) is based in the Department of Occupational Therapy, a context in which the focus is on how people live, adapt, cope, and change.

Thus, best practices in describing and assessing QOL either explicitly include the importance of spirituality or imply it under other domains. All three do not seem to draw upon any in-depth research into understanding *and* experience of spirituality nor assessments of its importance to individuals and families, with the result that they are more narrow than necessary. In the terms of some current parlance, they are "thin" rather than "thick" constructions of spirituality and thus limited in understanding the importance of spirituality, religion, or faith in many people's lives.[26] To state it in more "scientific" terms, they do not capture the breadth and depth of ways that the spiritual journey of identity, community, and meaning impact personal and social health, history, understanding, social connections, and transformation.

SELF-DETERMINATION AND PERSON-CENTERED PLANNING AND SUPPORTS

A social model of disability, rights, and QOL all have in common a fundamental commitment to the dignity and worth of individuals with disabilities and their families. All lead to, and advocate for, the central importance of the individual and family in social policies and community change as well as their importance in the evolution of what we now call "person-centered" and "family-centered" supports and services. "Self-determination" is a core policy value in services and supports for people with disabilities around the world, and especially so in Western culture. Person-centered planning began before self-determination became such a buzzword. Models of person-centered planning arose because many people believed that other systems of assessment and planning were more "professionally centered" and "system centered," rather than addressing their own unique needs, gifts, and dreams. Typical assessment processes were and are primarily used to determine eligibility for services and to choose services out of available service options. They did not listen deeply to the fullness of people's lives or capture what was most important to them

At the core of person-centered supports and services are two simple yet incredibly profound and broad questions: "What is important for someone?" and "What is important to someone?" "Important to someone" can include all the services and supports necessary to help them live lives that are healthy, independent, productive, inclusive, and self-determined. "Important to someone" encapsulates wishes, hopes, dreams, values, meaning, passions, relationships, purpose, and more.[27]

The models and strategies of person- and family-centered planning often involve individuals, families, and their "important others" much more dynamically than do assessment strategies and traditional clinical planning processes. (Examples of the latter include individual education plans [IEPs], individual habilitation plans, individual support plans, etc.) Person-centered planning processes frequently start with a focus on the strengths and gifts of an individual. Their holistic value comes from the inclusion of both services and supports available through public health, education, and human service systems as well as those typically called "generic, natural supports": supports available in the context in which people with disabilities and their families live a major part of their lives, such as through friends, neighborhoods, associations, extended families, faith communities, civic life, recreation, and employment.

Thus, if someone's spiritual and religious life is important to them, the tenets of person-centered planning would say that this needs to be respected, honored, and addressed in ways that are chosen by the person and his or her family and friends. Spirituality should then be addressed whether or not it is recognized as a dimension of QOL or respected only because everyone has a right of religious freedom and practice. Statements of rights, including the right to practice the faith of one's choice, are often included in the policies of service and support agencies and sometimes posted on their walls, but little is done to turn that right into experience or practice. Models of person-centered planning and family-centered supports are thus all open to discussion about issues of spirituality and faith. None of the models address that domain, just as they do not explicitly address many other domains of life as outlined in QOL models, unless a particular person-centered planning process has made an explicit commitment to do so.[28] The common vision of the models is to explore whatever is defined as important to someone or to their family, with the result that the most important issues and areas for them will be addressed.

Some people and planning perspectives may wish to include spirituality and faith under the "important for" category of questions. Despite the expanding research that addresses the ways spirituality helps people in terms of physical, mental, and emotional health, I am not doing so here because that would fall too easily into stereotypes that spirituality and religion are mostly about telling people what to believe or do. "Important for" may include prescription medications to stay healthy, but prescriptions involving faith and belief correlate immediately with negative associations with spirituality and religion.

Those kinds of "you should" observations may simply be negative and unwanted, but they can also be abusive and wounding—for example, "You should pray more" or "Your faith is not strong enough." The historical development of the professional injunction to "avoid proselytizing" comes in part from those experiences. Those stories and experiences may also be a key reason for the professional reluctance to address spirituality at all, especially if professionals in human sciences and services have not had training in how to do so. That reluctance needs to be addressed honestly. To be fair, however, spiritual and religious disciplines or professionals are not the only ones who frequently fall into the temptation of telling other people what is important for them and what they should do.

The role and perspective of person-centered planning facilitators is crucial in terms of discovering what is "important to" someone. A growing area of research is the exploration of the importance of spirituality, faith, and spiritual communities of practice as described and reported by individuals and families. Thus, both supporting professionals as well as systems of planning and supports need to be prepared to address spirituality and to have some confidence in their capacity to do so. Spirituality can be addressed in ways that support someone's wishes and interests, but it can also be addressed by helping someone find ways and supports to counter and transform the impact of negative experiences of neglect, judgment, or exclusion in the past.

THE SPIRITUAL CORE OF KEY VALUES IN DISABILITY RIGHTS AND SERVICES

The current values guiding disability policy and supports come out of, and impact, our understanding of disability; the universality of rights in which people with disabilities are to be included; and the vision and commitment of so many people with disabilities, their families, friends, and allies of full inclusion and participation in their own communities and society. In the United States, those core values are embedded in the Developmental Disabilities Act of 2000 as well as in most mission statements for services and supports:

- *Independence*: helping people once considered totally dependent to become as independent as possible by recognizing strengths, enhancing capacity and ability, and providing environments in which independence can be lived and practiced

- *Productivity*: usually interpreted as having a job or, more broadly, becoming a productive and contributing member of communities and society
- *Inclusion*: enabling people to be included in all of the areas of community life in which they want to participate, beginning with the right to inclusion in education
- *Self-Determination*: listening to, and honoring, individual choices, preferences, goals, and desires
- *Cultural Competence*: respecting the fact that people live in and come from many cultural backgrounds, and being able to provide services and supports in ways that honor the mores of that culture as well as individual choices and preferences

Spiritual questions about what it means to be human are at the roots of each of those values: Who am I? (independence); Why am I? (productivity); Where do I belong, or, rather, to whom do I belong? (inclusion); What kind of control or power do I have over what happens to me? (self-determination); and Will my personal uniqueness and cultural heritage be respected? (cultural competence).[29] These policy values can all be strengthened and enriched by a deeper understanding of their spiritual roots and dimensions of experience.

CONCLUSION

Thus, the current models for understanding disability as a socio-ecological construct, the critical role of rights, the importance of QOL, the core policy and practice values, and the imperatives manifested in person-centered planning all go down paths that implicitly include, lead to, and beg for attention to the role of spirituality and faith. In fact, doing so would help these models, policies, and processes like person-centered planning to live up to their own goals of being holistic, multidimensional, and person centered. Spirituality as a construct can help professionals, allies, and caregivers to understand the deeper and broader meanings of what is important to someone and, hopefully, help us all recognize, honor, and address the ways that spirituality and faith can and do support the kind of valued and inclusive lives that everyone wants. The converse is true: Ff spirituality is seen as important to someone and their family or if it represents a dimension of life in which wounding or painful experiences have happened, then supports and resources can address each of those experiences if an individual or family wants to do so.

If we reverse the direction of moving from dimensions of disability to spirituality, and then seek to understand spirituality more completely, does it explicitly or implicitly deal with the "worlds" of disability? Spirituality is a dimension of life that is often experienced and expressed most intensely in times of crisis, finitude, and vulnerability. In other words, starting with defining spirituality, one ends up in a world deeply familiar to people with disabilities and their families. The result can also be a deeper and broader understanding of spirituality and of the ways that the spiritual dimensions of life may be understood and supported, for everyone.

3

Spirituality
From Meaning to Disability

Like disability, spirituality can also be thought of as a social construct—as a way of talking about a dimension of human experience. Like disability, spirituality covers a huge range of perspectives, theories, theologies, and experiences. Understandings of spirituality vary greatly by context, culture, period, and personal circumstance. Those understandings and definitions are also never ones that stand still for long, if ever, as multiple factors, including differences in epistemology—what does it mean to know and how does one know—lead to different or changing definitions and perspectives.

How then does spirituality relate to the two other major frameworks for knowing that shape the context of this book: religion and science? How have others in those contexts defined spiritualty? My own definition of "spirituality" comes out of my own experience in both of those frameworks in the "worlds" of disabilities. The definition focuses on identity and meaning, connection, and purpose—the foundations of the core values in the world of disability services: independence, productivity, and inclusion.

Most models and definitions of spirituality essentially try to conform to the methods of discourse, diagnosis, and treatment in the health and human sciences. These models have primarily evolved in acute care and mental health settings, not from asking religious communities, or even communities in general, what spirituality means to them. There, the models multiply geometrically, or, we might say in more traditional religious language for describing and defining spirituality, "tenfold" because of the current diversity of religious traditions and practice and the centuries of discourse about what is most important and meaningful in human life. Throughout history, communities have been the primary places in which suffering, death, limitations, and vulnerabilities occurred. In our times, particularly in Western societies, acute care and mental health settings are the primary places in which the vulnerability and limits of life are faced and dealt with in person. Those experiences are often hardest when they are unexpected, or, as we might say, unexpected but inevitable. In those worlds of vulnerability and limits, we are back in the realm of disability

FRAMEWORKS OF KNOWLEDGE AND MEANING

If spirituality, religion, and science are all frameworks for knowledge and meaning, how does spirituality relate to the other two? Multitudes of voices have been part of those discussions, which leads to another contextual question: Who's asking and why—for what purpose?

Spirituality and Religion

One of the most common responses to surveys or conversations about religion in our current times is, "I am spiritual, but not religious." While this sounds like a clarifying statement, in fact, it contrasts two words and constructs that are much more overlapping than separate.

The assumed difference is that one's spirituality is distinct from whether one is a practicing member of a particular religious faith or tradition. So, generally, spirituality is assumed to be a universal dimension of human life, whatever one means by that term, while religion is a spiritual form and tradition that is codified and organized around a particular set of understandings about God and faith, rituals, and practices associated with it—for example, what it means to be Christian, Jewish, Buddhist, Muslim, or Hindu, or one of any number of subdivisions within those broader categories.

Being spiritual does not mean that one does not believe in God or experience the transcendent or holy. That may be someone's meaning, but a frequent self-assessment is, "I believe in God, but I just don't like religious structures or organizations."

There was a time in history, not that long ago, when the two were seen as the same. Religion was spirituality. Spirituality meant religion. Before the Enlightenment, the distinction between secular and sacred was very hard to discern, if it was there at all.[1] The rise of science and philosophies relying completely on reason began to make that distinction. People might now consider themselves secular but still spiritual. "Secular" is often interpreted as neither spiritual nor religious, but others, including prominent scientists, may call themselves secular or scientific as well as spiritual or religious.

This discussion is not intended to grieve the loss of the time when religion and spirituality were seen as the same, partly because that statement also glosses over the great diversity in each category. There have been huge advances made in human knowledge and understanding through scientific, philosophical, and other disciplines. Rather, the point is that words have varied meanings in different contexts. The difference between spirituality and religion is sometimes described as the difference between a living spirituality or faith in contrast to an ancient or hardened dogma, doctrine, or creed. However, bodies of knowledge can also have their own dogma and core beliefs to which everyone is expected to conform. One of the great ironies of modern time is that a popular, politically correct secular view is that being religious means one is not open and free because one has to conform to the dictates of one's religious tradition. To refute that is then, of course, to violate the core norms or beliefs of secularism. Any body of knowledge can be used in dogmatic ways. Spirituality and religion exist on a continuum rather than demarcating separate spheres. Sometimes they are assumed to be one and the same, especially when the value judgment behind that assumption is that religion is bad, false, or irrelevant.

The *Oxford Dictionary* defines "religion" as "the belief in and worship of a superhuman controlling power, especially a personal God or gods"—for example, "*ideas about the relationship between science and religion.*" Related definitions mentioned are "a particular system of faith and worship"; "*the world's great religions,*" and "a pursuit or interest followed with great devotion"; "*consumerism is the new religion.*"[2]

The *Oxford Dictionary*'s summary of the origin of the word "religion" is more enlightening: "Middle English (originally in the sense 'life under monastic vows'): from Old French, or from Latin *religio* (*n-*)

'obligation, bond, reverence,' perhaps based on Latin *religare* 'to bind.' "
The parts of our bodies that help hold limbs together are called liga-
ments, a word coming from the same Latin *religare*. The parallels, or,
as it were, the "linkages," are obvious to the core components of my
definition of spirituality: identity, connection (including, but not limited
to, that of a divine presence), and purpose, including motivation, call,
or, as described in that definition of religion, obligation.

Why are those connections important? Too often spirituality is
assumed to be an "individual" perception or belief or part of one's identity. A more accurate definition gives equal power to an understanding
of spirituality as connection (i.e., bond) and as purpose or obligation.
Thus, both experientially and in terms of function, religion and spirituality are much more alike than distinct. In most cultures they are
seen as either equal or very closely aligned as dimensions of experience
that "hold together" both individuals and communities.

Spirituality and Science

There is simply no way to do justice to the rich and complex history
of the relationship between spirituality/religion and the sciences in
a small part of one chapter in a larger book when there have been
thousands of philosophers, scientists, theologians, and others who have
produced multiple writings and research projects on the topic. Rather,
let me make a series of points here based on both my own professional
experience bridging the perspectives of religion/spirituality and the
human sciences in the worlds of disabilities, as well as share some core
observations by others that have been helpful to me in my journey to
both articulate the differences between these worlds and bridge them.

First, as I have worked with people with disabilities and their
families in many kinds of settings, I have seen and heard people express
great appreciation for the new ways of understanding disability, its
causes, and ways of supporting and treating others—for example,
positive behavior supports, self-determination, and person- and family-
centered approaches. Their origins are primarily in the worlds of the
human sciences and secular policy development. However, those ways
of understanding rarely explain the love, despair, hope, faith, meaning,
core values, motivation, yearning for relationship and community, or
sense of purpose and commitment that I hear people describe as being

most important to them. That paradox is mirrored in the image of "scientist" or "professional" that makes those core dimensions of life very hard for professionals to acknowledge, much less talk about, in their professional work and services. The paradox is deepened when individuals with disabilities and their families describe those qualities as the ones they most value in professional caregivers.

Second, I have also seen, heard, and witnessed the effects of both "bad religion" and "bad science" on people. Both are arenas where families and individuals can end up feeling judged and victimized. Both are arenas that can hurt people by overpromising the success of particular actions or treatments. In one, an individual or family can be told that their faith is not strong enough or their prayers not faithful enough. In the other, they may be told they did not follow the treatment regimen as they should have, which meant they were at fault, not the regimen. Both have their own dogmas and zealots. The tragedy is also that individuals with disabilities and families can get overlooked and indeed wounded by what one might call the friendly or not-so-friendly fire within the two realms of religion and science (e.g., "This treatment is proven to be more effective than that treatment" or "You'd be better off believing this rather than that") or even more so, between the two realms (e.g., "Your faith is not that important" or, alternatively, "We believe that God will heal this particular condition"). In the midst of the battles of theory and theology, the real stories of individuals and families are not heard or honored, and are usually completely ignored or lost.

Third, thankfully, new forms of research and discourse have grown out of collaborative attempts to bridge those walls by recognizing the role of spirituality and faith in the lives of individuals and families, utilizing that knowledge in services, and researching the impact of spirituality through the lenses of multiple disciplines (e.g., medicine, psychology, social work, psychiatry, and education). Spirituality is thus used as a social construct with a new language that enables conversation and collaboration between the sciences (often assumed to be secular) and religion. That collaboration is strengthened when one recognizes that the two are based on different ways of "knowing" (epistemologies) and valuing.

There are three writers and thinkers who have been particularly helpful in shaping my own understanding. Rabbi Jonathan Sacks, the 2016 winner of the Templeton Prize in Religion, compares the two realms in a variety of ways in his book *The Great Partnership: Science, Religion, and the Search for Meaning*:

> Science and religion are two hemispheres of human thought. . . . Some forms of knowledge need detachment, others attachment, empathy, and relationship. . . . Science investigates, religion interprets. . . . Science is the search for explanation, religion is the search for meaning. . . . Science takes things apart to see how they work. Religion puts things together to see what they mean. . . . Explanations can be proven, interpretations cannot. Science and some forms of philosophy search for the universals, religion is primarily about narrative and story.[3]

Second, Parker Palmer, who writes about vocation, truth, and communication among diverse perspectives, notes that "truth," in the world of the sciences, is something that can be proven, at least under its standards for truth. A falsehood is replaced by a proven fact. In the world of relationships and other areas more connected to spirituality and religion, someone's truth may simply differ from someone else's.[4] "My truth is different than yours, but we both can be right."

Third, pastoral theologian and former psychiatric nurse John Swinton has noted that, in the world of science, good equates to "observable," truth to "measurable," and beauty to "replicable."[5] Likewise, Swinton and Pattison argue for understanding and valuing spirituality as a "thin, vague, and useful" construct about areas of life that cannot be scientifically "proven" per se but that need a space and ways to talk expressively and functionally about them.[6]

Note the parallels in these discussions about science and religion with arguments in the previous chapter about the construct of disability: (1) Is disability "real" or a social construct? (2) If it is a construct, does its definition and use meet the core value of "functioning" effectively?

Who Is Asking and Why?

Understandings of spirituality and religion most often depend upon the perspective of who is asking the questions and why. The parallel with the definitions of disability is also obvious. Is our understanding of disability shaped by systems of classification and services or by the lived experience and voices of people with disabilities and their families?

Quality of life is a way to get at that life experience, but who is deciding what domains or areas are included in that construct? Spirituality is also a construct that plumbs a number of important dimensions of human experience. But it faces the same challenge: How do people with disabilities and their families and friends understand spirituality and religion, and are they helpful ways of understanding and dealing with their own experience?

Returning to John Swinton, he and Pattison cite other writers and researchers in noting:

> Amidst the theoretical and professional debates about the existence or non-existence of spirituality, the fact that ordinary people, patients, carers and professional healthcare workers seem to find the language of spirituality both unexceptional and helpful is often ignored. . . . It seems to be the case that many people find this language functional and helpful, particularly during times of illness and duress.[7]

In other correspondence with me, Swinton notes that the same question of whether the language is useful and helpful could apply to other key quality of life concepts:

> Most of the key concepts we use within healthcare are pretty thin and vague: health, community, friendship, dignity, compassion, etc. Whilst they may be thin and vague, they can still be useful insofar as they raise our consciousness to certain key issues.[8]

A "thick" description, by contrast, would involve much time, care, and attention to the multiple ways that spirituality can be expressed in someone's life: beliefs, practices, and rituals, all of which would involve paying much more attention to what is important to the person whose spirituality is being discussed rather than the requirements of a system of care.[9]

In other words, whose reality counts? That question is in fact the title of a book by Robert Chambers, a researcher and educator who has spent decades in grassroots community development and qualitative research, a book that is focused on neither disability nor spirituality/religion: *Whose Reality Counts? Putting the First Last.* His fundamental premise is that the "reality" that often "counts" is the reality of the researchers, policy makers, or theoreticians who set the categories of what is important and what is to be measured. Helping individuals, families, and communities should go beyond the traditional moral, religious and public policy purposes of "putting the last first," that is, helping the marginalized to be included and their voices heard. Rather, the final steps should be "putting the first last," learning how to research and help in ways that empower, release control, and get "the first" out of the way of the people being helped so they can meet the goals *they define* as important.[10] The parallels to good person- and family-centered planning and care in the world of disability and health care are obvious.

DEFINITIONS OF SPIRITUALITY

With those explorations of the relationships among spirituality, religion, and science in mind, how then should spirituality be defined? Like disability, spirituality is a concept that has multiple and evolving definitions. Most definitions in the arena of human services and supports have come from practitioners and researchers seeking ways to address both spirituality and religion in health and human services—they are looking for a *functioning* definition.

Some are quite short. Chaplain and researcher George Fitchett and colleagues in acute care medical settings describe the spiritual as "the dimension of life that reflects the need to find meaning in existence and in which we respond to the sacred."[11]

The pioneering George Washington Institute for Spirituality and Health, headed by Dr. Cristina Puchalski, cites the 1999 American Association of Medical Colleges definition:

> Spirituality is recognized as a factor that contributes to health in many persons. The concept of spirituality is found in all cultures and societies. It is expressed in an individual's search for ultimate meaning through participation in religion and/or belief in God, family, naturalism, rationalism, humanism and the arts. All these factors can influence how patients and health care professionals perceive health and illness and how they interact with one another.[12]

Dr. Puchalski shortens that paragraph to a definition similar to that of Fitchett and colleagues:

> Spirituality is the dimension of a person that seeks to find meaning in his or her life. It is also the quality that supports connection to and relationship with the sacred, as well as with each other.[13]

My own definition is similar but first evolved out of the context of my early work as a chaplain. After I became the Protestant chaplain at the large Newark State School in 1975, I led a number of weekly religious services in different parts of the facility. I soon came to see the basic spiritual needs as celebration and belonging. Celebration meant a sense of identity that had meaning and value as well as the experience of being valued in a place where hundreds of people had been sent because they were devalued by the society into which they were born. One way to show value was celebrating the image of God in every person and God's love for every person. Besides trying to embody that in my personal relationships and in religious services that focused on God's love and celebrating the lives of my congregation, my first "objective" means of pastoral care was to structure my pastoral visiting around delivering birthday cards to my Protestant flock. Cards are simple, taken-for-granted expressions of worth and value to most of us, but they are conspicuous by their absence in large institutions: Who celebrates my birth and creation?[14]

Belonging was relationships—to God, to friends, to staff, to family—but few people with disabilities talked about the importance of "belonging at Newark." Celebrating belonging, as any worship service does, often felt like a countercultural activity. A sense of belonging was more obvious in its absence through discussions about lost contact with families and communities in which people grew up. After being at Newark, my second chaplaincy role was at Monroe Developmental Center in Rochester, a place where people with intellectual and developmental disabilities were being moved, or "repatriated" in the words of policy, from the old institutions in the country to new living opportunities in the community. Margaret, one of the older women who moved there from Craig Colony, an institution that primarily housed people with epilepsy or cerebral palsy, always assumed I knew her hometown in upstate New York where she grew up before being institutionalized: "You've been there, Bill. Right? You remember the Episcopal church there, Bill, on the corner. That's where I belong."

Seeing her Episcopal roots, we helped her link to a nearby Episcopal church, where she started attending. Passing me in the hall one day, she said, "I hope you are not mad at me. I am going to that church now [rather than the service we had in the center]." I never wrote the column I wanted to write to area congregations: "Please Come Steal My Sheep."

I began to hear and see people with disabilities talk about their spirituality and faith as something that brought purpose to their life. They wanted, and want, to make a positive contribution to the lives of others. Cathy was my first teacher. She grew up at the Newark State School and moved to a group home in Rochester in the early stages of "deinstitutionalization" and "repatriation." She told her story toward the end of the first inclusive ministries conference I ever organized. As she finished, in her halting voice, she said, "It is really important for you to be nice to handicapped people but it is more important for you to let them be nice to you."

Through these and countless other experiences, with the challenge of defining spirituality in a system of services that asked, at most, what religion someone came from in its initial assessment process, my own "functioning" definition of spiritualty evolved to include three primary dimensions:

1. Core values, meaning, and identity, including what is sacred to someone
2. Connections and relationships, to self, others, the sacred, time, and place
3. A sense of purpose, call, vocation or obligation, being able to contribute.

Spirituality as Meaning and Identity

What is most important *to* someone? That is one of the questions asked in good person-centered planning along with what is "important for."[15] What are their core values that they bring to their lived experience, help them interpret and cope with that experience, and change as experiences lead to revised meanings and values? A more religious way of asking the same question is, "What do individuals and communities consider to be most sacred and holy?" Matters of the "heart" and "soul" are also common ways of talking about things that are most important to us. "What God or gods do we worship?" is another.

The core value of people in most religious and spiritual traditions is that they are created in the image of God or with a spark of divinity in them. It is a value about the gift and worth of human life. The Judeo-Christian tradition also talks about that core ritual identity as each person being a "child of God." At the core, do people value themselves, and do they feel and know they are valued, just for who they are?

One paradox is that naming or describing that which is most important or sacred to us defies clear words. For example, in Moses' question to God, "Who can I say sent me?" God refuses to give a name other than "YHWH"—"I am who I am" (Exod 3:13-14 NIV). Finding words to talk about a feeling, belief, or experience very close to one's heart (another spiritual metaphor) is sometimes difficult because of both the meaning and emotions attached. The intellect or language cannot get at the depth of feeling and meaning. Stories, pictures, symbols, or music often do that more effectively.

Let me illustrate by describing two relatively simple and engaging exercises that I have used in training sessions. The first is to ask people to write on a page of paper, "I am _____." and follow that with ten adjectives, qualities, passions, or roles that say something about who they are. I usually rule out the use of careers or job roles, partly because so much of our identity in Western cultures is shaped around what we "do." As people share their list with the wider group, two things happen. People find out new things about others whom they thought they knew, and connections between interests, passions, or qualities always get made with others. Then the conversation livens up, and the stories begin.

The second exercise is one used in cultural competence trainings called the "Family Values Exercise." Ten core values are listed on a page: tradition (ritual), hierarchy, equality, education, independence, religion, food, love, work, money, and other. Participants are asked to prioritize them, from 1 to 10, with 1 being the most important and 10 least, first in their childhood, then again from their adult lives. The leader places cards with each value listed separately around the room and asks the participants to go stand on or near the one they listed as first. As those groups start talking, what happens is the sharing of stories about how that value was evident in their personal stories. Done a second time around core current values, the conversation shifts to what brought the change and how that value is evident.

A shorthand way of talking about this dimension of spirituality is, "What means most to you?" or "What do you put your faith in?"

Spirituality as Connections/Connectedness

If the core dimension of spirituality above is shaped around "Who am I?" then the second is belonging, the "Whose am I?" question. What or who provides the central feelings and experiences of connectedness for us? Those connections can be varied:

- *Connection to/with one's self*: Common adages include "To thine own self be true." "First of all, know yourself." Feeling disconnected from a sense of self is often a sign or cause of one form or another of spiritual and psychological stress, and sometimes of mental illness.
- *Connection to/with others*: Where and with whom are your most important relationships? Who are your friends or part of your family? What culture, or cultures, are parts of your identity?
- *Connection to/with the holy or sacred*: Do you have a feeling of connection with a divine power or with other things you consider sacred?
- *Connection to/with place*: What place or places are most important to someone's identity? Often it may be hometown or country. It may be to a place in nature, which is frequently the answer, along with religious settings, when one asks the question, "What are your sacred places?" It may be a place of pilgrimage.
- *Connection to/with time*: Depending on one's culture and particular experience, the value placed on the past, present, and future may vary widely. Different people can also experience time in different ways, a phenomenon that is receiving more attention in the world of disability.[16] The value placed on time and tradition varies greatly. A common way of stating this is, "Do you live in the past, or present, or future?"

Stated more simply, whom and what do you love? With whom or what are you bonded?

Spirituality as Purpose, Call, or Obligation

The third dimension is the "Why am I?" question. A core sense of identity, including a belief or feeling of being created by God or of creation as gift, leads to the question of "How do I respond?" Experiences of deep connection in any of the areas listed above involve a sense of bond, obligation, or purpose. For example, "Those people, that experience, that place, this understanding, led to my motivation to work for . . ." is often the way this is expressed. "I have been given, learned, or experienced something fundamental to who I am. I must respond. How do I respond?" "This is what I feel called to do." That sense of responsibility is the major foundation for moral systems that recognize both freedom to choose and the legitimacy of limits and boundaries.[17] Stated more simply again, What do you hope for, where does it come from, and what does it lead you to do?

Dealing with the "Why am I?" question is also often a lifelong journey, one that is intensified at times by the unexpected, especially in the negative sense—for example, the classic theistic question, "Why, God?" or "Why is this happening, now? It's not right!" The search for answers to all of these core questions, and the journeys embodied in doing so, illustrate two of the primary metaphors of spirituality: search and journey. Rainer Maria Rilke perhaps says it most succinctly in his famous quote in *Letters to a Young Poet*: "Be still towards all that is unanswered in your heart and try to love the questions themselves."[18] Those spiritual metaphors of search and journey also point to the reason that "story" rather than "fact" is one of the primary ways for communicating what one finds about identity, community, and purpose.

THE LANGUAGES OF SPIRITUALITY

The development and evolution of spirituality as a construct and language in human services, including research, assessments, and support plans, has been the context in which the definitions cited earlier as well as my own have developed. There are multiple others. The point is not which one is right, but rather that the language of spirituality has built pathways for partnership and collaboration between the health and human services on the one hand and the religious ministries on the other. It may be obvious, but worth noting anyway, that the language, images, and concepts of spirituality used by many religious traditions and communities can be much different. They both predate and have existed alongside philosophical and scientific modes of discourse for centuries.

The common perception is that the languages of religions are belief, doctrine, or dogma. In the *Oxford Dictionary*, "belief" has two core meanings: a profession of a truth or conviction as well as "trust, faith, or confidence in someone or something." The latter is much closer to the three dimensions described above. Tim Shriver uses a different word, "grit," to describe the essence of personhood:

> The word "believe" probably comes from the Old English *belyfan*, or "to hold dear," "to love." We almost always associate "believing" with something religious or spiritual, and maybe that's appropriate since the most central religious and spiritual experience is being in love. But the root of the word also helps explain the meaning of volunteering.[19]

He uses this definition to talk about what people really mean when they say they receive more in their "giving" than the person they are helping does. When he asks Special Olympics volunteers to elaborate on that statement, people have a hard time opening up. When they do so, it is usually in the form of a story.

The crucial point is that the primary languages of spirituality (and of many religions) are less ones of theoretical or religious precepts or doctrine, however they are assessed, than they are ones of story, poetry, symbol, music, ritual, drama, and the arts. These are also the languages of community and culture, languages that are partly conceptual but also languages of feeling, passion, metaphor, and vision.

For example, in 1986, I organized a conference entitled "Merging Two Worlds" in Rochester, New York, on building inclusive congregations and communities as individuals with disabilities moved out of institutions. Bob Perske, one of the first chaplains in the older institutions to write profoundly about the pastoral and spiritual needs of people with intellectual and developmental disabilities and their families, was one of the keynote speakers. He recalled that he had just been to one of the first self-advocacy conferences in the United States, this one in New Jersey. In riding around in vans with self-advocates, he noted the popularity and power of the songs they were playing and singing together. One of his comments to the conference was that if the "disability movement is in fact a movement, then it is the only real movement in this country's history that has not had a song, or group of songs." My college background in American studies immediately knew that was true. "What's our song?" became the image I used for a number of years to talk about naming and claiming the spiritual and emotional dimensions of commitment, caring, and social change in the arena of disability.

To cite another example, the artistic expressions and gifts of children and adults with disabilities are becoming more common and acclaimed. Sometimes the art speaks for children and adults who have difficulty communicating any other way. Their art builds relationships with others, creates community connections, and changes attitudes about people with disabilities. A slight change in a symbol, such as the current revision of the standard disability sign of a wheelchair in a stationary position to one in which the wheelchair is leaning forward, and in motion, can convey immense meaning.

The importance of these languages is also illustrated in the rise of the field of disability studies with its multi- and interdisciplinary lenses of exploring and describing the experience of disability through English, literature, art, history, anthropology, sociology, and other humanities. One of the important outcomes for people with disabilities, their families, advocates, and friends is that the language of disability is no longer limited to diagnosis and assessment, and the labels, if used, begin to mean much more than an impairment or deficit in functioning.

SPIRITUALITY LEADING TO DISABILITY'S DOORSTEP

While there are all kinds of meanings associated with spirituality and even more varieties of literature and practice, the definitions cited in this chapter have primarily come out of the acute and chronic care contexts of health and human services, not out of the contexts of disability services and supports. In those contexts, definitions have been developed by interdisciplinary responses to the spiritual questions, needs, and issues faced by patients and people being served, their families, their friends, *and* professional caregivers. Many of these situations involve life and death issues, health crises, accidents, and chronic disease and illnesses. Or, in other words, the definitions and their uses have come out of experiences in which limitation and vulnerability are being faced and experienced, situations that can lead to healing but also to death, further chronic disease, or disability.

Those situations also involve dealing with the unexpected, shattered expectations, and the intense struggle to deal with the transition between a "before" and an "after."[20] Life is not going as planned. The unexpected is suddenly here. The inevitable, though expected, is now immediate. Everyone involved may be reminded of their lack of power and control, the limits of our knowledge, and the simple fact of life's limits and vulnerabilities.[21]

Crucial questions get raised of what it means to be human and finite while also continuing to love and to hope. Needed services or helpers are not available or cost far too much. People may feel like core rights are violated. Core meanings, values, relationships, and purpose come to the foreground with the intensity of the experience stripping away the everyday habits and illusions that keep those questions at bay. Independence can become intense dependence. Assumptions get made on the basis of long-held stereotypes. Spiritual or religious beliefs get tested or raised in stark ways along a continuum of faith and hope in a divine presence and purpose to experiences of anger, lament, despair, and meaninglessness. Community and connections may become most important but also the hardest to maintain when people resist asking for fear of being a burden or because it can be very difficult for others to be truly present with those going through that kind of journey.

Many people with disabilities, their families, their friends, and caregivers would be tempted to say, "Welcome to our world." That world, as noted in the first chapter, is a world where denial of mortality is stripped away along with the illusions of control and the assumptions that someone "in the know" can fix it. One's body cannot be ignored or taken for granted at times when both physical environments and attitudes play large roles in the person's experience of illness or suddenly acquired disability. Identities suddenly or gradually shift, core values get tested, love and support by others becomes crucial, or tragic in their absence, and questions of purpose and hope stare you in the face.

But the worlds of limitation and vulnerability are also worlds where the people involved (the person, their friends, and caregivers) can demonstrate great resilience, determination, strength, endurance, and commitment. It is a world where spiritual dimensions of life often come to the fore with demonstrations of their power, either positively or negatively. It is a world where cure may not be possible, but "healing" or transformation of one's identity and relationships can indeed happen. Faith, hope, and love can become paramount.

Let me illustrate this meeting of spirituality with disability by sharing the thoughts of two authors, one coming from the direction of acute medical care and the other coming from the perspective of disability studies. Arthur Frank, a sociologist, uses the core spiritual concept of "journey" to describe these potential changes out of the context of his own experience and skills as a sociologist. In his first book, *At the Will of the Body*, he uses his sociological lens to analyze his own experiences with two life-threatening health conditions. The central theme in that book is the powerlessness that people feel when they are "at the will of their bodies" but also in a health system that too easily and unconsciously disempowers them even more completely in multiple ways.[22] In his second book, *The Wounded Storyteller*, Frank posits that there are two common narrative stories of disease, illness, and disability in our culture: (1) the highly publicized and valued narrative of cure—being returned to one's former health or self—and (2) the often hidden or assumed narrative of "chaos"—having one's sense of identity, meaning, community, and purpose blown apart, with no understanding of how one can carry on. Such a narrative would be evident in a statement like "I would rather be dead than disabled." In contrast to the two opposing narratives, he posits a third, the one of "journey." After the initial crisis, a journey of adaptation, accommodation, and transformation can lead to a revised and renewed sense of identity and purpose, a resilient coping with "the new normal," and, often, a sense of gratitude, not that the disrupting event happened, but what it forced someone to confront, learn, and do.[23]

Tom Shakespeare, a leader in disability studies in the United Kingdom, talks about this as the "disability paradox" when people with disabilities report a quality of life as good as that of many others without disabilities. "Normal" assumptions would see that as highly implausible. He cites the concept of hedonic adaptation, the way in which quality of life, after a trauma, can return to near, or in fact beyond, what it was when the trauma happened.

> To be born is to be vulnerable, to fall prey to disease and suffering, and ultimately to die. Sometimes, the part of life that is difficult brings other benefits, such as a sense of perspective or true value that people who lead easier lives can miss out on. If we always remembered this, perhaps we would turn out to be more accepting of disability and less prejudiced against disabled people.[24]

CONCLUSION: MORE ACCEPTING AND EVEN MORE APPRECIATIVE

Spirituality, like disability, is also a lens or construct for looking at core elements of the human experience. One could call it a "social construct," but, as with disability, the real experiences and dimensions of spirituality are not just constructed by the environment in which one lives. The conditions we label "disability" can often be very real experiences of pain, suffering, and problems that "typical" persons do not have to deal with on a regular basis. "Typical" or "normal" is also a construction, arising in the mid-nineteenth century as a statistical average of qualities that made up the "average man."[25] Recognizing that we all have limitations is not the same as a too quick or facile attempt to empathize by saying, "We all have disabilities." Both constructs can be judged by how well they function.

The construct and experiences of spirituality may also be most clearly felt and experienced in times of trauma, suffering, accident, or death, or, as Tom Shakespeare says above, times of lived vulnerability and limits. Spirituality, as it were, leads to disability. Thus, those who have lived and even flourished with disability and limitation may often have multiple kinds of resources, including spiritual, that can assist others confronting that world personally and existentially. One hope is that the majority of people who research and utilize the construct of spirituality in health and human services will include people with disabilities in those studies and their resulting constructs. One possible result is that they begin to see the ways that concepts of personhood, supports, rights, and the crucial importance of inclusive communities that come out of the world of disability might make significant contributions to a wider discussion and search for best practices in holistic supports for anyone.

The thesis of this book is that the reverse is also true, that disability leads to spirituality, and that the constructs and "worlds" of disability can benefit from more intentional inclusion of understandings of personhood, identity, meaning, connections, and purpose that come from the construct of spirituality, the traditions of faith communities, and other forms of spiritual practice. If those two worlds can fundamentally connect with a conviction and understanding that what it means to be human is "diverse in gifts, inevitably imperfect, inescapably vulnerable, and bound to one another by a moral fabric not of our choosing,"[26] then there is a foundation for dialogue that moves beyond stereotypes, expands and deepens both constructs, and enriches the experience of all involved.

II

SPIRITUALITY IN THE LIVES OF INDIVIDUALS
WITH DISABILITIES

4

Spirituality in the Lives of Individuals with Disabilities

One way to explore spirituality in the lives of people with disabilities is through the lens of each major "kind" of disability. That is not the approach taken here for a variety of reasons. First, disability and spiritualty are being explored with a focus on connections between and within those arenas, not about perspectives on spirituality related to different forms of disability (e.g., physical disabilities, blindness, deafness) and also not about different forms of spirituality. Second, there are many people with various forms of disabilities who are writing about their own spiritual or faith journey and their reflections on it. Their voices are the ones that should take the lead. Third, most of my own experience, learning, and growth has been in the world of people with intellectual and developmental disabilities, their families, caring professionals who work with them, and communities in which they live. Their voices are the ones that primarily inform this discussion. Fourth and finally, the model of spirituality that focuses on identity and meaning, connections, and purpose is not a spirituality primarily about disability or disabilities, but rather one that can be used with any person or group of persons, whether or not there is a disability.

When everyday people talk about spirituality, they do so primarily through stories. So, to begin, this is a true story, written as a young chaplain after one of the many "sacred moments" in my own pastoral, professional, and personal journey, this one from Rochester, New York, in the fall of 1980.

A ROSH HASHANAH BIRTHDAY

It was not such an unusual scene, I thought, for a temple. A little boy, a middle-aged woman, an old man, all gathered around the rabbi after the Rosh Hashanah service to examine the Torah. They touched, felt, looked, and wondered. The rabbi had spoken that evening of each of us recovering childlike wonder . . . wonder at creation . . . wonder at God . . . wonder at the gift of belonging to his people. As the rabbi pointed out the parts of the scrolls and its coverings, *wonder* was the only word for the expression in the boy's eyes as he gazed at the strange writing and at the two companions he suddenly found with him.

And I wondered, will he ever know? Would he, or anyone, know of the vast differences between them that simply melted away in the moments of that age-old experience? At that moment, they were tied together by a common tradition. Their journeys, which had been so different, were now one.

For the Torah had been brought at the request of Harry. Harry was the oldest of three, going on seventy-five. Three score and ten plus some, and still going strong. He had gone up to the rabbi after the service and said what he had whispered to me near the end of the service:

"Can I kiss the Torah?"

As if the rabbi had nothing else to do, I thought, for there were hundreds of people there. I thought to myself, *Kiss the Torah? Harry, let's wait till another time. Wait till we come back. It has gone well tonight. Don't cause a scene now.*

But the rabbi, with patience, had simply said:

"Let's wait a bit, Harry, till people clear out."

And we did.

While we waited, Harry introduced himself to the other rabbi.

"Rabbi, my name is Harry. I'm from New York City. My brother, he sent me to Craig Colony, and now I'm here."

I thought to myself, *Here we go again.*

Harry does have a story to tell, and it goes out to everyone he meets, especially if they are Jewish. Every rabbi who came to the center where he lives heard the story at the biweekly Oneg Shabbat services. And his story, according to Harry, is something like this:

I'm from New York City. My grandfather, he sent me to Hebrew
school. I was born in England. We moved to Argentina and then to
New York. My brother, he sent me to Craig Colony. I didn't have
no seizures. I'm seventy-five years old. My mother, my father—all
died. I don't have no sister anymore. My brother, he's in the Jewish
home, but I don't know where. The letters the social worker sent
all came back. But do you want to hear this. . . .

Harry will then launch into one of the Yiddish songs he knows
by heart or recite the blessing for the Sabbath. And he'll tell you his
grandfather taught him that.

If you stop to hear what he is saying, you realize that for Harry
the only real tie he has to his family is that he is Jewish. His only sense
of belonging is that he is Jewish. He is angry sometimes, but most of
the time he simply wants to tell you his story. He wants to see whether
you know anything about his people—whether you can help get the
connections reestablished—whether your story or your journey crosses
his. *I don't belong here*, he seems to say. *I belong with my people. But
I don't have any people.* From England to Argentina to New York to
Craig Colony to Rochester. . . . *A wandering Aramean was my father.*

Harry's story, on this eve of Rosh Hashanah, was stopped only by
an overprotective chaplain, who cut in to tell the rabbi something of
the significance of the night for the second member of the trio whose
members stood looking at each other over the Torah. While Harry had
perhaps often been to temple as a child, from what Sally told us, this
was the first time she had ever been. And Sally was fifty-one.

Sally. Talk about endurance, about struggle, about patience, and
you simply have to meet Sally. She is not a person many people find
it easy to meet. The barriers she faces are too often barriers that other
people look at—and then run away from.

One barrier is that she is in a wheelchair. Many never see the person
after the wheels.

The second is the reason she is there: cerebral palsy, with severe
spasticity. It is a big nasty word that simply means she cannot control
her arms, legs, and head like others can.

The third barrier is the hardest of all for us who rely on words.
She cannot talk. She can mumble, she can murmur, she can sing, she

can pray, but the words are not our words. The ability to enunciate as others do is not there. But does she ever understand!

Sally understands. She knows what you are saying. She knows what you mean. She understands people, for she observes, watches, and listens. She knows that life can be pure hell. She knows the world is not fair. She knows that she has had to suffer, in almost geometric progression, because of her handicap. I will never forget having to help her control her arms and head as some struggling doctors at a local hospital tried to get a tube down her nose to get a specimen to test the degree of her pneumonia. In a world that too often defines dignity in terms of the degree of self-control, Sally did not stand a chance.

But dignity is what she has: the dignity of a soul that has overcome despair and overcomes it daily, the dignity of a spirit that never dies, the dignity of a smile and sense of humor that are humbling, the dignity of a curiosity that is forever on the prowl, and the dignity of a faith that literally holds her together.

Every single time in a year and a half that we had arranged something for Jewish clients, Sally was the first one there. *My soul thirsts for God.*

Every new event—an Oneg Shabbat service, a Hanukkah party, a Passover Seder, a folk dance at the Jewish Community Center—she reveled in them. *Yea my heart is glad in him.* When she sings, as when she prays, the physical effort is twice ours, the words unintelligible, but the beauty is there. *He put a song of praise in my mouth, a song of praise to our God.*

And this evening, finally, was the first time she had ever been in a temple. Why not before? Who knows? Unable? Unwilling? Unconcerned? Unsure? On whose part?

Certainly not Sally's. I had found myself unsure in the year as we moved toward the possibility for her. I knew she would live it, but would she be welcome? Would people see Sally inside, not outside? Would people stare at her, or at me? Who was I protecting?

Wait for the Lord, be strong, and let your heart take courage. When I finally got my courage together and the gates of the temple seemed open, thanks to a caring rabbi, I finally told Sally we might be able to go to the Rosh Hashanah service.

Her response made every possible and foreseeable indignity on my part seem so small. She jumped at my words with heart, soul, mind, and body. *I waited patiently for the Lord, he inclined to me, and heard my cry.* People often say that people like Sally will receive the rewards for their suffering in heaven. But, for Sally, life is now. Believing is now. Belonging is now. The rabbi spoke that evening of being Jewish, meaning being more than what one believes. It is also the feeling and reality of belonging. She also spoke of being Jewish, meaning being a *choosing* as well as a *chosen* people. Sally chose. Sally knew. Sally waited. And Sally triumphed. The rabbi at the pulpit and the Rosh Hashanah card in everyone's pew both said that Rosh Hashanah was an evening commemorating the birthday of the world. It was for Sally's world. *I believe that I shall see the goodness of the Lord in the land of the living,* says the psalmist. If it happened once, it can happen again.

So there we were. Harry. Sally. Naomi, beaming with pride because of her mother in the choir. Mark, saying all the words at the end of the sentences of the prayers, three seconds behind us, but saying them. Two Hillel students had also come with us, one of them away from home at Rosh Hashanah for the first time. An Old Testament professor, the husband of Sally's recreation therapist, read the Hebrew to her during the service. And me. What a motley band.

And there was the little boy. Now, at the end of the service, as the rabbi brought the Torah out, she helped Sally to touch and feel, and let Harry hold. Some other adults saw the scene and brought over the child—round face, wide eyes, blonde hair. They said he was from Russia and that this was the first time in his life of eight years he had even been able to be at a service in a temple. He and his family had been forced into exile from their home in order to be free to be who they are. Harry . . . coming out of decades of exile—finding a bit of who he was. And Sally, in bondage, but yet free . . . celebrating who she was, has been, and hopefully, will be. Differences in ages, nationalities, and abilities melted away in a moment when their journeys were truly one, bound together, as they have always been, by a single story: *I am the Lord, who brought you out of the land of Egypt*; by an ancient scroll: *My delight is in the law of the Lord*; and by a common song: *Let the people praise Thee. Let all the people praise Thee. Amen!*[1]

SPIRITUAL DIMENSIONS IN THE LIVES OF PERSONS WITH INTELLECTUAL AND DEVELOPMENTAL DISABILITIES

In this story, as in their lives, Harry and Sally illustrate the three core dimensions of spirituality and the interplay among them. For Harry, his core identity was centered on a search to reconnect with the stories, songs, and symbols of his childhood. He always wanted to tell anyone (especially a new acquaintance) where he came from because he wanted to see whether they would recognize any of his stories, names, or songs, clues that might help him reconnect with his past and community. Harry was in his seventies, but he had the energy and drive of a much younger person. He believed he had been sent away for no apparent reason from his people in New York City to Craig Colony, an institution for people with epilepsy about forty miles below Rochester in upstate New York. He moved from Craig to the smaller Monroe Developmental Center in Rochester and then to a group home in the community. He knew this was an opening and an opportunity. Unfortunately, the connections with his family had long been lost in a vast bureaucratic system, one that had urged families in the past to "institutionalize and forget." That same system was now focused on getting people "repatriated" in large numbers from the old and larger institutions into "the community," though not necessarily their community of origin or of choice.

Sally's intellectual ability was much stronger than Harry's. You knew she understood what she heard and what you said. But she could not talk like Harry. It took much longer to make sure you were on the same page with her. An early wooden version of a communication board with holes and pictures she could hit with her thumb was one way of liberating her mind and spirit. I never learned much about her childhood, but it was clear her core identity as Jewish was the one thing that she clung to and yearned for in a world that had misjudged her time and time again.

Harry and Sally both illustrate the ways that the core spiritual themes of identity, purpose/calling, connections, power/control, and cultural tradition interact with the fundamental policy values of independence, productivity, and community inclusion. Their lives also illustrate the ways that spirituality connects directly with the constructs or understandings of disability, rights, and person-centered planning. The table below outlines some of these connections.[2] A quality of life framework and analysis should include all of them.

VALUES, SPIRITUALITY, AND PRACTICE

Fundamental Human/ Spiritual Question	Core Spiritual Theme	Policy Value	Practices
Who am I?	Identity/ meaning	Independence	Person-centered language and planning; enhanced growth toward independence
Why am I?	Purpose, calling, vocation	Productivity	Employment, volunteering, making a difference
Whose am I? Whom do I belong to? (Also closely related to culture, below)	Community connection	Integration/ inclusion	Community inclusion, participation, least restrictive environment; citizenship, friendships
Where have I come from? Who are my people?	Cultural traditions, preferences, ways of understanding	Cultural competence	Person-centered planning, connections, honoring choice and uniqueness
How do I shape my own destiny? Why do bad things happen?	Choice, control, power	Self-determination	Advocacy, rights, empowerment

Let us turn now to the first three dimensions of spirituality: identity, purpose, and community connection and some of the ways they are expressed and experienced in the lives of people with disabilities, particularly intellectual and developmental disabilities.

Identity and Spirituality: "Who Am I?"

Any response to the fundamental question of identity, "Who am I?" or "Who are you?" is tied up in the ways our identities have been constructed in the personal and social contexts in which we live. The World Health Organization's model of disability says the same thing. Identity is shaped by experiences with family, community, cultures, and systems in which we grow up and that surround us, full of expectations, projections, stereotypes, beliefs, and cultural norms.

For Harry and Sally, their identities had been profoundly shaped by their spirituality, but that had been superseded by a cultural and historical context in which people with disabilities were institutionalized either for their own protection (e.g., a "colony for epileptics") or for the protection of their families, to ease the burden of caring for someone who had multiple caregiving needs or was assumed would never develop. Although this may sound callous, Harry and Sally were lucky in comparison to so many who were institutionalized early in their lives, because they both had experiences that shaped a fundamental part of their identity as Jewish, an identity they knew they shared with millions of others without disabilities. Being Jewish provided both an anchor and a hope. So many other institutionalized people did not have the opportunity to know the roots and communities from which they came. Their primary identity became institutionalized as "resident" or "patient," an identity conferred by others marked by conformity to rules, practices, and expectations without opportunity or permission to practice choice, discover passions, and grow into who they could be. Compliance, rather than choice and community, was the norm. A woman named Mary, who was in one of the institutions I served as chaplain, said it quite poignantly: "I learned you can say too much in this world. People don't like if you talk too much. You get in trouble. So I changed. Now I just be quiet. I should know, dear. I am eighty-eight years old. I learned that when I was fourteen."

Compliance still can be the primary concern of community-based service providers. There are at least two spiritual consequences. First, a primary focus on compliance often leads to an organizational culture based on fear, making it hard for anyone to flourish. People with disabilities whose lives are primarily lived within community service systems face the same risk of having to conform to organizational norms and policies as do those living in an institutional setting. This is simply because serving people together in residential or program groups makes it very hard to provide true person-centered services and supports. Second, people with visible disabilities living in integrated community settings also face the daily struggle of negotiating the same currents of compliance all of us face—the currents of expectations, projections, and cultural norms through which we encounter others. Having a visible disability can make that much more difficult in a culture focused on appearances of perfection. Surviving and thriving takes both a strong sense of identity and the support of others.

For example, Wilfredo Gomez, a Latino man with cerebral palsy, in an article "When Strangers Read My Body: Blurred Boundaries and the Search for Something Spiritual," describes his experience of dealing with strangers who feel that his visible limp entitles them to relate to him in ways that often involve spiritual themes. After telling a stranger that he was not a Bible salesman simply because he was disabled and carrying books and notebooks, the stranger gave him a blessing as he departed. Gomez writes:

> Experiences such as these . . . are an ensemble of others' attempts to construct my body linguistically, spiritually, and physically. . . . Some strangers conflate my physical disability with other emotional, cognitive, psychological, or learning disabilities. What goes unsaid speaks volumes: the assumptions, expectations, prejudices, dominant narratives, language barriers, and behaviors that already seem to frame the extent and context of these interactions, even before they occur. . . . The odd and frequent interactions I have with strangers leave me reflecting on how disabled bodies are often dismembered by others, however unintentionally. They leave me wondering what, if any, religious or spiritual base do my interlocutors subscribe to? Do they perceive me as lacking a spiritual or religious base? Do they assume that I have a religious or spiritual base? . . . I do have a spiritual base; however, I value the

space to explore and discuss my spirituality in my own time, rather
than in response to strangers' responses to me.[3]

For many people with disabilities, the responses by others based on
spiritual or religious assumptions are far less ambiguous and far more
hurtful. In the history of disability, spiritual and religious assumptions and beliefs have sometimes led to or sanctified reactions of pity,
fear, exclusion, and murder. Contrasting assumptions about disability
representing the presence of evil or the demonic vied (and still do) with
assumptions about identities as "holy innocents" or "eternal children."
Many people with visible disabilities and their family members can
recount their own stories of being approached by strangers who, on the
one hand, think they are helping by commenting on the specialness of
either the person with the disability or the parent or, on the other, feel
entitled to take the liberty to question why the parents allowed their
child to be born into the world.

There are at least two major dynamics at work in these kinds of
interactions: (1) the spiritual/religious/cultural assumptions and attitudes of people without disabilities used in their interactions with and
treatment of people with disabilities and (2) the impact *on* the spirituality of people with disabilities who are devalued on the one hand or
seen as "holy" or "superhuman" on the other.

With regard to the first, three core spiritual/religious assumptions
can be conveyed to people with disabilities and their families, according
to stories I have been told. The experiences have often happened to
them more than once.

First, there is the story that begins "You or your parents must have
done something wrong." That assumption can be stated explicitly or
implicitly even before finding out what might have caused a disability
or whether the question of "Why?" matters to the individual or family.
The default question, "Why are you disabled or different?" is often
more an issue for the stranger than for the person or family.

The second begins with the question of "Who sinned?" frequently
accompanied by faith-based prescription on how to fix it: "If your faith
were strong enough, or if you prayed hard enough, you could be cured
or healed." That can be followed, or preceded, with a request by a
nondisabled person or group of people to let them touch and "pray

over" the person with the disability. Harold Wilke, the clergyman born without arms who delivered the prayer at the signing of the Americans with Disabilities Act on the lawn of the White House, once told a story about a man with an obvious disability who had developed the perfect rejoinder to someone telling him, "If your faith were strong enough. . . ." The man simply replied, "If your faith were strong enough, you could cure me." (Note both the reversal of responsibility and power in that response as well as the sarcastic rebuttal.)

Third, at the other end of the spectrum, one of the basic assumptions running through many cultural and religious traditions is that people with a disability or their parents are "so special" and "inspiring," as "overcomers" or heroic role models. That feeling may be true for the person saying so, but it also quickly puts distance between the speaker and the person with a disability or family member. Overcoming one's disability or flourishing "in spite of the disability" then can become a common social narrative or expectation. Most individuals and families will say, if asked, "I don't want to be your inspiration. I am just trying to get by. Just let me be human." Stella Young, an Australian woman and comedian with significant physical disabilities, became an icon for her TED Talk in which she described that attitude as "inspiration porn."[4]

Other theorists and writers use different frameworks for describing some of the same experiences. Wolf Wolfensberger and colleagues, famous for the frameworks of normalization and social role valorization, outlined multiple ways by which cultural assumptions and practices devalue individuals by cutting them off from typical relationships and assigning negative deviancy roles and labels.[5] Both actions lead to multiple ways of "wounding" a person's identity. Those wounding experiences can include rejection; being cast into deviancy roles such as subhuman, menace, object of ridicule; scapegoating, segregation, loss of relationships and control; and impoverishment of finances and experience. Attitudes become stereotypes that lead to prejudices that, when embodied in policy and norms, become discrimination. Jack Nicholson, an emeritus professor of journalism, notes seven stereotypes often seen in media images or subconsciously reflected: "pitiable and pathetic," "super-crip," "sinister, evil and criminal," "better off dead," "maladjusted," "a burden," and "unable to live a successful life."[6]

These negative attitudes, expectations, and projections, many made worse by religious sanction, can impact one's sense of identity so profoundly that it often seems amazing when individuals with various forms of disabilities and their family members demonstrate by both their beliefs and actions the kind of positive outlook and determination shown by Harry, Sally, and countless others. Those of us without obvious disabilities wonder whether we could respond the same way.

However, a spirituality based on gifts, strengths, rights, and individual worth can be a strong or stronger force in claiming and shaping an identity beyond those negative norms. That spirituality is built on the core belief and value that every person and life has divine value by virtue of being created in the image of God or being a member of God's people. Every person is equal in the sight of the Divine (whatever name one uses for the sacred), and everyone should be treated in the same way you would wish to be.

The more "secular" version of that belief is that every human being is entitled to basic rights, respect, and equal opportunities for participation in human community. Every person has strengths and gifts as well as weaknesses and limits. Usually, those beliefs and values first become experienced and real in the love and care of parents, family, and close friends. The positive spiritual dimensions of identity and meaning can then be nurtured by the support of multiple others through valued relationships and through organizations and structures such as faith communities, schools, recreational programs, and other places in which people are included and supported in their discovery and development of their own unique identity. Stated differently, spirituality can also be utilized to help individuals and communities in shaping a different "construct" of what disability means to them as well as becoming an avenue and resource for an enhanced sense of quality of life.

One recent research study illustrates that very point. There have not been many research studies about how young people and adults with intellectual and developmental disabilities define the role of spirituality and faith in their own lives. Eleanor Liu, Erik Carter, and colleagues at the Kennedy Center at Vanderbilt University help reveal the importance of that inquiry in a qualitative research study asking young people with autism and intellectual disabilities to talk about their experience of faith and its place in their lives. Their core findings revolve around three themes: (1) the importance of expressions of faith in their lives (e.g., prayer, beliefs, congregational activities, rites of passage, social connections, and opportunities to serve); (2) the importance of faith and spirituality as a personal affirmation, a journey, a source of belonging and help, and a way to "go deeper"; and (3) the impact on their views of self by feeling known, understood, and accepted by God; the role of their disability in that identity; and the ways that identity can be expressed and used. The research team writes that the participants

> vividly spoke about the importance of faith in their lives. . . . Although it should not be assumed that faith is universally important to people with IDD, neither should it be assumed to be irrelevant. In fact, our study further highlights the importance of talking to young people about what matters *to them* in their lives and striving to support those things well. Our findings further suggest that faith may be expressed and valued in ways that are more similar than different among people with and without IDD.[7]

In a different form of research and writing, Karin Melberg Schwier describes the lives of twenty people with intellectual and developmental disabilities whose lives are "flourishing." Flourishing begins by finding what is *important to* people with disabilities by focusing on their "passions" in the context of supportive relationships. Through asking, listening, supporting, building on interests, having the will to chase discovered passions, and picking up the pieces when something changes, she outlines ways of helping individuals find out what means the most to them, what gives their life meaning, and what are the core pieces of their sense of identity.[8] Identifying and pursuing "passions" is yet another way that spirituality can be tapped in positive ways to help answer the question of "Who am I?"

From Identity to Purpose and Calling: "Why Am I?"

Discovering, shaping, and living out of a core sense of identity and meaning leads directly to a second dimension of spirituality: purpose, calling, and vocation. When people can find out who they are, what they love, and how they can use their core beliefs and passions, the right word is indeed "flourish." We can know and feel that in ourselves just as we can see and feel it in others, by either its presence or its absence.

The spiritual questions and journeys of purpose are lived out in the lives of people with disabilities in different ways, just as they are for anyone. Finding a sense of identity and purpose that can be lived out in vocation, employment, and contribution is one form of taking responsibility as "productive" citizens who make a difference and contribution to their community.[9] The shifting historical images of people with disabilities from outcast, deviant, vegetable, patient, or consumer to citizen, self-advocate, employee, or contributing member represent enormous social, cultural, and spiritual shifts in vision and understanding. In Sally's life, being and becoming Jewish was a core part of her identity, partly because her severe spasticity prevented her from "doing" much else, especially decades ago when assistive communication devices were not nearly as sophisticated as they are now. For Harry, his implicit and often explicit question was, "Why did I get cut off from the community in which I already had a role and purpose?"

The complex paradox of the "Why am I?" question for people with disabilities is that, while they may be trying to figure out their own sense of purpose and vocation, the power of their labels is such that others without explicit disabilities too often define that role and purpose as "being disabled," end of question. On the one hand, the assumption is that there is nothing someone with a disability can really do to be a contributing member of a community. One is a "consumer," not a producer or contributor. Judith Snow, a prominent disability advocate, organizer, artist, and community builder, talked about this phenomenon in a very powerful plenary presentation during the 2014 Summer Institute on Theology and Disability:

> Now [to] the concept of disability, some of the things that I am are a lack. They're a problem. They're something that's supposed to be fixed if possible, hidden sometimes, and at the very least considered to be a problem, something that shouldn't have happened. So, I'm sure others have had this experience, but a person who's been labeled, and certainly myself, we tend to go through life with people looking at us, and it's almost like they're not really looking at us. They're looking over our shoulder at somebody they think we should have been. So somebody's looking at me, they're seeing the person that

doesn't use a wheelchair. Somewhere in their mind they're seeing the person that they think I would have been if I didn't have spinal muscular atrophy, they're not actually seeing me. Because for them to see me is somehow not right, not bearable to them.[10]

On the other hand, the purpose of their lives can be interpreted, as Wilfredo Gomez said earlier, as a special vocation or role of helping people without disabilities to learn important lessons about their own lives.[11] The frustration with that assigned role is expressed by disability advocates, like the late Stella Young and others, who resist the notion that their purpose in life is to be someone else's inspiration. Later in her talk, Judith Snow said, with her great sense of humor and irony:

So I began to create a list of the various gifts that people talk about when they talk about being with someone who has been labeled disabled in some way. The first and foremost one, kind of the one that Enosh expressed, you might call gifts of hospitality, where the person is opening a space for deeper listening as well as opening a space for people to feel happier. Over all those years that I was exploring this particular approach, I'd say about 85 or 90% of the people that I talked to said that being with someone that had been labeled disabled in some way just simply made them feel happier. Now, I think if a company, if a corporation in North America ever caught onto this idea, you know there's a really simple way of making people feel happier, there might be a big turnaround in our economy, but so far nobody's caught on.[12]

Judith went on, with her own grace and insight, to note other things people say they have learned from people with disabilities, including "grounding" and "slowing down." Toward the end, she said:

In that world the concept of disability is very powerful. I expect to be able to say that I'm disabled in that world. I expect to be able to say I have certain rights based on the fact that my body doesn't work very well. But inside that kind of thinking I'm not ever able to move very far out of my place. And my place does not allow me to express my deep personal giftedness, or my deep personal relationship with life itself. In that kind of thinking what I am is exactly the replication of what the category says I should be, and nothing else is important in that kind of thinking. So I'm in a sense not a created being inside that thinking. I am just another piece of a machine.

So here's the tricky part. Both are true at the same time. I do live in a world that's about the law, and the categories, and structures. I'm also in a created relationship with the Creator of the universe. A personal relationship with the Creator of the universe. Both are true. So I am in fact both disabled and not disabled at the same time.

So for me the question is from which stance can I live my life most powerfully both for myself and for the community—or in other words for the church? From which position am I more able to contribute? More able to experience a fulfilled life? More able to encourage faith in the community? And more able to bring richness as a legacy beyond when I will personally be present in the world? I personally don't think disability is the position from which I can be powerful. I think disability is the position from which I can be controlled.[13]

Judith was also noting a second complex paradox about the "Why am I?" question. For many people without disabilities, as they think about people with disabilities, the *questions of purpose and vocation* are overshadowed by the *question of cause*. "Why am I?" gets drowned out by "Why are you disabled?" What caused the disability? Whose fault? That version of "Why?" looks backward while the "Why?" of purpose and calling usually looks at the present and the future. The latter can certainly include questions of "What have I learned or am I supposed to have learned because of my disability?" and "How has it impacted my sense of calling?" but many people with disabilities must deal so often with the reaction of others to their disability instead of being able to move to a conversation about preferred identity, interests, passions, being able to do what they love, or what they believe is their purpose. In other words, right after the typical social interplay of meeting someone, sharing names and where you live, assumptions about disability, explicit or implicit, impede the usual follow-up question, "What do you do?" because the assumption is "nothing."

Spirituality, Connections, and Community: "Whose Am I?"

Having conversations and opportunities to find and develop identity and purpose is not simply an internal process. That journey depends on relationships in which people are valued, listened to deeply, respected, encouraged, supported when the journey is not smooth, and celebrated when they reach goals or simply for who they are. The isolation and loneliness faced by so many people with disabilities can make that process very difficult. People around you who believe in you and who see your gifts and strengths as well as your limitations are essential.

The spiritual importance of connections can be seen in multiple dimensions of someone's life—to the sacred or Divine, to place, with culture, to one's history/time as well as to friends, family and other forms of community life. Depending on the person, each of these can be crucial in the "construction" of an identity in which disability is but one part, in having the rights to participate in community life, in maintaining ties to places and cultures that are important to someone, and, most importantly, at least through the lens of disability services, in enhancing individuals' assessment of their own quality of life. Having friends and relationships and a sense of belonging are the most consistently cited factors that impact quality of life in a positive way.[14]

That importance of community and belonging is the fundamental reason "inclusion" is the primary value in services and supports for people with disabilities and their families. Providing services "in the community" and enabling people with disabilities to use "natural" and "generic" supports are parts of the value and mission statements of multiple caregiving organizations and systems. However, one can be "in" the community but not be "part of" that community. Inclusion is too frequently and too easily defined as "where someone belongs" rather than the "To whom do you belong?" or the "Whose are you?" ways by which we have phrased the crucial value of community and connections. Having rights to participate can get you a space in a community setting, but rights only provide the opportunity for the development of relationships, connections, memberships, and roles that help one truly belong.[15] Beyond inclusion is belonging.

That is why helping or providing opportunities for people to explore each of the spiritual dimensions of connections mentioned above is so important. Planning discussions and supports should include the following:

1. Enabling people with disabilities, like anyone else, to have experiences or be connected to whatever they consider to be the Divine or sacred and to communities of faith or organizations

who share those same interests and beliefs. That can be expressed by the belief or actions that convey "I belong to God" or "I belong to [a particular faith community or organization]."

2. Finding the core interests and passions that help individuals develop a sense of their own identity and purpose and facilitating ways to connect them with other individuals or organizations whose passions or interests are the same (e.g., fishing, sports, music, volunteering, collecting, entertainment).

3. Determining what kinds of places are most important to someone and why. This usually is expressed as helping someone find a sense of home, but there can also be other places that people consider part of their identity and journey—"That's where I grew up" or "That's my favorite place to go" or "That's the place I feel most connected to the Divine."

4. Maintaining ties to the primary cultures of which one is a part, or wants to be, which includes customs, holidays, rituals, habits, foods, places, art, music, and more. Place and culture are also expressed in connections with family.

5. Honoring people's history and their own sense of time. Both remembering and hoping are fundamental expressions of human spirituality. Doing so speaks to the importance of helping to maintain long-term relationships, especially for and with people with intellectual and developmental disabilities. Their lives are lived primarily in the world of human services, where staff turnover makes long-term relationships extremely hard to come by.

These different ways of honoring the importance of connections and friendships point to the powerful potential of connections made through faith communities because all five of those kinds of connections can happen in those settings. In each of these kinds of connections, there is the opportunity for moving from relationships to real trust, friendships, and memberships where one can be known and valued for many parts of one's identity and story. Being known well is a deep and rewarding experience that most people value and need. Being known well means knowing beyond the surface of labels and stereotypes, whatever they are. Individuals can be known in a congregation or community as "that disabled person" but not known by their name or by the depth of their story. Our social addiction to surface identities and fame is at play here. Robert Raines, a noted Christian preacher and writer, said it most succinctly in a quote that has become a personal mantra in my own journey: "We all think we want to be well-known when what we really want is to be known well."[16]

CONCLUSION

Stories take precedence over theory in talking about spirituality, particularly in trying to explain a spiritual conviction or experience. Hopefully, this framework, or model, of spirituality will help many others to make connections to their own experiences and stories, or help to induce meaning from experience. The power of the spiritual dimensions of life can be evident in both positive and negative experiences and stories, and it is notable in the presence or absence of significant relationships. More stories will emerge in the spiritual dimensions of personal development, friendships, employment, caregiving, community building, and other dimensions of life.

Another paradox is that spirituality often gets described as values, beliefs, and concepts/constructions that generalize and cover multiple experiences in human life. But it is in the particularity of stories and experiences that we most feel attuned to spiritual experiences. General terminology can be used to talk about the importance of identity, core beliefs/passions, purpose and calling, and connections by using the languages of religion, the social sciences, laws and policies, and the arts, but we experience and know the depth of that importance in the stories of our lives and the lives of those whom we know. Describing spirituality in an objective, measurable sense is extremely hard, if not impossible, except through multiple forms of actions (e.g., "How often do you go to church, pray, etc.?") or by attitudes or beliefs that assume, rightly or wrongly, spiritual experiences associated with them. Like the concept of "flourishing," one might say, "I know it when I see or feel it," again, in terms of its power for good or for bad or its presence or absence. For example, Jean Vanier once shared the story of his visit to an orphanage for children with disabilities where he walked into a ward of eighty beds, and no one was crying. To cry means to hope for a response, hopefully of comfort, and to give up crying is to despair of relationship of connection.

Spirituality is observable and, indeed, sometimes replicable, when experiences and stories are connected and shared. Knowing somebody well, in the best sense of that term, also requires vulnerability and trust, perhaps on both sides. Those qualities are often hard to come by when people have been wounded by experiences and attitudes or by someone's perception of the roles they are expected to play. One common perception about the spirituality of individuals with intellectual and developmental disabilities is that they are so emotionally open or, stated differently, they are too quickly willing to be vulnerable and trusting, despite their painful experiences. A different framework might reverse that analysis and see that form of behavior as a huge thirst for real connection and relationship. The crucial antecedents of trust and vulnerability are keys to exploring spirituality not only with people with disabilities but also with their families. The difference is that most parents, who are usually people without intellectual disabilities, have the "typical" capacity to mask both distrust and vulnerability, sometimes because of bad experiences and at other times simply because of the necessity of getting on with the tasks of parenting and caregiving that face them every day.

5

Spiritual Development and Formation
From Child to Adult

One perspective on spiritual development and formation are the famous verses from the apostle Paul in 1 Corinthians 13:

> When I was a child, I talked like a child, I thought like a child, I reasoned like a child. When I became a man, I put the ways of childhood behind me. For now we see only a reflection as in a mirror; then we shall see face to face. Now I know in part; then I shall know fully, even as I am fully known. (vv. 11-12 NIV)

Hear the perspectives of four young adults with varied forms of intellectual and developmental disabilities on a panel at a conference in Portland, Oregon, entitled, "Treat Me as a Member, Not a Mission," in response to a question: "How did/does your disability contribute to your choosing the spiritual path you have?"

MAX: I chose the church I attend because I guess I don't get judged.

JADE: I knew that I wanted to believe in a God who saw my disability as I did. I do not want to believe in a God who pities me or puts me on a pedestal as society tends to.

PETER: My father raised me as a Christian. I was never a person to experience religion in public, but I did believe that God was in charge. As I grew up I moved toward the idea that people are in charge of their own lives, while I still believe in God. My father always said that I was here for a reason and it is because of my belief in this idea that I have survived and beaten the major conflicts that have been a part of my childhood.

ELEANOR: I was a semi-believer when I was a kid due to my families' beliefs, but I made a personal choice to become a full believer after high school. I've been through many obstacles and health issues from the day I was born, and it took faith and strength to keep moving forward and striving to be the who I am today. My faith has helped me see the person I can be despite all the challenges I face due to my disability.[1]

The spiritual growth and development of children and adults with intellectual and developmental disabilities has often been conceptualized through religious education for children, no matter the age. The young adults in the quotes above are certainly not talking in "childish ways." They, like other young adults with disabilities, have no desire to be treated as children, although they may have been conditioned to act that way through programs that equated mental and chronological ages.

Our core premise should be that the spiritual growth and development of children and adults with intellectual and developmental disabilities is just like anyone else's spiritual growth and development. That growth and development needs to happen in contexts that are "typical" and "normal" as much as possible. As for anyone, that development (1) starts in experiences in early childhood, nurtured through caring relationships within spiritual communities, and (2) needs to be addressed in age-appropriate ways as children grow into adults. Participation may call for creative communication and teaching strategies to enhance learning. A frequent outcome is that those strategies may be just as beneficial to "typical" children. Spiritual growth needs to be viewed as part of multiple dimensions of one's life (as it is for everyone) and as crucial at numerous times in one's life-span. The life-span approach parallels psychological theories of growth and development. As spirituality is intentionally nurtured in the context of relationships and community, one can then construct (and resurrect) a theological understanding of that journey through the concept of formation.

Spiritual growth and development can and does happen outside of communities of faith or religion, but the involvement of children in any culture's communal expressions of spirituality is essential to their growth and development. The anecdotes that come to mind are stories by Jean Vanier, founder of the L'Arche communities, among others, on his visits to large institutions where there were wards of children with disabilities, often in beds they rarely left. They had no significant early experiences of bonding and care, leading to behavior showing no "faith" or "hope" that anyone would respond.[2] A large unit called "Disney" in the Newark State School where I served as Protestant chaplain in the 1970s was not much different, but thanks to caring staff and a dedicated team of "foster grandparents," these kids did get out and up and received a fair amount of individual attention.[3] Early bonding first happens typically with one's parents and relatives. However, as children grow, spiritual growth and development through experiences of love and acceptance by others in a faith or cultural community is also critically important.

USING A "NORMAL" MODEL TO FRAME SPIRITUAL GROWTH AND DEVELOPMENT

A central assumption during much of the past fifty years has been that spiritual and religious education needed to look like "special education." Special education became the first true cultural affirmation that every child could learn and had the right to an education. Thus "special religious education" utilized strategies, resources, and practices from special education, which included segregated settings in faith communities that mirrored those same kinds of settings in public schools, because these children "obviously" learned in different and special ways.

A second, and related, assumption has been that religious education is seen primarily as individual understanding of the tenets of a specific faith tradition, or, in other words, as an exercise of reason and intellect. The focus was on special education tools that helped children learn religious and spiritual concepts—Bible stories, songs, or basic beliefs that more "typical" children learned. That belief about belief, so to speak, missed the ways in which spirituality is learned and developed through multiple forms of communication and communal relationships such as simple participation in communal events—singing, rituals, and habits of worship—as well as learning by observing and practicing. That belief particularly impeded spiritual growth and development when it came time for religious rites of passage in which the prevailing practice was that all children must learn to recite a creed, read and comment on a "Torah portion," understand what was meant by communion, or have enough intelligence to make a so-called adult decision. If young people could not demonstrate "understanding" in the traditional ways, then they were often denied access to participation in the rituals and traditions that defined full membership.

Those assumptions are changing rapidly, but they may still be encountered by parents and individuals working with children with intellectual and developmental disabilities. Educators and parents have learned that children with sensory and motor disabilities are perfectly capable of learning in "typical" ways. Children and adults with intellectual and developmental disabilities are often capable of demonstrating learning by behavior if not words. The demonstration includes their own unique insights; their own understandings of spiritual identity, faith, hope, and love; and their commitment to, and joy in, a community of faith.

In the past fifty years, theologians and social scientists have also developed theories of how everyone grows and develops, not just in the explicitly religious dimension. Psychologists like Piaget, Erickson, Kohlberg, and Kegan developed what are now considered iconic models of the stages and dynamics of human growth and development. In a parallel framework of religious development, James Fowler published his famous book *Stages of Faith* in 1981.[4]

The issue with James Fowler's framework is that it is very abstract and difficult to translate into practice. John Westerhoff's *Will Our Children Have Faith?* is a much more useful model for application to practice and ministry. Formerly a professor of religious education at Duke Divinity School, Westerhoff's book argues for a reinterpretation of our understanding and practice of religious education.[5]

Westerhoff's central thesis is that religious educators, beginning in the late 1800s, adopted the "school" model, in which "schooling" is the context for growth in faith, and teaching and instruction is the means. Thus, as already noted, the teaching of concepts and beliefs was most important, a very problematic proposition for some children with intellectual and developmental disabilities. Westerhoff suggests that actual learning takes place in all the experiences of a community of faith. The life of that community occurs in and around its rituals, its group experience with each other, and its shared action for and with others. Rituals signify the importance of order and predictability. Shared experiences are the ways by which a community relates to its members and then "images" those experiences, interpreting them in the light of its tradition and story. Action together is the stance of the community in relation to society and others.[6]

Using the term "enculturation," Westerhoff makes a plea for the thoughtful, planned use of all those components of a community of faith as the context for spiritual/religious education and growth. Faith is not simply knowledge; rather is it "an action which includes thinking, feeling, and writing, and it is transmitted, sustained, and expanded through interactions with other 'faithing' selves in a community of faith."[7] His fourth chapter, entitled "Life Together," outlines a model of faith development. It came from his observations and synopsis of individual stories and accounts of life and growth in faith. He cites four "styles" of faith, purposefully using "styles" rather than "stages": experienced faith, affiliative faith, searching faith, and owned faith.

Up until age six or seven, children first *experience* faith. What matters most is the experience connected to the words of faith, not the words or concepts themselves. Those experiences are provided by the communal environment and interaction with others in which children are surrounded by love, acceptance, affirmation, and celebration.

Around ages six or seven until sixteen, give or take, children begin to consciously *affiliate* with their faith community. Affiliative faith is characterized by (1) a sense of belonging to a community through participation in, and contributions to, its life; (2) a dominance of affections, through music, drama, storytelling, whereby one experiences wonder, mystery, fear, joy, and the like ("a religion of the heart"); and (3) the sense of identity that comes from the authority of the community and its story—not the individual. One is to learn and internalize the story of the community. That story provides one's identity; for example, "I believe this because I am Jewish and that's what Jews believe."

As one moves into adolescence and young adulthood, one frequently begins to *search* for answers to new questions. That searching is characterized by the growth of doubt and critical judgment, experimentation with different traditions and religious alternatives, and an enthusiastic commitment to all kinds of persons and causes. To use oversimplified stereotypes, one may illustrate the differences between affiliative and searching faiths by contrasting the "hometown church" with the "college chapel."

Finally, as one grows into the adult years, one begins to form one's own individual sense of spiritual and religious identity. *Owned* faith is a way of saying, "This is my story, my spirituality/faith. I own it and I am owned by it." An owned faith is characterized by a willingness to witness in word and deed, a realization of the importance of community, the search for such a supportive community, and often a renewed emphasis on spiritual habits and practices like prayer, worship, and ritual.

In a key metaphor, Westerhoff asserts that the four styles are not stages or a process. He compares the relationship among them to differences between small and large trees. Imagine a tree with one, two, three, or four rings, with each style being added over the one before:

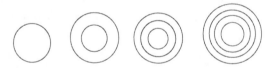

FIGURE 5-1. *The Four "Styles" of Faith*

The implications are fourfold. First, small and big trees are both full and whole trees. A small tree is just as much as a whole tree as a large one. Styles of faith are complete and whole in themselves. One grows to fulfill potential, not to be "bigger than." Affiliative faith, for example, is just as much faith for that person as owned faith is for another. Second, like the parable of the sower and the seed, growth comes from having the proper environment and is arrested if the proper experiences and relationship are not present. Each tree does its own growing. We do not control it. Third, growth is gradual, not rushed. Finally, growth never eliminates previous rings—one does not lose nor can one wipe out earlier faith experiences/styles and the impact they had. In addition, one does not lose the needs met by the different styles.

Westerhoff's model is particularly useful for envisioning the spiritual journey of children and adults with varying levels of intellectual disability. It frames growth and formation in ways that move beyond reason and understanding as the primary goal and indicator of success.

EXPERIENCED FAITH

Being included in a nurturing environment is crucial. All children need a place where love, trust, acceptance, hope, and celebration are experienced and felt when they are young. The learning of songs, stories, and symbols may be an outcome, but it is both the experience and expression of spirituality and faith in the company of other children and adults that is most important. Touch can be crucial. People with intellectual disabilities who are sometimes labeled as having a "mental age" of less than five or six can and do participate and respond in their own ways with clear excitement and joy in those kinds of environments. As they grow older, they still may respond to, and enjoy, participation in environments where those same experiences can be found, even if their level of support needs are still labeled as severe or profound, and one is unsure of their intellectual understanding.

Most, if not all, faith communities do not say participation by children at this age, or this style of faith, is not important, with the implication being that real growth and learning takes place after reaching an "age of reason." Rather, a community's act of faith embodies the importance of including children in the life of that community. Many faith traditions have rituals of blessing, dedication, or baptism of an infant. Those often involve a pledge by the wider community to share in the responsibility of raising this new "child of God." Thus, the primary focus of inclusive faith communities should be that all children (and adults) have the experience of being included in this kind of loving and faithful community. In the famous words of Jesus to a disapproving crowd of adults, "Suffer the children to come unto me." "Suffer" I interpret as "Sit on your expectations about decorum, importance, behavior, and learnedness, and let them be here!"

Many adults with intellectual disabilities have been described as having a "childlike faith" because of their level of intellectual development. Common stereotypes include "eternal children" and "holy innocents." The problem is that those stereotypes lead to low expectations. Adults with intellectual disabilities then respond to those low expectations with behavior like that of children rather than responding to expectations that they can learn and grow. Those adults may need simplified lessons, more experiential ways of learning, and different ways of communicating, but such teaching strategies do not mean that adults should be treated like children. Jeff McNair, a professor of special education who has done extensive work in religious education with people with intellectual and developmental disabilities, notes that a faith community should treat anyone in ways appropriate to their chronological age, not their mental age.[8] For example, Jade, one of the panel members in the opening quotes, said she did not want to be pitied or put on a pedestal.

The questions of how to include people with profound levels of intellectual disabilities is one of the perennial challenges facing communities committed to inclusive spiritual supports. One of the answers is the simple importance of friendship.[9] Other strategies come from a very creative process for adults with severe and profound disabilities to tell their own story and work with symbols, pictures, music, and styles of communication.[10] As John Swinton notes, that process takes a true "space to listen" to the various ways that individuals communicate.[11] Authors like Jean Vanier, Henri Nouwen,[12] and Christopher de Vinck[13] write about the profound power and impact that persons who communicate very little can still have on the spirituality of others. Rather than seeing such a person through the eyes of despair, their perspective is one of seeking to understand and appreciate the mystery of the person within while also utilizing communication strategies that are adapted to that person, without being or sounding childish.

A "childlike" understanding of faith, or an "experienced" style of faith, also does not preclude unique insights and questions. Almost everyone who has worked with children and adults with severe or profound intellectual disabilities can tell stories about what one might call a "flash of brilliance" that can come from their own unique perspectives. One of the most powerful stories I have ever heard came from a parent describing her experience of searching for a church home after a move from Pennsylvania to South Carolina with their "moderately retarded, micro-cephalic daughter" who was now a young woman. After trying several churches, including one with a youth or young adult group where something happened that was the opposite of welcoming, the daughter came home with her parents one night and said, "No more church!" The mother admitted to me that she took on her maternal authority by saying things like, "We have to find a church home. We need to be able to worship God." Whereupon her daughter remarked, "Well, it may be God's house, but he's not home." There are just as many on the "positive" side of inclusion. Kathleen Bolduc, the Presbyterian mother of Joel, her son with autism, recounts multiple experiences in Joel's upbringing in their congregation in which atypical behavior and statements led to profound moments of revelation for many present, including one in which he burst back into the sanctuary just before communion after a bathroom break saying, "Wait for me! Wait for me!"[14]

AFFILIATIVE FAITH

As children grow with age and experience, the next style of faith in the Westerhoff model is one in which they affiliate with a specific faith tradition as part of their developing identity. They learn many of the basic tenets of that community and tradition. They will claim an identity as Catholic, Jewish, Muslim, and so on. Their own beliefs are ones learned from the community. Authority rests in the designated roles within that tradition and in the beliefs of that tradition. The focus is more on obedience and emotions, with intellectual learning focused on the tenets of that tradition.

This style of faith, and its typical age range, is usually the time that someone goes through a rite of passage into the "adult" community of faith—confirmation, bar or bat mitzvah, adult baptism, and the like. For example, I grew up as the son of Southern Baptist missionaries. Our family was frequently in church in a variety of cultural contexts. When I was six, I "went forward" in the Baptist tradition of making an affirmation of my faith in Jesus and asking to be baptized. Truth be told, I had almost no intellectual understanding of what I was doing. For me, as for many others, rites of passage are ways of claiming that one is growing up and is entering (or wants to belong to) the adult community of faith. The community expects that ritual for you and invites you to be guided by your family and the tradition in doing so.

The involvement of children, young adults, and adults with intellectual and developmental disabilities highlights at least four crucial dimensions of these transitions. First, when a child, person, or family is not welcomed or invited or is denied the opportunity to participate in those rituals of transition, the pain experienced by individuals and families can be intense and long lasting. Just ask any group of families with children or adults with most any kind of disability, and a significant number of them will share those negative experiences, especially if you are a trusted and safe listener. A Roman Catholic mother told me that when her son was refused first communion because of his intellectual disability, "When they rejected Michael, they rejected me."

Second, the converse is also true. When a community of faith essentially says, "We will figure this out and make it happen," those rites of passage can be wonderful opportunities to build relationship and to help someone be known to the wider faith community. Those occasions can have profoundly positive impact on individuals, families, and congregations. The documentary *Praying with Lior* tells one such story about Lior Liebling, a young man with Down syndrome and his bar mitzvah, a story about a rite of passage celebrated by the synagogue that had raised Lior in its midst and recognized his particular gifts.[15] The Archdiocese of Newark is one place where children and young adults anywhere on the autism spectrum are welcomed and enabled to go through rites of passage such as first communion and confirmation by having religious education teachers collaborate with professionals who know and use applied behavioral analysis to help each person learn how to participate to the best of his or her ability.[16] This kind of program is also a prime example of the ways that the worlds of scientific, educational, and spiritual/religious understandings of disability can collaborate.

Third, when clergy and congregations are sensitive enough to realize that many adults may not have had the opportunity or invitation to participate in a rite of passage, age does not make a difference in the power of its impact. Rabbi Evan Jaffe, the longtime, beloved rabbi at the Jewish Community Center in Flemington, New Jersey, had a part-time role as Jewish chaplain at a nearby residential institution. Years ago, he decided to help each person in his charge learn as much as possible in order to go through a bar or bat mitzvah if he or she chose to do so. I was present at one bat mitzvah in which the retired parents and siblings talked about the profound meaning of the ceremony for them because they "had given up on their community of faith recognizing their child."

The fourth implication is that this style of faith illustrates the importance of an affiliation to the development of one's sense of identity. Calling oneself Jewish, Baptist, and so on, is usually a typical, valued identity in a community. That identity is frequently accompanied by new forms of participation in a spiritual community such as using one's gifts, helping others, or taking some role in a congregation. Those all contribute to the dimensions of spirituality of meaning, identity, purpose, and connection—"I am Muslim and I belong." "You are now Muslim and you are part of us." When others see individuals with disabilities taking part or being given a part in their community, perceptions often change because they see ways that people with disabilities are givers as well as receivers, responding to their own sense of call by using their gifts and interests in service.

The importance of the first two styles of faith and spiritual development points to the importance of experience and practice. Every faith community, or indeed cultural community, has its own "culture," often with unspoken expectations, rules of behavior, and traditional or habitual ways of doing things. Westerhoff framed the process as "enculturation," a term that can apply to many forms of spiritual communities. The autism community talks about the importance of learning "the hidden curriculum" in any social setting. Using other language from the world of behavioral sciences, these are "functional skills" or, one might say, "membership skills."[17] Those unspoken rules and rituals may not be known until they are broken. Learning that curriculum takes more practice than intellect. Practice is aided by inclusion from one's early years—having multiple opportunities over time to learn from the ways that hidden curriculum is taught and modeled by both adults and peers.

SEARCHING FAITH

In teenage and young adult years, many people who have grown up in communities of faith or in other cultural forms of spiritual communities and networks often begin to question the beliefs or traditions in which they have been raised. In my experience, many teenagers and young adults with intellectual and developmental disabilities have their own journeys of searching and questioning. For a first example, the panel of young adults who were quoted at the start of this chapter talked about their own spiritual searching and journey. In other parts of their conversation, they noted the importance of spirituality as part of their own identity:

> JADE: As a member of my church, I know that I have great potential and a personal relationship with God. When Jesus suffered in the garden of Gethsemane, He knew all of the afflictions of mankind, including mine. This means that God knows what my life is like as a person with a disability. I was given this disability to gain experience here on earth, and I'm expected to enjoy my life. My mission on earth is to advocate for other people with disabilities so that they can be happy. Disability is just a way of life for those who are born with it. One day, I hope it's kind of mundane.

> PETER: I see myself as a bit different and a bit weird, but in actuality, I'm just Peter. I'm as normal as I need myself to be. I'm myself and no one else.

> ELEANOR: My life was up and down with confidence and self-esteem, but as I got older and hung out with those that accepted me for who I am, I saw God through them, and I knew I was on the right path in life. My disability makes my faith stronger, because without it I wouldn't be here and as healthy as I am.

> MAX: My faith gives me a lot more confidence in myself.

They also responded to other questions related to the importance of their faith/spirituality, how faith helped them to cope with their disability, and the ways they were involved with their own faith communities.[18]

A second example comes from a qualitative research article by Erik Carter and colleagues involving twelve teenagers / young adults with disabilities, many of them with autism. The four primary findings were (1) the importance of faith in the lives of the young people, expressed in ways that are more similar than different for people without disabilities; (2) the importance of prayer as spiritual practice; (3) the positive impact of faith and congregational involvement; and (4) their positive self-perceptions in the context of their faith.[19]

OWNED FAITH

Those quotes and research point to the understanding of faith by the young people involved. They had now chosen to believe and practice in ways that we describe as growing up. They sought to live out that faith in their own lives and in their faith communities. They noted the importance of spiritual practices for their own identity and support.[20]

Some people with intellectual and developmental disabilities may never go through a time of searching that can lead away from a faith given to one that is clearly "owned." The temptation is to think that people with more severe levels of intellectual and developmental disability may not have intellectual ability to question, search, and make their own choices. That assumption should be explored critically and carefully. People with more severe cognitive limits may not have had opportunities to participate in relationships or faith communities in which they have been welcomed participants instead of people to be cared for. Other people may have had very negative experiences that have led them to associate spirituality or faith with exclusion or rejection. Finally, there is limited research on the spiritual lives of people with more severe cognitive and communication limitations, but that does not mean an absence of anecdotal accounts of relationship and experiences reported by others that testify to the spiritual gifts and life they have encountered in those relationships. One needs only to go to the multiple stories coming out of the L'Arche communities and the work of Jean Vanier to illustrate the phenomenon[21] and to theologians such as Hans Reinders who have written about theology and profound disability.[22]

John Swinton and colleagues in the United Kingdom have been leaders in demonstrating how this kind of research can be done. In several projects they have used qualitative, participatory research methods to explore the spirituality of persons with severe or profound intellectual disabilities. In one of their projects and reports, called *Everybody Has a Story*, their key findings include the following: (1) People with intellectual disabilities often do not have relationships in which others take significant time to listen to the complex ways they may communicate. (2) They are rarely given the choice and opportunity to enter those kinds of relationships, either in spiritual communities or elsewhere. (3) They "have an intuitive sense of their inner being and an urgency to narrate their life story to others. The expression of a person's inner spirit is fundamental to their psychological and spiritual wellbeing." (4) Activities that utilize both multiple communication strategies and an investment of time point to the eagerness to share their own story, to encounter another, and to be engaged in a spirituality that is more one of being and relationship than of mind and ability.[23]

Story may well be a key framework for describing spiritual growth within a never-ending story whereby one first experiences the community's story, learns the origin stories, finds one's place within that story, perhaps leaves it behind to try others, and then, eventually, claims the story as one's own. In fact, story and theological reflection are the only ways one can capture the depth of those experiences.

SPIRITUAL AND FAITH DEVELOPMENT: FORMATION AS THE LENS

The crucial importance of relationship, friendship, careful attention, and community noted by both Swinton and Westerhoff moves us away from seeing spiritual development as a primarily cognitive process. Rather, the deeply historical concept of "formation" is a more accurate framework to use in describing and understanding spiritual development. Formation comes from religious communities (i.e., religious orders of priests, monks, and sisters) as well as early understandings of professional formation and apprenticeship. Formation focuses more intentionally on identity, relationship, mentorship, openness to call and vocation (or purpose), as well as acting together in community. Formation is also closer to the Latin root of the word for education,[24] *educere*, which means to "lead out," a sense of journey and empowerment rather than an imparting of objective knowledge or the acquisition of specific skills.[25]

When most of us describe our own spiritual journey and development, we may talk about changing beliefs and practices but even more so our relationships with the people who have been mentors, teachers, and guides in the context of a caring community. The importance of key relationships and friendships cannot be overestimated for anyone, including people with disabilities, and especially people with intellectual and developmental disabilities. Inclusion then becomes imperative, with its intentional focus on enabling and sustaining relationships for people who have often been left out of those opportunities where they are valued and mentored. Thereby, they have opportunities to learn by cognitive skills as well as by watching, modeling, and practicing in the context of caring individual and communal relationships. In those relationships, the inner life, emotions, stories, symbols, rituals, and traditions can be experienced, heard, seen, expressed, learned, and practiced.

A second critical reason for utilizing the concepts and practices of formation in understanding spiritual development is that it also provides a framework for interpreting and understanding the ways in which caregivers and friends of people with disabilities often describe themselves as *being formed* by these relationships and friendships. Formation thus allows for the ongoing discovery of truth in the context of authentic relationships, including the formation of professionals in caregiving relationships. Formation provides a context for talking about professional commitment to calling as well as an opening for honesty by professionals about the ways they are shaped by the people whom they serve and who may call them "friends."

CONCLUSION

There is both promise and problem in using any kind of developmental framework to describe and explain spiritual or psychological development. The promise is that it can provide adults in a wide variety of teaching, caring, and leadership roles a way to interpret and guide behavior as well as to build communities of practice, as it were, in which children, young adults, and adults can learn and grow. If one compares Westerhoff's notion of "styles" with other models of human development, such as those in Erikson, Piaget, and Kegan, there are overlapping similarities in which their perspectives complement one another.[26] If these theoretical frameworks are seen for what they are—constructs that guide understanding and behavior—rather than as objective reality, then their gift and power is enabling teachers, mentors, leaders, and friends to meet people wherever they are in the integrity and wholeness of their identity and journey. The question yet again is whether a given theory or construct functions effectively for all involved.

The problem with developmental and stage theories is that they frequently become ways of comparing and valuing one stage over another. Even more problematic, human beings quickly begin to believe that they can control those steps and stages. Creating environments in which people have the resources and relationships to learn and grow can then turn into systems that assume the capacity to process people from one place to another and, as it were, turn them out as "finished products" on the one hand or cast them out as "defective goods" on the other.

Those human tendencies exist in religious and spiritual communities just as they manifest themselves in educational institutions and human service systems. There is less danger of doing so if those communities are indeed focused on the spiritual components of life (more so than the physical and psychological) in which one can be known and cared for while also knowing and caring for others. The reason is that assumptions about truth as observable, measurable, and replicable can more easily lead to the temptation to build a controlled process. Most technological advances in fact depend on that way of defining truth, but not so in spiritual formation.

Religious and spiritual systems can also, in fact, become controlling systems. However, when they do so, it is usually more explicit and obvious. Claims of absolute truth can be countered by other interpretations within a given tradition as well as by scientific and other forms of knowledge. Thankfully, there are also religious affirmations about the humility that should frame any assumptions about the human illusion of controlling growth. The apostle Paul, for one, says it succinctly when talking about who gets the credit and power: "I planted the seed, Apollos watered it, but God has been making it grow" (1 Cor 3:6 NIV).

6

Spirituality and the Transition to Adulthood

Spirituality and transitions are inextricably linked. If we see spirituality as journey, journeys are from one time to another, one place to another, one state of being to another, one identity to another, one age to another, and multiple other forms of changes in one's life. There are spiritual dimensions of important life transitions such as birth, adolescence (with typical rites of passage in spiritual communities), moving into adulthood, marriage, parenthood, major geographical moves or career changes, major health issues, retirement, aging, and end of life. All along the way, there will be other transitions in relationships as loved ones move, leave, or die. Transitions involve loss, gain, and adaptation. They can be called "liminal" spaces and times, an "in-between" earth and heaven, times in which core spiritual issues and feelings rise to the fore as one may feel uprooted from the "normal" before settling into something new.

People with disabilities and their families, like everyone else, experience most of these transitions. In its life-span perspective, the Missouri Family to Family Project notes, "Throughout our lives, we face questions and search for answers that will assist us on the journey to a meaningful life. This is true for everyone, especially for individuals and families that experience a disability or special healthcare need."[1] Their model cites six major stages: prenatal/infancy, childhood, school age, transition, adulthood, and aging / end of life. Note that in their six stages, as in much of the world of services and literature for families with members with disability, the word "transition" means *one* major life period: the journey from school age to adulthood.

Why? For most "typical" young people and their families, that period entails some anxiety but also excitement as they usually leave home, go to college, or find a first job, all ways of moving into the expected social roles of adulthood that blend independence with responsibility. That may be the journey for young people with sensory and motor disabilities, but for many families with children with disabilities, especially those with intellectual and developmental disabilities, *transition is a crisis.* It means a move from "entitled" participation in school and education to a life where there are no guaranteed entitlements, services, or programs. It is a time when questions of capacity, ability, and support get raised yet again as people deal with decision making, where to live, what to do during the day, and who pays for the needed supports. Using the words of Hans Reinders again, it is one more example of moving from "before" to "after."[2]

In this case, however, transition is not the before and after an onset of disability, but before and after the end of school, a transition that often kicks up both new and old questions of identity, purpose, and community: "Who am I?" or "Who are we now?" "What now?" "Where are supports?" "What will I/we do?" That's why the word "transition" has come to mean what it does in the worlds of disability. It is also why the role of spirituality and spiritual supports needs to be explored and utilized to help someone grow from being perceived as a child to being perceived as an adult in the lives of congregations and communities.

SPIRITUAL SUPPORTS IN TRANSITION AND VICE VERSA

As "typical" young people grow up, finish high school, and go to college, find a job, and move out of the house, anxieties and celebrations are both part of the process. In the United States, for example, think of the usual anxious rituals of searching for a college and then waiting to hear from both the admissions and financial aid offices. It is also a time of celebrating admissions and choices by family, friends, and acquaintances, including the recognition of admission, graduation, and transition in social, spiritual, and cultural communities. The excitement often masks the anxiety of separation by both parents and young people who are moving into new contexts where they begin making friends all over again. If someone is staying home and getting a job or going to a college or trade school while living at home, it is still a time of transition into new environments, relationships, and, eventually, employment, usually followed by moving out of the family's home "to be on your own."

In both scenarios, new expectations arise as the long-range questions of vocation, job, career, and calling rise to the fore. The actual experience of making choices and decisions as well as taking responsibility for them can be very different than the anticipation and dreams one had for doing so. Our culture says those are the lessons of "growing up" and "finding one's self" in the transition to adulthood, a process that may last much longer than expected. Both young adults and parents may need a variety of supports in this process of taking on new identities, losing, adding, or altering community relationships and developing both the personal focus and skills related to purpose and direction.

Thus, it is a time of spiritual searching and questioning while one acquires new freedoms, opportunities to make choices, and responsibilities. If a young person has been part of a faith community, it may mean questioning the faith tradition in which he or she has been raised, trying or moving to new faith communities and traditions or none at all, or moving into new roles within those communities. Hopefully, young adults will feel ongoing interest in their journey from their faith and cultural communities and a sense of welcome and support when they are "home." It may mean finding new mentors and guides as they search, experiment, and grow.

Granted, the expectations of this transitional journey are very generalized and may not fit what happens to many young people and families. But for young people with intellectual and developmental disabilities and their families, they may not fit at all. Depending on the level of disability, there are very different assumptions about capacity for independence and fewer options for moving away from home. Rather than decreasing responsibilities for supporting their child, parents often become more responsible because their child / young adult is no longer in school for most of the day. A young person with a disability may have older siblings who have left home and gone on to new lives or younger ones who leave while they are still at home. Young people with disabilities often have fewer opportunities to be with peers if they and their families cannot find programs or jobs that enable them to be out of the house. Thus, they have fewer opportunities to make choices, find new friends, and try on new roles. Ideally, in school systems, planning for the transition has started as early as age fourteen. The latter years of school, which can be till age twenty-one in their case, may involve community-based job training opportunities that lead to employment possibilities upon graduation, but that is certainly not a guarantee.

If young people with disabilities and their families have been part of faith communities, other dynamics may come into play. I have been involved in helping a congregation think through the question of whether a young person with a disability, who had grown up in a youth group, should continue to remain in that youth group as he moves into his early twenties. Individuals and their parents may prefer that option because it has been such a valuable experience. However, questions arise when all of a young person's peers have moved on. That young adult may not have had the same kind of relationships with the younger teenagers moving up into the youth program. That concern can get heightened as the young adult with the disability grows older and the age gap grows wider. A congregation may feel like continued participation in the youth group is inappropriate but it has not thought through what it could do. For individuals and parents, even the act of raising that concern may seem like taking away valuable supports while offering nothing in its place. Just as in a school system, situations like these call for proactive transition plans to prevent reactions to a de facto situation that has gotten very awkward.

How might that happen? An ideal scenario might look something like this.

――――――

A young person with a disability has been included in religious education, youth programs, and other parts of a faith community from the beginning. She has made friends with peers and with others in a congregation. She has had the opportunity to prepare for and go through appropriate rites of passage that happen in the teenage years. As conversations in the youth group begin to turn to what its members are doing after graduation from high school, the congregational and youth group leadership know that this transition time may be a hard one, especially for the young person with a disability and her family.

The leadership does not try to protect that young person from these discussions but rather begins a process of talking with the family to plan together what might happen that would help their daughter transition into new roles in the faith community as an adult member.

In addition to being aware of the life-stage transitioning tools for families with children with disabilities, the leadership offers to be part of transitioning planning that is done with staff from the school system. If the latter years of high school involve job training and community-based opportunities to try different kinds of jobs suited to her interests and skills, the leadership can work with the family to utilize the social capital (i.e., networking power) of the congregation to help find community opportunities they can connect to school personnel, job coaches, and others working with the one "aging out."

In addition, they know two kinds of planning and support strategies that come out of the worlds of disability that could be utilized in the context of the faith community. The first is using one form or another of person-centered planning, which can be done with an individual, her family, and others who know her well.[3] That planning process might address the overall transition of this young person and her family as she graduates, or, more specifically, the transition that could happen within the faith community. The focus is on affirming the move into young adulthood and exploring new, adult-oriented roles within the congregational setting for participating in the community and contributing to it—taking on adult volunteer roles, participating in young adult activities or women's groups, and the like.

The second tactic might involve the development of an organized circle of support within the congregation that would work with the individual and family to carry through with the person-centered plans and adapt them as appropriate. That circle of support should be seen as a way for other members of the congregation to work together in a meaningful strategy of support, one that can focus on new opportunities but also on building new relationships. There is no one way to run a circle of support, so it could be fairly informal or more structured, like the model in the Mennonite booklet *Supportive Care in the Congregation*.[4] In that model, the circle is organized for the long haul. It may change membership as people come and go, but it is a form of commitment by a faith community to support an individual and his or her family over time, through transitions to possible jobs, a supported living program outside of the family home, and changes in the family system.[5]

———

The importance of that scenario is that a family is not left alone to fend for themselves as they move with their son or daughter through these transitional years to adulthood. The value of sustained friendships and supportive relationships over time is immense. A parent of a young woman with Down syndrome once told me about their daughter's transition through the help of their congregation. As their daughter moved into her teenage years, the parents realized that they had been overprotective. They then worked with the church staff to help their daughter become part of the youth group where she began to do things apart from her family and to gain skills in relationships and independence. As the daughter moved into her young adult years, the church helped them to find a faith-based residential provider. Their daughter was then able to move out of the family home, just as most of her peers had done, but stayed connected to the church. The mother concluded her story by saying that their faith community had provided the context where they could begin to let go, to help their daughter become more independent, and to move into adulthood, all with the support of the congregation.

The connections and community were maintained, albeit changed, and the congregation provided a context in which core issues of identity (independence, choice, responsibility, etc.) could be worked out as well as the development of adult ways to use and contribute her gifts in response to her own mix of interests, passions, and call. To change the language back to the world of disability services, the core issues being worked through were independence/self-determination and productivity (employment), both with the help of the connections in her congregation. Faith communities are largely an untapped resource in this area of policy and practice.

INDEPENDENCE AND SELF-DETERMINATION:
PRINCIPLE AND PARADOX IN TRANSITION TO
ADULTHOOD

The values and principles of independence and self-determination drive much of the policy and practice for public and private supports for people with disabilities. They are values that Western societies take for granted for its citizens, in theory, if not always in practice.[6] Independence and self-determination were not part of disability services until the disability "movement" began in the middle of the past century. The social assumptions—the social model in play at that point in history (primarily the medical model)—assumed that people with disabilities could not be independent. In the case of people with intellectual and developmental disabilities or mental illness, they had neither the capacity nor the right to self-determination.

Acting on the values of independence and self-determination does present spiritual and theological paradoxes. A total focus on independence as the primary value can ignore the ways in which all of life is both dependent and interdependent. As with any paradox, the spiritual task is to live with and between the balance of what appear to be opposites. The choice is not an either/or but a both/and or, in this case, an "all three/and." A spiritual and religious perspective would state, "We are all dependent creatures, dependent on the God who has created the world, but called to respond independently and collectively to the gift of that creation in ways that recognize our profound interdependence with all of creation."

The concept and value of self-determination faces the same critique. The spiritual dimension of identity and meaning affirms the importance of being able to make choices that are true to one's interests, passions, and values, but, from the perspective of the spiritual dimension of connection, none of us is completely self-determined. We are shaped and bound in a web of complex relationships with others and our environment. From the dimension of purpose, a spiritual/theological perspective would say that each of has a unique vocation, call, or path that is also gift, not completely of our own choosing: "Did I find my vocation or did it find me?"

The values of independence and self-determination have been explored from many perspectives and issues without ever considering their application to people with disabilities. One recent example is surgeon Atul Gawande's recent book, *Being Mortal: Medicine and What Matters in the End*.[7] The book begins by critiquing the ways the medicine has taken over the period of aging and end of life, resulting in paternalistic systems that take away personal choices by making people into patients and residents of nursing home, where their lives are determined by others for their own "health and safety." The capacity to shape the end of one's life in ways that affirm one's identity, connections, and sense of purpose is simply lost or greatly limited. Alternatively, medicine has another extreme of simply "informing" patients about diagnoses, treatment options, and implications, and retreating to the stance of autonomy and independence that says individuals are totally responsible for their own choices. Gawande believes that people want guidance rather than being controlled or being left alone. He argues that people do not need to sacrifice autonomy or the capacity to shape their own end of life story just because they need help.[8]

Gawande advocates for "a better life" and way of handling aging than simply a denial of mortality. That happens, he says, through being able to let go, have difficult conversations, and shape caring supports that respect people's desire and capacity to shape their own story and life until the end. He notes that there is no such thing as complete freedom. We are inherently dependent on others, forces, and circumstances beyond our control. Gawande also cites philosopher Ronald Dworkin on autonomy as the responsibility to shape our own lives "according to some coherent and distinctive sense of character, conviction, and interest." He then writes, "All we ask is to be allowed to remain the writers of our own story."[9] In the last half of the book, he explores systems of care such as the original versions of assisted living, Bill Thomas' Green House movement, and hospice care in which policies and practices are built around individual wishes and values for maintaining what is most important to them in their final days. Life is meaningful, he notes, because it is a story.

The paradox here is embracing and managing our inherent dependence while also trying to "remain the authors of our story." Being the author of our story may be ultimately an illusion based on the ideal of autonomy, one that disregards the ways that our own stories are bound up in others and theirs in ours. If that is true, it still does not diminish the values of independence, self-determination, and the "capacity to shape one's own story," especially in the face of social models and systems that have acted as if people with disabilities and those nearing the end of their lives are totally dependent and have no ability to indicate their choices or preferences. In fact, those values have arisen as a rallying cry and countercultural antidote in the face of those authoritarian and patronizing systems that too often separate individuals from the possibility of living their story in accordance with their own values, relationships, and purpose.

I was part of several initiatives in "self-determination" right after the turn of this century. People with intellectual and developmental disabilities had been moving out of institutions for forty years. A wide diversity of community-based programs had grown up that supported individuals and their families while also providing varied forms of residential options, mostly group homes or supported living options. "Self-determination" arose because most services were "slots" in day or residential programs that someone had to take and then fit into those programs. Person-centered planning and self-determination became ways of shaping supports and services to fit the person, rather than the other way around. They both give individuals and families much more control—the capacity to shape their own stories, especially when the self-determination model included the possibility of individual and family control over public funding allocated to provide those services and supports along with the power and responsibility to hire their own staff.

The Robert Wood Johnson (RWJ) Foundation piloted the first self-determination initiatives. Their four principles of self-determination were freedom, authority, support, and responsibility—individuals with their families had the freedom to choose what services and supports they wanted and how they were to be developed or delivered, the authority to approve the use of the funds allocated to them through a fiscal intermediary, and the responsibility not only to use those funds wisely but to contribute to the community through employment, volunteering, and other channels. In fact, "spiritual communities" were cited as a primary venue not for supports but for making contributions to one's community.[10]

In New Jersey where I worked, a small planning grant from the RWJ Foundation led to a statewide pilot of a self-determination initiative for one hundred individuals and their families. In this early model, funds were allocated based on needs and supports assessed by a planning team that included individuals, families, support brokers, and state personnel. Once the budget was allocated, the individual and family were responsible for working with the support broker to develop the planned supports. They had the authority to approve use of the funds allocated to them.

There was tremendous excitement, energy, and commitment unleashed by this vision and pilot through the power to shape supports around an individual's needs, strengths, and dreams. The Essential Lifestyle Planning process captured both what was important to someone and what was important for them.[11] The pilot was not problem free. It was very hard work for everyone, but its capacity to recognize and honor individuals' identity and values, their sense of purpose and dreams, and to build onto the current relationships with family members, friends, and other community connections enabled very meaningful lives and great loyalty to the "program." For me, the "spirit" of the pilot was exciting in multiple ways, one of them being the opportunity to include and involve people's spiritual life and community if that was their choice.

Some might quickly question the capacity of individuals with severe intellectual and developmental disabilities to make the choices necessary in that process. Capacity is, however, not simply a legal term for autonomy and rights. In this process, the individual and those who knew him or her best were at the heart of shaping the plan and subsequent supports. No matter what level of intellectual capacity individuals have, those closest to them know their preferences, things they like and don't like, and have the capacity to interpret preferences and choices from ways that the individuals are able to communicate.

Those convictions have become the foundation of a relatively new legal principle and process called "supported decision making." Supported decision making has been developed in parallel with the UN Convention on Rights for Persons with Disabilities. Supported decision making is an alternative to guardianship and limited guardianship, both of which have the possible outcome of decisions being made by a guardian that does not respect the needs, wishes, and preferences of the individual. Supported decision making, on the contrary, respects a person's autonomy, will, and preferences by recognizing that all persons have legal capacity and the right to exercise their choices through accommodations and support in partnership with a group of *trusted* supporters.[12]

Supported decision making is based on the social model of disability rather than a medical model. Rather than using the "best interest" model of guardianship, supported decision making is based on the "best interpretation of will and preference":[13]

> In my opinion this approach does not deny that in certain situations somebody else and not the person concerned shall formulate decisions. However, the tool that shall be used when it comes to these kinds of situations is not the "objective best interest" test but rather the "subjective best interest" test. While the former test is based on what others think to be objectively the best for the person concerned, the latter test is built on the respect for values, faith, will and preferences of the person concerned.[14]

Both self-determination and supported decision making thus have spiritual and theological foundations as well as legal ones. My reasons for describing them in some detail is directly tied to the ways in which individuals, families, friends, and caring communities, including faith communities, can support young adults with an intellectual and developmental disability as they move into adulthood. Both explicit and implicit circles of support based on compassion and friendship have great potential to empower and support an individual with a disability by respecting and honoring their spirituality, that is, their sense of identity, meaning, preferences, connections, and purpose. A community's faith tradition already calls upon its members to recognize each other's uniqueness as a child of God, their interdependence, and the resulting injunctions to respect, care for, and love one another. Thus, a community of faith can be an unparalleled source of support in collaboration with other public and private supports for individuals with disabilities and their families.

CONTRIBUTION AND EMPLOYMENT

Person-centered planning, spirituality, and theological traditions all affirm that an individual has gifts and strengths as well as needs for support. In the public arena, that belief translates into helping young adults entering adulthood find a job or another way to contribute to the wider community by taking into account their passions, dreams, and sense of purpose. In a religious and theological context, it means all people are called to use their gifts in service to others and the ongoing care for the world that God has created. In other words, the call of most spiritual and faith traditions is not just to care for and support those with needs or who are marginalized, but also to recognize that those individuals with disabilities are likewise challenged to respond to God as faithful followers or disciples. Many people without obvious disabilities will testify to the profound contributions that people with disabilities have made to their own lives. Many people with disabilities, however, also want the opportunity to use their own talents and interests to make a difference, as well as help support themselves, by contributing in socially valued ways to the wider community that go beyond helping others to work through personal questions and issues about disability.[15]

The social coin of contribution in most societies is through a job, defined in disability policy as the value of productivity. For most adults, having a job is central to a sense of identity and purpose. The question "What do you do?" follows most introductions. Having a job, being needed, making a difference, being productive, earning a living, providing for others—all make a huge difference in our self-esteem, our sense of hopefulness, and our identity as citizens and members and managers of many other identities (e.g., religious, cultural), roles (family, community), and vocations. As Frederick Beuchner famously describes our life journey, "Neither the hair shirt nor the soft berth will do. The place God calls you to is the place where your deep gladness and the world's deep hunger meet."[16]

SPIRITUAL AND RELIGIOUS FOUNDATIONS OF WORK

There are deep spiritual and religious understandings of the importance of work.[17] The biblical tradition starts with God at work, producing one thing after another, creating the world in six days. On the sixth day, in this first chapter of Genesis, God created man and woman in God's image, to "rule over" and "have dominion" over the earth (v. 26 KJV), phrases that in Hebrew can also mean "take responsibility for" or "manage." On the seventh day, God rested. However one interprets the Genesis story, it is a story of work as creation, care, and responsibility, an expression of the bounty and "goodness" of what was created, and a recognition of the sacred rhythms of work and rest.

In the second chapter of Genesis, commonly called the second creation story, the order is a little different. God created the garden of Eden and put man in the garden "to till and keep it" (v. 15 RSV) After Adam and Eve are expelled from the garden, they are told that they must work, only now it will involve more travail and suffering than it did before their disobedience. In the Jewish tradition, we are called to the work of *tikkum olam*, repairing that breach between God and humankind.

The Hebrew Bible continues to tell the story of a God working with God's people, redeeming them from work as slaves in Egypt, and continually inviting them to be faithful followers, stewards, partners, and collaborators in God's ongoing act of creation. In an economy that was primarily agrarian, farmers (employers) were commanded to leave a tenth of their field so that the "widow and orphan" might harvest their own food.[18] When the dream of a return from exile in Babylon was foretold, the vision was that everyone returned, including the "blind" and the "lame."[19] Everyone belonged. All had a part. To be faithful meant integrating that faith in the realms of daily personal, civic, and economic life. For the prophets, one of the core indicators of a righteous society was the way that society treated those who were marginalized.

In the New Testament, the call to faithful service by Jesus goes out to everyone. In the parable of the talents, the question was not how many talents you had but what you did with them.[20] The apostle Paul wrote of the gifts of every single person, every part of the body of Christ having value and being inseparable from the whole, noting that everyone was called to be faithful stewards of the gifts and talents that God had given them.[21] Like the prophets in the Hebrew Bible, he noted the extra care and attention that needed to be paid to those considered to be the "weaker members of the body" (1 Cor 12:12-26) In fact, the "lesser parts" may be the most important.

As with the prophets, this biblical tradition envisions a community where everyone has a place and sense of purpose. The whole community takes special responsibility for ensuring that those on the margins have that same opportunity. In other traditions, there are similar injunctions. For example, in Islam, "With works comes dignity . . . no one enjoys a meal more than a person who actually gives their time, effort, and labor to go out and to provide a way to take care of themselves and their families."[22]

From Faith to Work

Faith communities base their vision, service, and outreach on scriptural traditions and community needs. The possibilities for concrete and practical forms of support depend only on the vision, commitment, and gifts of other members. Several "employment ministries" have grown up around the United States to help unemployed members or others in the community find jobs.[23] Most of them have not included people with disabilities but could do so. The Putting Faith to Work project is one that specifically focused on congregations as a resource for helping people with disabilities find jobs.[24] These scenarios and examples came out of the project:

- As a person with a disability grows up in, becomes included in, or returns to a congregation after an injury, clergy and others can get to know the individual's need and dream for a job or way to contribute to the community. A small group or existing ministry within a congregation responds, gets to know the individual, and works with her on her interests, passions, gifts, and dreams. In other words, they help a person define her own sense of vocation and calling. Then they begin to utilize all the members of the congregation (employers and employees and people connected to many others) to help this young person find an opportunity. This is not an employment program per se. It is about helping one of their own find a job and transition into adulthood.
- In a Pennsylvania congregation, a job coach working with a young man with autism who loved power tools talks to the teenager's pastor. They come up with a way for him to use a leaf blower to help care for the church grounds. He becomes so good at it that a local landscaping crew notices, leading him to a paid job.
- A veteran returns home with a physical disability, one that perhaps keeps her from doing her previous job. How might the community of faith rally to help in that transition and

work with her to find a job that fits her gifts and interests? They involve another congregational member and a contact with an employment counselor or job coach to help plan together the pathway to work. If there are specific skills she needs to learn to return to work, then she turns to other members of the congregation for mentorship or someone who can help her learn these skills.

- A young adult with spinal cord injury knows neither how to develop a resume nor how to dress for interviews and work. The support circle could approach employers in the congregation or members of their team to help him learn these important skills.

- An older man transitioning from a state developmental center is excited and eager to give back and assimilate into the community, despite being labeled "not capable of competitive employment." With the assistance of support staff, he gets connected with a local parish and begins volunteering his time to organize and inventory food pantry items. In time and with the appropriate assistance, he develops other skills, including bagging/boxing items and assisting persons in the community as they come weekly to get food items. Through the volunteer work, he secures a job at a local grocer. Eventually, he encourages the grocer to contribute monthly to the food pantry in order to feed more people.

- A circle of support in a congregation essentially becomes a board of advisers for a young man with a disability in a congregation who wants to set up his own microenterprise. They do so, enabling him to sell art works and cards and more for years, with the members revolving as on any other board of directors.

- A twenty-two-year-old man leaving high school for the world of adult services is kicked out of his sheltered workshop for inappropriate behavior. He is then kicked out of two-day programs for similar reasons. For the next year, he spends his days at home with only the companionship of his support staff. The staff discover that he loves cars, being around cars, and most of all, cleaning cars. He begins cleaning and monitoring (state vehicle regulations) the agency vehicles. Members of his support team know that other members in their congregations work for car dealers. They talk with them and together, working with the dealer, work out a part-time job for him detailing cars and keeping the vehicle bay clean. From this connection, another opportunity at a sister dealership opens at which a mobile crew is paid to clean the mechanic bays and customer service area three days a week.

The power of a congregation to help someone find a job is based on the capacity of congregations to gather around someone who needs support, to listen, plan, and then utilize the social capital of the whole congregation to help find opportunities. In social capital theory, a congregation is full of employers, employees, and volunteers, all who know other people in the community and thus are a networking powerhouse. If a person and congregational team working on employment need the help of public services and vocational programs, they may have members in their congregation or a partner in the world of human services who can help them negotiate bureaucracies, benefits, and red tape. That faith community can be an effective advocate for needed supports. There may be public supports available such as transportation or an ongoing job coach that could help, but red tape seems to have tied that up. So they decide to talk and advocate with local agencies to help get those supports lined up while they work on finding the right kind of job opportunity.

Employment for people with disabilities is usually seen as the responsibility of the public sector, not the private or the religious. Most people, though, find their jobs through connections. The possible number of ways that faith communities could assist young people with disabilities or adults transitioning back into the workforce after acquiring a disability is as varied as the stories of individual people, specific congregations, and the communities in which their members live and serve. This kind of support or ministry depends on realizing and enlisting the social capital that exists in a congregation. These possibilities can find their theological foundations in both "liberal" and "conservative" faith traditions. The tools are these: exploring and finding identity, passion, and meaning, combined with one's sense of call, dream, or vocation, and then building and working with the potential connections that are often just waiting to be asked or invited. Those tools, in other words, are another version of tapping spirituality and faith to create new opportunities for people to become contributing members of their congregations and communities.

CONCLUSION: TRANSITION INTO AND IN COMMUNITY

Most of us who face one kind of difficult transition or another fear the loneliness in that transition more than the transition itself. Having a companion, someone who shares your story, someone on the same journey makes a huge difference, whether in a serendipitous encounter, a support group or network of others who have been there (or still are), or friends, family, and others in your community. It is a theme versed repeatedly in songs and religious traditions. Think of the famous American spiritual that captures that image "Jesus walked this lonesome valley. He had to walk it by himself. Oh, nobody else can walk it for him. He had to walk it by himself."[25] The Twenty-Third Psalm is one of the most beloved and well-known passages in the Bible because of its assertion that "The Lord is my shepherd" even when "I walk through the valleys of the shadows of death, thou are with me!" (Ps 23:1, 4 KJV).

For individuals with disabilities of all kinds and their families, finding others "who are with me in the journey" can be a struggle all by itself. The reflexive action of most others, even the organizations designed to support them, is to "do something for them." Those services are crucial, but they often lead down prescribed paths. The value of having friends and companions in both body and spirit who are willing "to be with" individuals and families while they all find the right things to do is priceless. Faith communities have a largely untapped potential to help people with disabilities and their families through the transition from young person to adult, from student to employee, and from participant to community contributor. They can do so by helping individuals and families negotiate the paths of transition that may also involve separation and letting go. A community can support and guide in whatever way appropriate to a person's level of expressing choices and decisions. Finally, they can help a person they have come to know as one of their own to find the confidence and opportunities to use their gifts to contribute to the community in which they live.

Transition does not have to be such a lonely journey.

7

Spirituality, Aging, and End of Life
A Paradox of Loss and Celebration

The spiritual needs and gifts of people with intellectual and developmental disabilities stand out with a stark clarity in the years of aging and end of life (just as they do for most everyone), with the corresponding issues of handling grief and loss throughout one's life. Until relatively recently, these needs and ways to support individuals with intellectual and developmental disabilities during these transitions have not received a lot of attention. It means dealing with two of the major areas that professionals and caregivers have found hard to address: spirituality and death.[1]

There are at least three reasons for that reluctance and difficulty. The first is the question of what we as caregivers and friends believe about both. Dealing with death and end of life issues and the spiritual issues involved is at once profoundly individual and communal, personal and professional. It is an area that cannot be explored without raising our own experiences, thoughts, feelings, and beliefs regarding death and end of life issues. Thus, it calls for both human and professional sensitivity and skills at their best: being able to support others when there are so many questions, feelings, and different traditions while recognizing the ways our own journeys shape our ability and skill to walk alongside others both into and through "the valley of the shadow of death."

The second reason involves the common perceptions (or misperceptions) about the capacity of people with intellectual and developmental disabilities to experience and understand both spirituality and death. Spirituality has too often been equated with the capacity to reason. Thus, likewise, many have believed that a lack of capacity to reason makes it difficult for people with intellectual and developmental disabilities to understand death and concurrent experiences of grief and loss. The truth is that most everyone struggles with understandings of death, grief, and loss, so the real question is not whether people with intellectual and developmental disabilities experience and understand these core parts of the human experience but how they do so.

The third reason involves our beliefs about professional roles and how we live out those roles with people when they grieve, age, and face the end of their own lives. Along with family, professionals have often been the primary (if not only) people in relationship with many who have intellectual and developmental disabilities, not counting their peers. Some of those relationships last for a long time. They are highly valued by individuals, their families, and many professionals, often characterized by an unspoken sense of mutuality. As people age, deal with grief and loss, and die, the challenge for professionals is to be present with and for others in ways that may feel more like family and friend. If the role or image of a professional becomes an excuse for distancing oneself, then it becomes an unjust and tragic denial of relationship—unjust because the professional person assumes the sole power to do so, and tragic because the human intimacy of shared grief and support is lost to both.[2]

DENYING DEATH OR DEATH AS DENIER

In older systems of care that took place in institutional settings rather than the community, end of life and death had its own real and symbolic impact. In my first job as Protestant chaplain at Newark State School in upstate New York, death in the facility was often a reminder of the loneliness and loss of all connections and community. It was not infrequent that chaplains and social workers received calls from relatives saying, "Would you please inform _____ that their mother or father died?" (Sometimes followed with a next phrase, "several months ago.") I have never forgotten one of my first funerals, in one of the facility chapels, with four male residents present (being a pallbearer was the best-paying job on the campus) and one staff member sent from the resident's living unit. Doing that funeral seemed to make no sense, since funerals are really for the living, unless one took a justice perspective—this person deserves what we would do for anyone else. Those experiences certainly highlighted the cultural abandonment of the residents in the institution, an end of life congruence with a life-time cut off from family and community even when that was cloaked as the best of professional, social, and family care. One symbol of that abandonment was the circular, numerical markers at the institution's cemetery in the place where headstones should have been.

When families did become involved at the time of death, their grief was shaped by the history of ambivalence, uncertainly, love, emotional wounds, and loss. I remember two experiences in particular: (1) the shock and pain of one family when I took them to see the grave in that otherwise lovely rural countryside with the numerical markers and (2) the rage of a family who tore into a young physician trying to explain to them the death of their daughter from ingesting a rubber glove because of her pica behavior. I did not understand the depth of their anger, especially since they had been very infrequent visitors, until I realized they were essentially yelling at the doctor who caused the intellectual disability by misuse of forceps during delivery. Twenty-six years had been stripped away, and they were right back at the trauma of her birth.

The whole institutional system was based on a denial of the experiences of loss. Parents were encouraged to send children to institutions and forget about them, a loss that arose each time there was an experience like those above. But deaths also became evidence of abuse and neglect in institutional care. At Newark, the people who lived there hated to go to the "hospital unit" because so many of their friends who went there never came back, nor were their deaths acknowledged and mourned. That fact of institutional life led to use of deaths as an indicator of quality of care, which continued as the system evolved into community-based supports. That indicator became part of the argument about which setting was better, that is, which had lower mortality rates?

In current community-based systems, the loneliness at the end of life is still too often a reflection of loneliness during life, evidence of disconnection that can happen even while living "in the community."

One of the troubling calls I used to receive in my work at the Boggs Center in New Jersey was when an agency contacted me because of a relatively sudden death in a group home. The agency would be seeking any kind of help from someone experienced in dealing with grief and intellectual disabilities. I had that experience and did a regular workshop for community staff in this area, but the problem, from my perspective, was that I was usually a stranger, not a local clergyperson, congregational member, or hospice chaplain who already knew the person, his or her friends, and the staff. Those situations sometimes involved conflict between relatives and the direct care staff, with each making assumptions about the other's lack of care and concern. All that complexity sometimes gets even more compounded when routine medical care becomes an end of life issue because community-based health-care systems, hospitals, and doctors do not know these patients either, or when assumptions about quality of life end up impacting decisions about treatment that might be routine for someone else.

If independence, productivity, inclusion, and self-determination are indeed the values we hold dear and that shape policy and practice, then it is not hard to see death and end of life as the antithesis, the denier of the values we follow as well as of the people that we cherish. Aging and end of life is a destroyer of independence, often taking people who have been striving for more independence their whole lives onto a "downward" path toward dependence and loss of identity. Everyone struggles with productivity and purpose as they retire and move into old age and the final stages of life. The difficulties in service systems to enable people with intellectual disabilities to choose the equivalent of "retirement" are well known to professionals and others who work in these settings. Aging, infirmity, and, for sure, death take one away from participation and community. They raise the questions around "Why?"—the "Why?" of illness and loss, the "Why?" of death itself, questions that challenge any assumptions we make about self-determination, much less personal and professional power and control.

GRIEF MULTIPLIED

The emotional and spiritual impact on caregivers, whether direct care staff, families, or professionals, can even be more intense in a modern system focused on growth, development of potential, and progress.

Expressed feelings may cluster around a sense that death is a double injustice—"Why did she have to die? She already had the bad luck of having a disability. That was enough to deal with, why this?" Death becomes the ultimate "unusual incident," and the system responds with questions and investigations about cause and responsibility. Too often the staff being questioned experience a hidden assumption that it was someone's fault. When abuse or neglect is involved, that investigative system gets reinforced. In either case, the "grief" of suspicion, investigation, and paperwork gets piled on top of, and mixed in with, the need to grieve in more typical ways, making effective grieving and spiritual support even harder.

Addressing the grief and loss with other "consumers," family members, staff, and friends also has other challenges. One challenge is that far too many staff and agencies report the experience of having a family member call to inform the agency that someone's parent or sibling has died, but also expressing their desire that the person served by the agency not attend the funeral. Staff and family alike make assumptions about the capacity of a person with intellectual disabilities to understand or to handle what is happening, ironically at a time when everyone might be struggling with those questions. "He can't understand" overlaps with "We don't want to cause him more pain," with the result that no one makes a real effort to address the grief involved. A second challenge comes from finances and waiting lists. Systemic pressures in human services also lead to an inherent push to move on and to fill the empty bed or program slot, thus not giving anyone the time to recognize and feel the empty places in homes, programs, and hearts.

Unrecognized grief, unaddressed grief, in Granger Westberg's classic phrase, is "grief denied, but only delayed, and grief delayed is grief denied."[3] Ken Doka and others refer to it as "disenfranchised grief," a description that can apply both to a refusal to name and recognize the feelings[4] as well as to the lives of people who are already marginalized. Grief denied or delayed can then be acted out in behavior, on the part either of individuals with intellectual disabilities or of staff whose unresolved grief can lead to disillusionment and departure. In the face of all the problems of staff turnover and change, it is easy to forget the profound and deep connections that exist between many staff and people with intellectual disabilities. Dealing with death is often a very new experience for younger staff or an extra challenge to an agency when their staff members come from many different cultural backgrounds with varied ways of understanding death and varied cultural rituals for grief and mourning.

Outlining these issues is not meant to imply that there are not examples of very positive strategies to address grief and loss, and powerful stories of the ways agencies and staff have worked together to treat individuals, friends, families, and staff with loving care and respect. Those stories are increasingly true when people with intellectual and developmental disabilities have grown up as visible parts of their community in schools, faith communities, recreational programs, Special Olympics, and other areas of community life. There may be a whole army of friends and community members who have had a stake in seeing someone get as many opportunities and as much support as possible. It is not unheard of for hundreds of people to show up at funerals of children or adults with intellectual or developmental disabilities.

Leaders in designing person-centered planning and training personnel in its use are recognizing its potential for shaping a much more effective and humane response to aging and end of life issues, just as our society is learning that planning for end of life issues is a way to address both anticipated and unanticipated issues as one approaches death.[5] That kind of planning is even more important for people with intellectual disabilities, given the health-care challenges they may face as they get sicker or have a terminal illness. They confront a bigger health system focused on healing, fixing, and curing, one in which death is also seen as the enemy to be held off and one in which disability may be viewed as evidence of medical failure or a "fate worse than death." To use a metaphor from literature and film, those currents in health care have the makings for a perfect programmatic and spiritual storm, one in which people with intellectual disabilities and their caregivers can get tossed about and overboard quite easily. Anticipating a storm and planning for it is thus crucial. Specific planning activities around end of life issues, such as using supported decision making, advance care directives, do not resuscitate orders,[6] and even preplanning of funerals become ways to think about medical treatment and funeral plans as well as to remember what has given a person's life meaning. These plans can be a guide to how those around a person can honor those values, and that person, in, throughout, and after the final days. In other words, rather than seeing old age and death as a denier of the core values of a service system and of one's spirituality, they can become a time to honor them even more deeply.

AGING AS AN HONORING AND CELEBRATION

In recent decades, there has been an explosion of research and resources related to spirituality, aging, and the end of life, although not much of that has focused particularly on the arena of intellectual and developmental disabilities. There has been an intense focus on issues in aging in intellectual disabilities as more effective care helps people with intellectual and developmental disabilities live much longer lives. In the past fifteen years, attention to end of life issues and the emotional and spiritual issues in dealing with death and dying has increased.[7] Even so, there can be a tendency by many to assume that "special" people might need "special ways" to deal with grief, loss, and aging/ end of life issues. One way to affirm the common humanity of people with disabilities is to start with research and resources from the wider population—"What do we all do?"

In a resource manual entitled *The Challenges of Aging: Retrieving Spiritual Traditions*, the Park Ridge Center looked across spiritual traditions at the core spiritual tasks of aging as envisioned or lived out in different religious and cultural traditions.[8] Five "unique" tasks of aging were identified:

1. Reaffirming covenant obligations to community
2. Blessing—How have our lives been blessed or a blessing to others? Where do we now give our blessing to younger generations?
3. Believing and practicing honor toward those who are aging, treating them with dignity, respect, and appreciation
4. Maintaining faith in the face of loss and grief
5. Reconciling discordant experiences—letting go, reconnecting, and forgiving

Those tasks of aging provide a very useful framework for our thinking about how we might support people with intellectual disabilities and their significant others as they move toward the end of life.

Covenant Obligations to Community

Our systems of supports and services have valued community inclusion while also struggling to make that real. As people age, the questions to ask are, "Who is part of someone's community—who are the key people with whom they have been connected? Is it family, direct care workers, professionals, individuals with whom they live, friends, or others in the community? What communities of faith, work, residence, and shared interests (e.g., sports, hobby clubs, etc.) have been part of in their lives? What has been important to them? What might the person we are supporting want to do with those current and past connections? What might those community members want to do in relationship to the person who is in the final stages of life? Are there ways that those relationships involve a sense of covenant, of wanting to maintain a connection even toward the end or wanting to do things one feels obliged to do, or wants to do, before it is too late?"

Exploring those questions could lead to a wide variety of responses. It might involve looking through picture albums or getting pictures of old friends and important places. It may mean revisiting places where one grew up or lived. If early enough, it may mean thinking about ways one can still begin a connection to groups in which one has wanted to participate. In retirement, many "typical" elderly persons pursue an interest or hobby that they have long wanted to do. In Ira Wohl's film *Best Man*, the sequel to *Best Boy*, his intellectually disabled cousin Philly, in his seventies, has his bar mitzvah, an event that creates a whole new set of relationships and community for him.[9]

Reunions are one of the most typical cultural acts of renewing and remembering past acquaintances. They are not usually part of the lives of people with intellectual and developmental disabilities. Many of us have class reunions, military reunions, and school reunions. Many of the adults whom our system currently supports lived together in institutions before moving to community settings. Service systems have been so focused on helping people move away from institutional lives that the questions of maintaining relationships with past friends and staff, or of reconnecting with them, are rarely asked. We forget that they may remember. The potential of reunions for aging adults with intellectual and developmental disabilities is significant, given the importance of relationships in their lives. In less dramatic ways, there are now wonderful stories of agencies that honor the wishes of someone's friends in a group home to visit a sick or dying friend in a nursing home or hospital on a regular basis if they can no longer stay in the residential setting or with their families.

Giving and Receiving Blessing

The act of asking for a blessing from one's elders, or the opportunity to give one's blessing as an elder, is an ancient spiritual tradition. It is not a ritual and language commonly used in our Western world, but everyone can recall elders who were crucial because of how they treated us in life-affirming ways. In disability services, that could also happen, but it depends upon our own creativity. For example, we are already getting better at identifying key strengths and gifts in the people we support. Many of us, in whatever kind of caregiving role, have had our lives profoundly impacted and blessed by people with intellectual disabilities. But we rarely tell them so in ways that come out of established relationships. People with disabilities are increasingly reacting negatively to the kind of attitude or expression that says far too quickly, "Oh, you are such an inspiration or blessing!" Their term for that, as noted earlier in the book, is "inspiration porn." A sense of blessing that comes out of a long-term relationship is far different.

One of the tasks of aging and the final stages then, if not earlier, is for us to let people know the gifts and strengths we see in them and how their lives have blessed us. A chaplain at Eastern Christian Children's Retreat in northern New Jersey, a small residential facility for adults with multiple disabilities, started ritualizing the act of recognizing gifts by giving a certificate of appreciation during the annual planning meeting. Using his own observation, his conversations with staff, and simple certificate templates from Staples, he produced individualized Certificates of Appreciation and presented them during the meeting. The impact on family, staff, and "consumer" was often profound as the "system" recognized and validated someone's gifts and impact on others as well as discussed the individual's needs and goals. At least one family said, "I have never been to one of these meetings and had someone tell me about the ways my child has contributed to their life."

Second, beyond our affirmation of "their" blessing to us, how might we help them give a blessing to others in the final stages of their life?

What might someone want to do for someone else? Or if we indeed have moved to being able to help individuals and their families think about advance care directives or funeral planning, what might they want to "will" someone or some organization? Does someone who is terminally ill want others to have a possession that might help them remember the relationship? For example, a sensitive parent of a person who died in a New Jersey group home remembered to ask the staff and fellow residents whether anyone there would want a possession for a memento. Indeed, one of his best friends wanted his friend's Yankees baseball cap. Think about the potential meaning for someone being able to make those decisions before his or her death, knowing that death was coming. It is a perfectly normal way of saying goodbye, expressing thanks, and giving a part of oneself—a blessing.

Restoring Honor in Aging

"Honor your father and mother, that your days may be long on the earth" is one of the Ten Commandments. Up until the "youth culture" took over, honor toward elders was much more prevalent, but it is still there, in many, many ways. Community elders, grandparents, and senior members of congregations: there are many ways in which the honoring still takes place.

How then might service systems in developmental disabilities embody that attitude and value rather than seeing aging individuals only as a new set of problems? It is first an attitude of respect, honoring people's choices, perhaps figuring out ways to let people do things they want to do even if it is programmatically inconvenient. Many support agencies are working on ways for people to "retire" if they so choose. Maintaining vocation or employment goals even if someone does not want to do them or because that is the only option are both unimaginative and antithetical to the values of choice and self-determination.

Other strategies could involve helping people write and develop their life story, a process that has received much more attention in Europe than in the United States. Most of the people supported by agencies have long medical or treatment records. How might staff, families, or volunteers help turn those into life stories, with pictures of people, places, and events that one can see, review, and show to others? These can be stories of evolving identities, meaning, connection, and purpose. How might systems revision "aging consumers" as "survivors" and "veterans"? Many have survived decades of programmatic changes, moves, staff turnover, and more. Could we tap those individuals, and their stories, to be part of training programs to help new and younger staff learn more about the history of services and supports? We all want our stories to be useful to others. Finally, as in the task of giving blessing, can professionals and caregivers figure out ways to tell people who are aging and moving through the end stages of life what "they" have meant to "us"?

Maintaining Faith in the Face of Loss

This is a time of life to pay special attention to spiritual beliefs and practices. That is as simple and as hard as ensuring that people can practice their own faith and develop relationships with spiritual leaders and communities. Clergy and other counselors can assist in areas where professional staff may feel uncomfortable, such as helping people prepare for death through prayer and scriptures; daily or weekly rituals; and engaging in rituals of loss, mourning, and remembering such as ensuring that individuals can participate in funerals and other rites of mourning for their friends or family. As appropriate, we also honor individuals by giving them the opportunity to deal with their own anticipatory grief. Creative resources such as the Books Beyond Words series use adult-appropriate drawings to tell the story of what may happen as someone's parent dies or when they face major health issues.[10] If people have not had the opportunity or support to develop a relationship with a faith community or other social and cultural networks, and it is their desire to do so, this is surely the time to do so, both for the individuals themselves and then for supports to friends and staff during and after death.

Reconciliation

The final spiritual challenge of aging is reconciliation, dealing with discordant experiences, things that people may want to say or do with others before it is too late. Some of the strategies mentioned also address this. By helping people to tell their own stories, in pictures and words; by helping people reconnect with distant family members, former staff, or old friends; by visiting or reuniting with special places and experiences; and by helping people be "at home," wherever that is, our service systems can provide opportunities for people to address old questions and feelings. When I was chaplain in a residential facility, I often had the opportunity to participate in someone's funeral. When asked to do a eulogy, I often tried to weave together the unique qualities and strengths of someone's life so that staff and families could see the person, and each other, in new ways by realizing how much their family member, or "their" consumer, had touched others. The question for me is how we might help that kind of sharing to happen before someone dies, so the person feels and experiences the emotional and spiritual resolution.

All five of these spiritual dimensions of aging are evident in a graphic that came from a spiritual assessment process done by a clinical pastoral education student of mine in New Jersey working at a community-based agency. She trained and worked with the staff to have conversations with everyone in their residential programs about what was most important to them. Using a Wordle graphic, in which the larger size of fonts reflects frequency of word use, this is what they found.[11]

Is God in nature?
My Mom died.   Who will watch my cats?
I miss my friends at Woodbine. My Pop-pop died.
I really, really miss them.   What is cancer?
Where do people go when they die? I can't talk to my friend in Ancora?
Why does cancer kill a person?   I'm shy. How can I see my friends from New Lisbon?
I need help to get there.   I don't like to think about Woodbine.
My best friend doesn't live here anymore. I know I'll never be able to drive.
My best friend died. I need a friend to sit with.
My Mom's in Heaven. I can't live alone anymore.
Where is Heaven? I need someplace for my kids.

FIGURE 7-1. *Assessment: Spirituality and Aging*

Note that most of these responses are about the loss of past connections, worries about what will happen as they age, wondering who might help them if they go to a faith community, struggles in the past and present (Woodbine and New Lisbon are two residential institutions from which many people had come), remembering and honoring experiences and relationships in their lives, and others.

ANTICIPATORY GRIEVING: MAKING SPACE

If we pay attention to the spiritual tasks of aging, then we have already made major strides toward assisting individuals and their friends with planning for the last part of their lives and anticipatory grieving. There are new curricula and resources to support training and educational opportunities about death and loss.[12] We can also recognize that there are multiple teachable moments when end of life questions and issues can be addressed. Television shows, news about deaths of famous people, or deaths of family members of both staff and consumers all provide opportunities for people to discuss questions and feelings and to discover what individuals may or may not need or want as they think about their own end of life.

Agencies can provide staff in-services on dealing with death, grief, and loss. For many staff, simply talking about end of life, grief, and loss is not easy. These in-services may provide a beginning while also outlining policy and planning by the agency. Inviting clergy, hospice chaplains, or other counselors to do those in-service trainings would also help develop relationships between the staff and community resources who could be called when they are needed. Training can also provide a time and place for staff to talk about how they might support each other when one of the people in their care is dying. Figuring that out and sharing the care helps avoid the kind of resentments that can also happen in families when one or two family members feel like the rest of the family has been neither present nor supportive. This is even more crucial when professional staff come from multiple cultural and faith backgrounds. The team can then understand the ways that the cultural traditions around death and mourning of the individual and family, as well as the team members, can be recognized and respected.

As already mentioned, building relationships with local resources is crucial so they are not strangers when called in to comfort staff and the people in their care. When that is not the case, for example, and a clergyperson who does not know the person or much about intellectual disabilities is called in to perform a funeral, there is a very real chance that the service will not be conducted in ways that honor the person or meet the needs of the individuals involved. In Syracuse, New York, for example, the regional developmental disabilities service office developed an active grief response team that included clergy and professionals from other disciplines to respond to individual situations and to provide training and consultation.

When possible, staff should plan for times of loss, grief, and aging with individuals and their families. That can involve end of life planning processes,[13] but it can also involve collecting information on a family's experiences and traditions for handling loss and grief when the individual and family begin their relationship with the agency. One such process is called a "loss assessment."[14] Those discussions can also be an opportunity for an agency to lay out its policies and practices— telling families that when someone close to the individual dies, this is what the agency tries to do, this is how staff will help, and these are the reasons why they believe it is important for people to participate in the rites and rituals that allow for grieving and support.

WELCOMING AND SHARING THE GRIEF

The primary spiritual challenge to caregivers is to recognize and welcome grief before someone's death as well as when death happens. Grief can be expressed in all kinds of feelings and all kinds of behaviors. The biggest danger is ignoring or suppressing grief, simply because it is one of the most normal of human feelings and experiences. When I served directly as a chaplain, staff would ask me about individuals who frequently talked about the death of a relative or pet, even though it happened years before. They wondered whether that ongoing discussion was evidence of their inability to understand death or deal with it. At first I wondered the same thing, but I came to recognize that those questions and feelings were one way of asking and saying, "Who have you lost?" At one level, beyond all the labels and disabilities, we are the same. At another level, it may have been an indication that they were not able to participate fully in the rites and rituals of grief—the typical ways of "acting it out" that we have in every culture and faith tradition, such as the rituals around death or memorial rituals like visiting a grave or lighting a candle.

Thus, our challenge is to create safe places and opportunities for people to share, live out, and address their own grief and loss. There are at least four key strategies for provider agencies and professionals to use for people in their care.[15] First, provide accurate and honest information to friends and staff, with enough time and support by others to help process that information. People deal with feelings and questions in very different ways and at different speeds. There is no one way that "it" should happen. Deal with the questions and feelings that people have, not those we might think they should have.

Second, enable maximum involvement in the social and spiritual activities surrounding death. That means doing what we need to do to enable people to participate in wakes and funerals, visit cemeteries, write cards, and participate in memorial activities. If family members have concerns, help them to know that staff will provide supports. If people cannot participate in those activities, or even when they can, agencies may also organize an additional memorial services and other activities within a group home, day program, workshop, or entire agency. One of the services I remember most fondly is the one where a young girl's classmates and friends helped make the flowers out of colored paper.

Third, be mindful of the primary supporters in someone's life, and keep them connected to them. When we grieve, we do not turn to everyone. We turn to the people we trust most. Do what is needed to support that supporter, as they provide the anchor for a person during the hardest times of grief. Finally, maximize the opportunities for the expression of grief and condolences. As already stated, cards, gifts, planting trees, cemetery visits, anniversary rituals— these are all typical channels for expressing grief and condolences. One great irony, in my experience, is that we who worry about the capacity of people with intellectual disabilities to handle grief and death often discover that "they" are better at doing so than we are, or that they do or say things that are profoundly helpful to others. Grief is not often resolved quickly. People with intellectual and developmental disabilities often learn more slowly. Thus, opportunities for expressing grief may need to go on for years, just as they do for many of the rest of humankind.

CONCLUSION: ENDINGS AND BEGINNINGS

The crises and challenges presented by end of life experiences for people with intellectual and developmental disabilities are also opportunities for developing and celebrating a wider network of caregiving relationships, finding creative ways to share and to support each other in times of loss and death, and honoring both the common and unique qualities that individuals with intellectual disabilities share with others. Those times can provide opportunities for the best of what it means to be professional—chances not to fix and cure but to journey with others, to deal with the tough questions and feelings that disability and death raise for us, to recognize and celebrate those holy moments and miracles of accomplishment and growth, to recognize and give thanks for the meaning and gifts that others have brought to us, and, at times, to sacrifice and go beyond the call of duty and role for the sake of others.

For both individuals and systems, good endings can become good beginnings. The tragedy is often not in the death itself but in the fact that individuals' unique identities, gifts, passions, connections, and sources of hope and purpose were not recognized and recorded earlier in their life so that, by the time of their death, no one really knows their life story. Their stories have been forgotten even before they die. Mourning can lead to remembering and renewal to live and care in ways that matter most. It can help us all remember that every person has a unique story, even though that story can get hidden behind labels and systems. In each of the major spiritual traditions of the world, new life and meaning comes in and through the journey of facing death. Perhaps, if "we" let "them," people with intellectual disabilities can be our companions and guides on that journey as well.

III

SPIRITUALITY AND FAMILIES

8

Spirituality and Families
Beginnings and Journeys

Invite a group of families who have children or adult members with disabilities to tell some of their faith stories (church, synagogue, mosque, depending on context). They will never give lukewarm answers. If the families trust you and each other at some level, that is, no one is going to report on them or judge them, and the questions are open ended— the stories will flow. Some families will talk about how they have had excellent, but not always smooth, support from their faith communities or other sources of spiritual support. Other families may share experiences of what could be called a "neglect" of expected or longed-for care from clergy, congregations, and others. The word "neglect" is too tame when they recount experiences of feeling unwanted, rejected, or hurt by actions or words by clergy or members of faith communities. When others blame the parents for a child's disability or prescribe that more faith will lead to healing, the more appropriate word is "abuse." Telling those stories takes trust and courage, especially if the experiences are recent, raw, or unresolved. Other families may say that their faith and spirituality has been very important to them, but that they have given up on finding the spiritual support that they had hoped for from their faith community.

Lest one think that neglect and abuse are unique to faith communities, be assured that is not the case. In a recent study involving five hundred families in Tennessee, Erik Carter and colleagues at the Vanderbilt Kennedy Center discovered that the expression of spiritual questions, needs, or interests are also ignored by other sources of support designed to help families with disabled members. The researchers found that spirituality was an area most families considered important in their home life: family prayer, scripture reading, and other rituals and practices. However, a much smaller percentage of families had the experience of having those needs and interests recognized and honored, either by their faith communities or by public or private services and supports available to them. In organizations whose policies and practices are predicated on "person- and family-centered care," no one asked about their spiritual interests or about possible ways they could help families find the appropriate spiritual supports if they were interested.[1] That failure violates the very tenets of person- and family-centered care.

Families and advocates are changing this picture. An increasing number of families are now making the first moves—asking, advocating, and writing blogs, articles, and books about the spiritual journey of their child and their family. More service agencies are recognizing the power and impact of good spiritual supports.[2] Advocacy and training within faith networks are leading to creative congregational responses and deeper theological exploration of the experience of disability. One now can name almost any form of support that has been important to families with children with disabilities and then find a faith community, somewhere, that has figured out how to provide it.

The diversity of family cultures, spiritual and religious traditions, and types of families simply means that there is similar diversity of spiritual responses and ways by which families address the spiritual dimensions of becoming parents of a child with a disability. The same goes for relatives of a person acquiring a disability. The starting place is usually at the beginning, with their discovery that a child or loved one is or will be disabled. The initial journey is often through a cloud of shock and trauma. Any event that results in unexpected and unwanted changes to a course of expectations, like a sudden change in the parents' image of an expected child, usually involves a journey through variations of the "What?" "Why?" and "How?" questions of their past, present, and future. In my forty years of listening to, and reading, family stories, there is no normal time span for that journey. Most families do emerge in ways that get beyond the question of "Why?" to reframed expectations of their child and of their identity as parents. Their core values and ways of finding meaning may change, as well as their sense of purpose. Relationships with others can change as those others support them (or do not) in dealing with cultural stereotypes, expectations, and the realities of disability and parenting.

Issues related to spiritual supports for families occur over the lifespan, just as they do with anyone else. However, disability can focus and heighten questions and issues in ways that make them difficult to avoid. The best help comes from open-ended questions with a willingness to take the time to listen to their unique story, wherever they are in the journey. Listening to family stories was where and how my journey as a clergyman in this arena began. Like other clergy and helping professionals, I sometimes failed to listen deeply enough to take the time needed, and rushed in too quickly wanting to help. A parent recently noted to me, "Just be fully present to another being without judgement . . . that's the gift we need to cultivate, and it doesn't come easily. . . . THAT might be the place to put all of our human nonhelpful offerings." If one assumes that families are the experts in their own story, they are usually quite willing to forgive.

IN THE BEGINNING

For most parents, their story begins with the discovery of the fact that their child has or will have a disability of one form or another. Or, in truth, their journey begins with the decision to have a child or the discovery that "we" are pregnant. That all happens in an environment shaped by varied levels of hope, love, relationships, personal and cultural identities, values, and their own dreams or sense of vocation and calling as a family. Those stories will be very different, but almost every one I have heard or read is a profound experience of vulnerability and unexpected change. Listen to at a relatively new one in some detail. Jason Whitt, a young professor of philosophy and theology at Baylor University, wrote about his family's story in 2015 in an article published in the *Christian Century*. He and his wife discovered, very shortly before their daughter was to be born, that there were "issues." In his own words:

> In June 2009, after eight months of routine pregnancy, a sonogram revealed that my wife's amniotic fluid was low, requiring doctors

to perform a C-section and bring our daughter Camille into the world. We were assured that the baby was fine, but then, within 24 hours of her birth, we learned that she had breathing difficulties, was smaller than expected (3 lbs., 10 oz.), and needed to be taken to another hospital.

Thus began a four-week nightmare of traveling 45 minutes each way from our home in Waco to the neonatal intensive care unit at Scott and White Hospital in Temple, Texas. We soon discovered the horror of the NICU for parents. Physicians who work in the NICU do not see "normal" children and don't assume "normalcy." They assume *problems* and are on a constant search to discover them. While this pursuit is medically responsible (there is a reason that a child is in the NICU, after all), my wife and I found ourselves inwardly and sometimes outwardly pleading, "Please, can't she just be who she is? Must we assume the worst?"

Each visit brought a new concern from her doctors. We'd hear: "Her head is too small." "Her fingers are too long." "Are her ears rotated just a little too much?" "Is one eye lower than the other?" "We need to do an MRI." "Her kidneys worry us." Guessing what they might posit next filled us with dread.

We weren't ready to be parents to a special-needs child—that was a club to which other people belonged. This was early in our journey with Camille, and we needed simply to be her parents—to love her as the beautiful child we saw. Wrestling with special needs and genetic syndromes was not something we could comprehend.

But over the coming months we slowly accepted Camille's condition. When Camille missed developmental milestones we began to acknowledge that she would not be like other children. We became open to genetic testing, moving from not wanting to hear anything into a compulsion to find answers. One geneticist sanctimoniously called it our "diagnostic odyssey."[3]

"Odyssey" is a very appropriate metaphor for that journey, one that recognizes that answers of any kind are not easily found and the journey is often a long and stormy one. "Marathon" is the metaphor used by Ann Turnbull, a special educator and national leader in family support, to describe her family's journey in raising Jay, a young man with multiple intellectual and psychological disabilities. Rud Turnbull, her lawyer husband and Jay's father, noted in an e-mail discussion his own interest in mythology:

> The role of Greek myth as explanation for the fact of disability, when other explanations do not satisfy the existential queries about "why me"; and the importance and role of dignity as a tool for constitutional interpretation and accountability and outcomes measurement. The interest in myth arises because families resonate with myths; they understand their lives as Sisyphus or Hercules.[4]

The "Why?" questions take so many forms. In a short, dramatic documentary in the 1980s, *Mother Tiger, Mother Tiger*, the mother of a child diagnosed after several months of unexpectedly slow development asks a series of angry questions directed toward God, including "Why me?" "Why our child?" and "Why not someone else's?"[5] The question can take the form of interrogating professional caregivers about missed warnings or what the doctor or hospital might have done. Is it a "personal test," "punishment," "your family's fault," "my fault," or "a blessing"? Who had the control and power to prevent this from happening? Whose fault is it? When the "Why?" question is experienced at those existential depths, the responses are usually, on the one hand, anger at someone or something else or, on the other, shame and guilt about what one might have personally done. The feelings are all profound spiritual questions that impact core identity and meaning, purpose, and how to respond and cope.

JOURNEY AS A GRIEF PROCESS WITH CAUTION SIGNS

The family journey has also frequently been compared to a grief process in which one's expectations and hopes are shattered with subsequent stages of mourning, searching, and adapting. The analogy can be a helpful one to parents and families over time, though not necessarily in the moment. There are at least three cautions that bear discussion and exploration: the double-edged constructs of the grief and loss process, the potential for analysis to become self-fulfilling prophecy, and the multiple ways that the "Why?" question can be asked and answered, if it can be or should be.

First, diagnosing someone's feelings as a grief process can be a way of easily distancing one's self from feelings and experience, on the part of both parties. Grief process frameworks can be helpful to caregivers as well as individuals, but not if they are used as a way of assuming

someone can control the feelings or process itself. Berating yourself
or being told you should be at a particular stage of grief simply adds
to the frustration while also avoiding vulnerability or pain that you
may be feeling. The crucial actions needed are voicing and listening.
Rather than "diagnosing" shock, denial, anger, bargaining, depression,
and acceptance, as in Elizabeth Kubler Ross's well-known stages of
grief,[6] a simpler framework of response questions gets to the heart of
the experiences: "It can't be!" "Why?" "Whose fault?" "What can we
change?" and "How do we go on? What do we do next?" Individuals
and parents may confront and ask those questions in multiple verbal
and nonverbal ways.

A perspective that is particularly helpful because of its simplicity is
from therapist Patrick O'Malley in a *New York Times* Op-Ed column
about working with a woman who had lost a baby. He first comments
on the problems with the classic stages model of grief:

> That model is still deeply and rigidly embedded in our cultural
> consciousness and psychological language. It inspires much self-
> diagnosis and self-criticism among the aggrieved. This is com-
> pounded by the often subtle and well-meaning judgment of the
> surrounding community. A person is to grieve for only so long and
> with so much intensity.

In line with my conception of story as one of the languages of spirituality and community, O'Malley then talks about a "story of loss with
three chapters." Chapter 1 is about the attachment that has been there
before a loss, the bonds built by their unique relationship. The degree of
attachment is directly related to the intensity of grief for most patients.
"I often tell them that the size of their grief corresponds to the depth of
their love." Chapter 2 is the death event, which can throw the person
experiencing the loss into chaos and a sense of uncontrollable feelings.[7]
Then chapter 3, he notes, "begins after the last casserole dish is picked
up, when the outside world stops grieving with you."[8]

The crucial role that a grief framework or process should be able
to play is that it enables a listener or counselor to be more fully present
to a person in mourning. Pastoral theologians talk about this as "a
non-anxious presence."[9] Grief or loss are not predictable processes that
one can control.

The second caution comes from the fact that assessments can sometimes become self-fulfilling prophecies. In the1960s, psychologist Saul Olshansky developed the construct of "chronic sorrow" to talk about the feelings and lives of parents of children with disabilities.[10] Again, that construct *may be* a helpful term for some families when they experience recurring feelings of grief or the memories of the feelings of their diagnostic odyssey as they face some new event or crisis impacting their child or family. But families have a vast range of feelings, including gratitude and joy. If a caregiver assumes chronic sorrow, that can become a self-fulfilling prophecy by way of shaping what they look for and ask about in conversations with families. "Chronic sorrow" was challenged by Ann Turnbull and colleagues at the Beach Center when they began to explore the "positive contributions" that families described in their stories about the impact of their child on their lives.[11]

Both constructs, chronic sorrow and positive contributions, point to the influence of environmental or social constructs and the history of understanding the journeys of families. Olshansky's article was published in 1962, around the beginning of the end of the professional and cultural exhortations to families to institutionalize their child with a disability and, sometimes, just forget about them. Doing so did not avoid chronic sorrow. In fact, for many families, institutional placement was a trauma that left a silent and deep well of unspoken sorrow. By the 1980s and 1990s, children and people with disabilities had legal rights to be part of community life. Advocacy efforts were led in large part by families, beginning with those who founded the national Association for Retarded Children[12] in the 1950s and strengthen greatly by the Kennedy family in the early 1960s. The result was an explosion of expectations and requirements for community support and participation, along with ever-growing networks of families supporting one another.

The third caution is that there are also multiple answers to the question of "Why?"—a question that can get asked at many different levels. The important task is to help families find their own answer to the question as they are asking it. Sometimes there are clear causes of the physical roots of a disability, increasingly so as more and more genetic factors are discovered and named. There is growing awareness of environmental factors and toxins that can cause a disability. Scientists and researchers also help us become more aware of the interaction between genetic makeup and environmental impact. For example, Down syndrome has a clear, definite cause, but early intervention, inclusive supports for child development and education, and higher parental and social expectations have led to accomplishments and capacity that were considered impossible when I began my career in the 1970s. The scientific answers to the "Why?" question are still a mystery in many types of disability, with autism as a prime example. The question, however, is just as much about the philosophical, emotional, existential, and spiritual pain, if not more so.

Those questions and potential answers have been explored for centuries by religions, philosophers, theologians, and cultural traditions. The issue of theism, or the "Why?" question, is not only occasioned by the birth or diagnosis of a child with a disability or an accident leading to an acquired disability. Rabbi Harold Kushner generalized the question to everyone out of his training and his personal experience of having a child with a very rare disability when he wrote *When Bad Things Happen to Good People*.[13] Most people would cite the title of the book as *Why Bad Things Happen to Good People*. The difference between "When?" and "Why?" is a striking example of our modern assumptions about control and invulnerability.

I met the parents of a young woman with Down syndrome early in my career who trusted me by sharing their very different experiences with "Why?" The mother had read the book *J.B.*,[14] a modern poetic and dramatic interpretation of the biblical book of Job. "I read it over and over again," she said, "until I realized he never got an answer to the question of 'Why?' He transcended his need to know." The father shared a journal and story he had written in which he struggled with the despair that other families have also reported, fantasizing that perhaps the best thing he could do was to kill his daughter and then himself. By the time I met them, their daughter was thriving, and they were impressive parents and advocates. That fantasy, however, is acted out far too frequently, especially by a single parent dealing with the toughest question cited by many families, "Who will care for my child after I am gone?"

In that same decade of the 1970s, I found a model for addressing the "Why?" question that has been helpful both to me and to families, seminary students, professionals, and others with whom I have shared it. David Patterson, a chaplain who worked with children with cerebral palsy and their parents, wrote one of the first early books dealing with spiritual and religious issues in being parents. In a chapter entitled "Finding Help through Your Faith," he used a diagram to explore the potential spiritual and theological responses to a life event experienced as painful. The horizontal axis below indicates whether God is or is not the author, that is, the cause. The vertical axis indicates how the suffering is experienced.[15]

FIGURE 8-1. *Spiritual and Theological Responses to Pain*

Starting from the bottom left corner, and going clockwise, if God is the author and it is harmful, then suffering is experienced as retribution, punishment to me for something. For example, a parent must have done something wrong in the past for God to have given them this child, or, for an acquired disability, "I had it coming." Moving to the top left, if God is the author but it is experienced as beneficial or helpful, in either the short or long run, then this pain and suffering is redemptive. It is "God's will for my own benefit." Next, in the upper right-hand quadrant, if God is not the source but the meaning of the events is still perceived as beneficial, then suffering can be providential—"God did not cause it, I did not want it, but my life has been changed for the better because of it, or "I have felt God's presence and strength in so many ways. There have been so many gifts coming out of it." Finally, if God is not the source, and the pain and suffering, such as the birth of a child with a disability, is perceived as harmful to the child or the family, then suffering is absurd. Then there is no lesson except seeking to eliminate the causes and ameliorate or fix the results.

Several reflections follow from the diagram and biblical passages quoted by Patterson. The first is that all of us, at one time or another, may attach those theological meanings to experience. Second, there are passages, people, and stories in the Bible reflecting every one of these questions and responses, whether one considers them answers or not. Said another way, they are all faithful responses. Third, and most important, there is no single or right answer or response; it depends on the person, context, faith tradition, and culture.

The primary lesson is to listen to how a belief or answer functions for someone. For example, someone who says, "This is God's will" can mean very different things. For one person, that may mean that there is a purpose in this struggle and journey even though he or she does not know what it is. For another, it could mean, "God did this to me. I don't know why. I am angry about it, but who am I to question? I just have to accept it." In the first example, the answer serves as a pillar of hope. A counselor might disagree theologically, but he or she should be very careful about saying something like "I don't believe God works that way" without offering some other pillar or foundation to stand on. For the second, too many people and families feel that one of the unwritten rules related to suffering or trauma is that you should not question God, much less be angry. Then, an effective and helpful response is to explore why they think that is the case and illustrate alternative responses in scriptural stories and writings.

FROM BEFORE TO AFTER

Thus, one of the helping strategies for a wise friend or counselor is to explore the assumption that one cannot question God, particularly if that person is from a Judeo-Christian tradition. The Bible is full of stories, psalms, and indeed whole books (e.g., Job and Lamentations) in which people are questioning why something has happened to them or to their people. The Hebrew Bible is a story of a relationship and journey,[16] both of which involve questions, arguments, and hard times.

Theologian Hans Reinders, like my parent friend in North Carolina, writes that the question of "Why, God?" never gets an answer acceptable to most people. Searching for an answer can be a diversion from or a part of the process of lamenting and mourning.[17] Jesus' words in the Beatitudes, "Blessed are those who mourn, for they shall be comforted," are about not the comforters or the answers but the appropriateness and necessity of mourning.

Theologian and ethicist Hans Reinders calls this the journey "from before to after" in the experiences of both parents of children with disabilities and family members of people who have acquired a disability from a traumatic brain injury. He points out that people going through that kind of traumatic journey of adjustment and coping may not feel any sense of providence or presence until afterward, looking back. Then, they might see that their spirituality, faith, or God (or that expressed through the act or words of others who helped them) was part of what gave them strength to cope, to come through, and to keep going.[18]

The crucial supports that enable resilience, adaptation, and moving ahead can involve personal factors, beliefs, and the attitudes and actions of others. For many families, the primary supporters turn out to be other families. Families can be connected quickly through networks like Parent to Parent and caregiving professionals who recognize the multiple kinds of resources that other parents can provide.[19] What others say to parents and people going through that kind of trauma and struggle is not as important as their presence and willingness to listen, unless it is one or another of the multiple euphemisms that get said too quickly and do anything but console. The arena of disability seems to be rife with what can only be called well-meaning but stupid, or insensitive, comments. Carol Levine, an expert who works in the area of aging and caregiving, and who has a brother with a disability, has her own list entitled "The Top Ten Things Caregivers Don't Want to Hear . . . and a Few Things They Do." Number one, higher than some others like "I know just how you feel," a cautionary note for everyone who tries to bring God into the picture too quickly, is "God does not give you more than you can bear."[20]

The metaphor of unexpected journey is also the key theme in a short, classic essay that is iconic in the world of families with children with disabilities. Emily Kingsbury's *Welcome to Holland* is the story of someone packed up and in the air on a long anticipated flight to Italy that instead lands in Holland, a very different destination than expected.[21] Currently, many more families and parents are writing about their emotional and spiritual journeys in print and online forums, all of which can be incredibly valuable resources to family members as well as to those who support them.[22] The caution, again, is that every situation has its unique qualities. The effectiveness of any written resource may depend on the place where parents are in their journey.

CONTINUING THE STORY OF CAMILLE AND THE WHITTS

There are so many stories of families who do not receive the kinds of supports they could have used or wanted in this journey "from before to after." Likewise, there are multiple stories of receiving harmful responses from others that were intended to be helpful.[23] But there are now more stories and examples of families getting the supports they need to help with the inherent resilience and strengths they may already have. Those positive stories are important to hear. The Whitt family story with Camille and their church, quoted earlier in the chapter, continues:

> What we discovered is that Camille is a mystery. . . . She is pro-foundly intellectually disabled and will never talk, walk, or eat on her own. Parents of special-needs children are confronted with a future that seems both ominous and cut off from them. They also confront painful isolation. For us it began with the stark realiza-tion that all the dreams we had for our daughter had vanished. . . . The birth of a special-needs child is experienced first as tragedy. Parents are at a time of life that's supposed to be joyous but are instead grieving a future that seems like a nightmare. How can a parent express these feelings to another without appearing cold and heartless? Often parents are cut off from others because par-ents of typical children can't understand the challenges and fears these parents experience. . . .
>
> Special-needs families also find themselves isolated in a privileged status that's given to them by well-meaning but misguided fellow Christians. Every special-needs parent I've spoken with has heard, "I couldn't do what you're doing. You are such special people. God

chose you because he knew you could handle it." We've heard this more times than we care to remember, and we always bristle at the statement. Special-needs parents don't want the pedestal. These statements imply that we never have a bad day or moments of bad parenting, frustration, or breaking down in tears.

When someone declares us "special," he or she is suggesting that there is an alternative—that it would be acceptable to refuse to receive our child. As Christians my wife and I do not believe this. Instead, we believe that we are called to love and care for the children God gives us. There is nothing extraordinary in this. We don't want to be held up as super-parents or heroes for loving our children; we want to be recognized as *parents*.

As they do for any family at our church who has a newborn, church members coordinated and brought over meals twice a week. . . . We received them for months and finally had to request that they stop. Our congregation wanted to support us, and the most tangible way to do that was to offer food. . . . I realize now that it wasn't about the meals. Bringing food was a way for our congregation to celebrate Camille's birth. As I noted earlier, many parents experience the birth of a special-needs child as tragedy, and celebration rarely is part of the family's first days together. Yet our church was willing to go through the actions of celebration. They rejoiced for us even as we struggled to make sense of a world that had turned over.

The birth of a special-needs child is initially experienced as tragedy. Parents grieve lost dreams, dread an unimagined future, and are frustrated by a new world that they never imagined. Yet for most families the grief is transformed into an experience of great joy and blessing. Families begin to recognize that they might not have the child they imagined, but the child they have becomes a source of joy and deep love. We missed celebrating Camille's birth, but we don't miss any opportunity to celebrate and rejoice in the little girl that she is now.

As important as the meals were, we could have easily slipped back into isolation if that had been the end of our church's outreach to us. Thankfully, a church family that we only knew in passing drew us out. Rachel Craig called us with an open invitation: we were welcome at their house for dinner every Tuesday night—no strings attached. If we needed to eat and run, that was fine. . . . For the next year and a half we spent almost every Tuesday evening at the Craigs' house. Two other families were also regulars. At those meals we found much-needed community. Tuesday evenings were a space where Camille wasn't different. She was loved and embraced by everyone there. When we arrived someone would hold her so we could eat and have adult conversation. With the families that encircled us we could share frustrations and fears as well as joys and hopes. Conversations didn't have to remain safe and superficial. We breathed deeply and let down the walls that we'd erected to protect ourselves from the perceived judgments and evaluation of our parenting efforts.

Then our church began to work to create space for Camille. We belong to a smaller church that doesn't have a dedicated special-needs ministry. When Camille was a baby it was natural for her to be with other infants in the nursery. The workers listened carefully as we explained what she could and couldn't do, as well as the best ways to hold her and engage her. Each Sunday morning they welcomed Camille; they never suggested that she was in any way a burden and were genuinely excited by her presence.

When Camille grew too big for the baby room we were concerned. Other children her age were walking, but since she couldn't we feared that she wouldn't fit in with other toddlers. But the volunteers encouraged us to bring her, and although she stayed in her stroller she was included in activities. Despite the fact that she couldn't use her hands to create it, Camille had her own work to take home just like the other kids. Each week one of her teachers completed the class activity and put Camille's name on it so that we knew she was an important part of the class.

The pattern has held as she's graduated to older classes. Camille enjoys her time in Sunday school, and the other children see her as a part of the class. One Sunday I came in and saw a three-year-old talking to the teacher while unconsciously resting her hand on Camille's leg. It was clear that this little girl regarded Camille as her friend and was showing her affection by a simple touch. Even as boundaries are broken for our family in these acts, more boundaries come down for other children and adults as they learn to embrace a special-needs child.

Our church has also recognized our needs during worship. The children's area is crowded during the worship hour, and my wife and I felt that it was a burden to leave Camille (with her large stroller) there during worship. So we either missed worship or sat with Camille in the narthex, trying to listen to the service through speakers.

To draw us out of our exile, our children's minister began a group known as Camille's Companions. Each Sunday a volunteer sits with Camille in the narthex so my wife and I can take our son into the service. Sometimes these companions bring their own children to sit with them. After services we find a group of teenagers gathered around Camille talking to her and holding her hands. These are children of Camille's Companions who have come to know Camille and see themselves as her friends. Again, what was done as a means of meeting one of our needs has transformed how the teenagers and adults in our church perceive those with disabilities. By looking for ways to make a place for Camille and offer community to our family, our church is discovering that Camille offers gifts back to the body.

Community is important for our family. We need community to embrace us and draw us out of our lives into the larger church family. My wife and I need it. Our son needs it. Camille needs it.

We've also learned that our church needs Camille. Too often well-meaning followers of Christ see those with disabilities, particularly children and adults with intellectual disabilities, as objects of care. Able-bodied Christians determine to care for "the least of these." Rarely are those with disabilities seen as persons with spiritual gifts who have something to offer and from whom other believers might learn—it's easier to give to those with disabilities than to receive from them. Yet Camille has shown that she is ready to share her gift of joy. Her companions say that it's impossible to be sad around her, and some add that their time with her is the best hour of their week.

We're not the only family with a special-needs child who is hungry for community, but other families may not know what that community might look like. Our churches must become places where they find welcome and an embrace that breaks down their isolation. Our congregations need this too. When we fail to bring families and their children with disabilities into the life of the church, the church misses out on gifts that the whole community needs.[24]

The story speaks both for itself and as a sign of hope that more families are beginning to share similar stories about the response by their faith communities and others to their family's journey.

AFTER AND BEYOND

The challenges for parents and families go on in a myriad of ways
as children age, all of which can include both spiritual questions
and supports:

- Parents experiencing increasing pressure on their time and
  parenting skills because of the sheer amount of caregiving
  responsibilities. If they have difficulty finding appropriate
  social supports, or material supports such as insurance, then
  stress and fatigue can come out in many different ways. Respite care can be very hard to find.
- Problems in an extended family if there is not the expected support or, even worse, if there is blaming because of the disability.
- Questions that may get raised as a family hopes and plans
  for the key religious rites of transition, such as baptism, first
  communion, confirmation, bar and bat mitzvahs, and so on.[25]
- The varied issues a family may face trying to find the right
  educational environment for their child or the right kinds of
  specialized services. That also pertains to religious education.
- The despair and loneliness felt by children with disabilities
  and their parents when their child is not invited to birthday
  parties, has few friends outside of school, or is shunned or
  bullied because of the disability.
- Children with disabilities moving into their teen years when
  typical questions of identity and social connection become
  even more heightened by the presence of disability.
- Siblings who may be struggling with their own journey because of the care and attention needed by their brother or sister.
- Parents struggling with their children's behavioral issues and
  acting out at whatever age and in whatever place, including
  their faith community.
- The huge questions that teenagers and parents face as their
  child with a disability transitions or ages out of the school
  system, which is obligated by law to include them (an entitlement), to an adult service world where that entitlement

disappears, compounded with all the questions of independence, employment, social roles, and more.

- Parents struggling with issues of sexuality and disability being lived out by their children.[26]
- The ongoing question that most families carry with them
  from day one: Who will care for our child after we are gone?[27]
- Transitions out of the home for an adult child, if there are
  viable options in a time when funding for public residential
  supports is getting even tighter.

At any point, a new crisis or transition can kick up older memories
and feelings. Professional caregivers can also cause additional grief
when they do not seem to see and understand a child as the parents
do, or by those who discount parental input and opinion.[28] In a recent
series of e-mails to me, Betty Pieper, a longtime parent advocate in New
York, wrote about her son Jeff and professional services:

> I've found an inverse relationship in respect (lack thereof) to the
> length of time/duration of caregiving and the intensity of com-
> mitment (with similar credentials or "better" credentials than
> those in paid, clinical settings) for those of us who spend our
> lives in home environments. Maybe a bit of ageism mixed in,
> but the past year when Jeff was hospitalized for a long time, and
> assaulted with horrible "care," we were subjected to phenomenal
> disrespect and arrogance. Even worse than the early days, which
> were never good. . . . I haven't mobilized energy and focus to
> know what best to do about it. . . . I did get and internalize three
> hundred pages of records. I mostly spend time with Jeff at the
> group home or struggling through the weekend with him here
> at home. Now that we are seventy-two and eighty-two and his
> care is complex, let alone the fact that he bears no weight and
> needs our lifting to position him in his molded (scoliosis) insert.
> It is daunting but he is almost always optimistic/courageous and
> even his rigid autistic ways demonstrate true determination to
> live life his way.[29]

One of the best recent models for framing the kinds of family support needed over time was developed by Shelli Reynolds and colleagues as part of a project called the National Community of Practice for Supporting Families of Individuals with ID/DD and its Life Course Tools.[30] She sorts supports in three major areas:

Information and Training Supports	Emotional Supports	Instrumental Supports
Discovery and Navigation	Mental Health and Self-Efficacy	Day-to-Day Needs
• Knowledge and skills • Information on disability • Knowledge about best practices and values • Skills to navigate and access services • Ability to advocate for services and policy change	• Parent-to-parent support • Self-advocacy organizations • Family organizations • Sibling shops • Support groups • Professional counseling • Non–disability community support	• Supports for the role of daily care/support • Respite/childcare • Adaptive equipment • Home modifications • Financial assistance • Cash subsidies • Short- and long-term planning with family

As Jason Whitt outlined in his family's story, their faith community provided them with many of these supports. There are stories of clergy and congregations helping in almost all of those examples listed. Faith communities around North America have become increasingly intentional about supporting families with children with disabilities. Families are often at the forefront of that development. To be sure, that is not the most common story and experience. No one congregation does all of them, but congregations and public support organizations can learn from each other and from the stories circulated in family networks. They also can learn how to refer to trusted community resources and partner with them in supporting individuals with disabilities and their families. Some families would prefer to receive support from their clergy or congregation rather than other nonprofit or government organizations. The Charting the Life Course project has several short planning guides listing key questions and issues that come up for families over the life course.[31] They mention spirituality and faith communities explicitly as one of the key sources of community-based supports. Other families might say that the spiritual supports they have needed and received have come from many sources other than those provided in their faith community, particularly networks or connections with other families.

CORE COMPONENTS OF SPIRITUAL SUPPORTS AND THEIR IMPACT

So what is central to spiritual support of parents and families, by clergy, friends, and, indeed, other kinds of professionals?

Presence

Presence is the willingness and ability of others to simply be with parents and families when they are in crisis or when they are needed. Most of us prefer for support to come from an individual or group with whom we already have a valued and trusted relationship. Presence means the first stance is listening, not prescribing, fixing, or doing something. There may be many things to do and ways to help that emerge from compassionate presence, but the willingness by others to be with someone in a crisis and over the long haul is often the most appreciated support. It is the first step toward addressing many of the emotional and mental health needs as defined in the chart above.

Counsel and Guidance

This does not mean first of all professional counseling but rather guidance in the areas listed under "Discovery and Navigation" above. A mother once told me that her caregiving struggles led her to see a pastoral counselor. She reported, "He wanted to talk about my relationship with my mother. I realized I just needed and wanted some respite care!"

Counsel can also be guidance with emotional and spiritual questions or issues, through other parents, trusted friends, and professional caregivers. It can be simply listening to the questions and feelings, and then being ready, when families are, with stories and spiritual resources that may be of help. As I note below, it can also be a key resource in reframing the personal, social, and religious/theological constructs of disability that impact a given family

Advocacy

Advocacy that accompanies and empowers is definitely one source of spiritual support. In fact, advocacy has often had its foundation in faith communities, although not as often in relationship to disability as to other minorities. One of my favorite family stories came from a parent who talked about taking her minister with her to their daughter's IEP meeting.[32] She noted, "We got everything we wanted. . . . They thought he was our lawyer." It always gets a knowing laugh, but think of the power of having representatives from the congregations or spiritual networks accompanying a family as they face crucial times of planning, navigating educational supports and ensuring the needs and rights of their child are met.

Building a Supporting Community or Network

The church that surrounded the Whitt family in the story cited earlier is one example. It could include many of the supports listed in the third box in the chart above, "Instrumental Supports and Day-to-Day Needs." As psychotherapist Patrick O'Malley asked earlier, "Who is there and provides supports after the last casserole is delivered?" Informal and formal circles of support within a congregation or in partnership with other support organizations are both ways to meet individual and family needs and hopes. A community of support can also be one that works with a family for long-term planning around the question "What happens after we are gone?"[33]

Using the definition of spirituality described earlier and its links to the core values in current services, the impact of effective spiritual supports can be profound. First, think about the importance of the people or strategies that help parents (or individuals) as they work through the "Who am I / are we now?" questions toward new understandings of their child, their own identity, and what is most important and sacred to them as they go forward. Having a network and community in which their understandings of disability (i.e., social constructs) are much more positive than negative may be invaluable in helping families find new meaning and support. Jason Whitt noted the willingness of their congregation to embrace Camille as one of them and to celebrate her just as they would any other family member. If a family were already involved in a spiritual community like the Whitts', there would be expectations and hopes of response by that community. A welcoming, supportive response thus can be crucial in reframing personal and social attitudes and understandings (constructs) of disability. In the Toronto quality of life model, the impact can be on the "being" and "belonging" of the person with a disability and their family.[34]

Second, reflect on the ways that supports provided in the times, roles, and areas we have listed might impact both versions of the "Why?" question: (1) the question of why this happened and (2) understandings of the parental role, vocation, and calling. For some parents, the presence of a child with a disability leads to new visions for their life's calling. The opportunity to raise a child with other children and families in an inclusive congregation or faith community that celebrates presence and growth through typical rites of passage also provides another context for "becoming" as outlined in the Toronto QOL model.

Third, a supportive community, whether congregation, parent group, neighborhood, or human service organization, helps answer the question, "Whose are we?" Acts of reaching out, welcome, and inclusion, along with the opportunity to use one's gifts in service to others, taps the power of spiritual supports to help individuals and families *belong*. The inherent social capital that results from that belonging in a faith community and other support networks also has the power to help open doors to belonging in other parts of a community. The experiences of being known and loved for who you are and feeling "at home" are, as the credit card commercial says, "truly priceless."

CONCLUSION

Both the construct of spirituality and the experience of spiritual supports can thus be crucial components of a family's adjustment to having a child with a disability or to a disability acquired at any age by an individual or family member. Spirituality really has no equal as a framework for understanding and dealing with grief and loss. Spiritual and religious understandings of divine presence, personal identity, meaning, purpose, and a community of support shape so many cultural contexts. That is one reason for the extensive discussion at the beginning of this chapter of the initial adjustment that families have to make and the ongoing questions they encounter.

Starting from the more secular family support framework developed by Shelli Reynolds and colleagues, there are multiple ways that spiritual supports and communities can be a significant source of support for families. Professional service providers can utilize spiritual assessments to open those possibilities, but simple conversations and a professional willingness to work with clergy and congregations can also open those doors. Doing so requires care, sensitivity, and skill, for two important reasons. The first is the prevalence of unhelpful spiritual or theological euphemisms and the negative experiences of many families. Second, though, exploring a dimension that taps into core beliefs, feelings, and the very heart of one's experience has a great deal of power that needs to be used carefully and wisely.

When spirituality is used sensitively, and with commitment to the long range as well as the crisis periods, its power can be profound. Another of my favorite stories also involves Rud and Ann Turnbull, their son Jay, and their daughters. They worked very hard to build many community supports with Jay, including an inclusive church in Lawrence, Kansas, where Jay was a valued member.[35] They also built an intentional circle of support that helped their family with the planning and coordination of Jay's supports.[36] After one of those meetings, Jay's sister Amy came out with the exclamation, "It's awesome to be surrounded by people who are not sorry for what you cannot do." That line became a song through the gifts of my seminary classmate, songwriter and singer Tom Hunter.[37] It would be hard to find a truer line about acceptance, inclusion, celebration, and belonging.

9

Respite Care
A Sabbath for (and from) Caregivers

One of the biblical questions I sometimes ask when giving presentations about scriptural traditions and disability is, "When is respite care first mentioned in the Bible?" Occasionally, someone makes the connection and answers, "Genesis, chapter 1: 'After creating and working for six days, God rested.'" The significance of a Sabbath was built into the very fabric of created life by a story that recognizes and divinely sanctions the need and, indeed, necessity, for a time apart, a day of rest as well as one of reflection.

Exploring the spiritual roots of respite care also means looking at the services and supports for and with people with disabilities and their families, which are changing in the face of person-centered and community-based supports. There are multiple options for creating respite programs that call for collaboration among many potential community partners: medical and service systems, recreational programs, faith communities, parent organizations, and both the public and private sectors. But respite care is also an area that calls us back (or forward) to a vision of community in which people and families support one another in neighborhoods, extended families, and other informal networks. Respite can involve professionals, but almost anyone can be involved as a form of hands-on, concrete support for a caregiver. Respite care may be both a focused form of support and care as well as a by-product of other activities that give individuals and their primary caregivers a chance to be apart from one another.[1] When carefully thought through, respite care can also be an opportunity to provide support in ways that can lead to ongoing relationships and friendships. Those relationships not only take place "in the community" but also help build community itself. Tackling the issues of finding and developing respite care options leads directly into questions of identity, responsibility, self-care, asking/receiving, trust, and community. It is a form of care that is ultimately about sustaining ongoing care and creativity rather than fixing family problems. All of us may be able to imagine being in that position at some point in our life's journey if we have not already been there.

CAREGIVING FAMILIES AND RESPITE CARE

For many "typical" families, parenting and caregiving responsibilities on top of job and career pressures lead to more than enough stress. That's true even with the diverse strategies that many families use to find additional caregiving supports: day care, after-school programs, swapping care time with other families, using grandparents and relatives, activities and programs that involve children and elderly parents out of the home, babysitters, play time at someone else's house, sleepovers . . . the list can go on and on. In most Western societies, we are a long way from the origins of "It takes a village to raise a child," in which relatives, friends, neighbors, and elders lived nearby and could all keep an eye out for children and others who needed temporary supervision.

None of that is "typical" for families whose children or adult members need extra levels of care, attention, and supervision, especially when there are physical disabilities and chronic illnesses involved. "Twenty-four/seven" has become the mantra for always having to be "on" as a caregiver, with the "sandwich generation" describing the situation of families caring for children while also assuming caregiving responsibilities for their parents or elders. One of the ironies of the history of services in this country is that respite care first came into the awareness of professional services when professionals decided other professionals needed it when the deinstitutionalization movements began in the 1960s.[2] Hundreds if not thousands of group homes were developed for adults moving out of institutions, leading to a professional awareness that the staff needed breaks and time off, a need that had not been recognized for families caring for a child or adult at home. When inclusive education became an entitlement, those "typical" forms of parental breaks become even more important. When that entitlement ends and there are no guaranteed supports or services once a person with an intellectual or developmental disability turns twenty-one, then the caregiving issues become a crisis. That same crisis can happen when something happens to a primary caregiver that removes them from the picture.

The need for parents and caregivers to have a break, to have time for themselves or with other members of the family and friends, is ubiquitous. The flip side is that children and adults with disabilities of one kind or another also need to be with peers and people other than their primary caregivers. One parent writes about the importance of a week of respite after six months of intense care for their newborn daughter with a severe chronic illness:

> The week that our family stayed at the beach was the most wonderful gift during those six months. *It was truly a blessing not only for us but also for our daughter, for it gave us the opportunity to stand outside the situation and view it from a distance. It enabled us to review what had gone on before, to put things into perspective, to think and plan. We were also physically restored, and we were able to go on with much more strength for the next 12 months caring for our daughter.* Respite care was unavailable 11 years ago when we needed to cope with the challenges my daughter presented to our family. I had to make it happen [which she did by arranging an extra week stay in a hospital after one of several surgeries].[3]

Note simply the italicized sentences and the ways those "outcomes" are almost identical to the value of a Sabbath.

RESPITE CARE AND PUBLIC SERVICES

The initial respite programs that began were indeed just that: programs organized as services for families. Respite centers, in-home respite, and other models evolved that relied on public funding and supports. The prospects of being able to arrange an extra week stay in a hospital for respite care, like the parents did above, is now much more remote, given the costs entailed. In the 1980s there was a growing awareness that generic community services needed to expand to include children and adults with special needs because (1) specialized programs were too costly, (2) generic services demonstrated the capacity to adapt to other populations, (3) long-term social costs of being involved in specialized programs perpetuate differences, and (4) they strengthen support networks for all families in the community.[4] One could add the myriad of regulations involved in specialized programs as well as the increasing difficulty of finding direct support care workers.

There is now growing attention to the emotional, psychological, and financial costs of the rising levels of caregiving that are needed as more families deal with spouses or parents who are aging or have dementia. For example, as I was writing this paragraph, the e-newsletter *Disability Scoop* came with the headline "The stress of caring for a child with a disability may truly take a toll, with a new study suggesting that mothers of those with special needs see greater declines in memory as they age."[5] In the United States, the National Alliance for Caregiving compiles studies and resources showing the growing need for caregiver support as the baby boomers age as well as the economic value of the informal caregiving being provided.[6] More and more states have developed family support programs that include and offer some funding for families to pay for respite care services. Even with that support, families still describe respite care as one of their greatest needs but also hardest to meet in ways that match the quality of care they desire.

> As one parent put it, "Families need an uncomplicated, easily accessible means of arranging respite care to meet their wants and needs. When a potential pleasure becomes more trouble than it's worth, I give it up. I always measure the event against the complication involved in making it happen. Time off is no relaxation if I spend the entire time worrying if the kids are OK. I can't enjoy myself if I think they are unhappy, and certainly I can't relax if I'm not confident about the reliability of the person watching my children. I think many professionals are under the misconception that time away from the care of rearing a child with a disability is what I need to maintain my sanity. I need much more than time—*I need security that comes from knowing that the person I've left my son with is as capable as I am of providing for his needs. You simply can't relax and enjoy yourself and worry at the same time. It's peace of mind I need—not just time.*"[7]

Two paths can lead to that security and peace of mind. The first is through a focus on the right kind of professional training and caregiving skills, particularly if the respite care is being provided through an agency program. The right kinds of credentials are a path to helping families trust a respite caregiver, especially when the caregiver is unknown to the family. If a caregiver does not have confidence in a respite caregiver, for whatever reason, that anxiety may be alleviated by the level of trained competence as well as the compliance with the standards for the program.

The second path is knowing and trusting the person involved, whether or not he or she has had professional training. According to families I have known, they would much rather have support and respite from someone they trust and know well, perhaps someone whom they have helped to train, rather than from a stranger, no matter how well qualified. That can also be an issue for the child or adult being cared for—a friend or someone well known can be a relationship that is valued and looked forward to rather than having to adjust to a stranger and new caregiver.

THE SPIRITUAL FOUNDATIONS OF RESPITE CARE

Thus, one core spiritual dimension of respite care is that of relationship—knowing substitute caregivers and trusting them. Spiritual and faith communities are potentially excellent sources for respite care because people tend to trust family, friends, neighbors, fellow congregational members, and other people they know personally. Trust has had the chance to develop over time. Faith communities may also have the capacity to link and address needs related to people with congenital, acquired, and aging disabilities, three areas where the primary caregivers may need respite care but must then find support from three different kinds of social service systems. That is one of the reasons that state-funded services who may provide similar services are sometimes referenced as "silos."

Even before finding a trusted care provider, the first task is helping families recognize their own need for respite care, or simply a time for themselves. That can mean dealing with their own self-image and how they cope with both internal and external expectations of being caregiver. It also means believing that time for self-care is a necessity as well as a gift. Giving ourselves permission to seek respite care means dealing with the complex ways by which we both give and receive help and support in our society.

Three of the primary self-images and values in Western societies are being competent, being responsible, and being in control. Internal and external expectations combine so that one is to be competent at both work and at home. Not only am I to be competent in tasks of work, caregiving, and parenting, but also it is my responsibility as parent, son, daughter, spouse, or sibling. "That's what we do in our family." Often it is expressed as "That's the mother, daughter, or wife's responsibility. I must then show to others that I have all those tasks and duties under control without it being too big of a deal."

This is where the image of the "supermom" or supercaregiver gets born. Caregivers may just feel like they are doing their best to get by while others look at them and say, "I could never do that." Or, "I don't know how they do it all." For the caregivers, what they commonly hear is, "You are such an amazing parent (wife, daughter, husband, etc.). You are so special." When I have been able to talk honestly with 24/7 caregivers and ask whether they have heard people say that to them, a frequent response is a finger in the mouth imitating a gag reflex. "On the contrary," parents and caregivers say, "I am not special. I am just doing what I have to do" (or "am supposed to," "want to," "am expected to," "been asked to"). I have heard parents say, "I end up feeling like I can't snap at my kid or respond in ways typical parents do when frustrated, exhausted, or upset." The images of parents as "supermom" or "superdad" (likewise, spouse, son, daughter, etc.) evoke many of the same issues for caregivers as does "super-crip" for many people with disabilities. The expectations lead to the internal pressure to overcome all the issues being faced without putting too many demands on others or making too many requests of them.

If caregivers then need help, they first need to recognize it to themselves or others and then possibly deal with their potential guilt (or anger) in having to do so. One of the ironies I have encountered in caregivers and professionals alike who love and work with people with limits is that we are reluctant to admit and accept the fact that we also have limits. A second is that the need for self-care should seem both obvious and important. In the Jewish and Christian traditions that I know best, these two ironies can be addressed by some honest exploration of scriptural stories, passages, and images. Begin with the creation of the Sabbath, a divinely appointed day of rest, reflection, and renewal. Whatever one believes about the creation story, the origin of the Sabbath is a recognition of the deep human need to step aside from normal routines and the tasks of working and living. Worship is but one dimension of that need. If God needed to rest, then maybe I do as well.

Move on to the many figures in the Bible with limitations, to those who were called sinful because they did not recognize their own humanity, and then to the writers of the Psalms who both plead for relief (121) and celebrate stillness, restoration, finding refuge and sanctuary, and being cared for (23). In the New Testament, Jesus modeled a need for times when he could "go apart" (Matt 14:23; Luke 5:16), as well as offering himself to all "who labor and are overburdened, and I will give you rest" (Matt 11:28). The ways in which the people of God are called to care for and with one another as well as "the least of these" (Matt 25:45) is a theme throughout the Bible. A motto of the respite care movement partially embodies some of these scriptural injunctions: "Asking for help is a sign of strength."

St. Bernard of Clairvaux, one of the early church fathers, has one of the most profound and piercing explorations of the dynamics of care for others and care for self. There were, for him, four levels of love, framed in terms of love of God or others and oneself. In the first, one loves oneself for the sake of one's self, which can also be self-centeredness, pomposity, or glorification. In the second, one loves others (or God) for the sake of one's self, a very "normal" human transaction whereby we care for others in hope of receiving something in return. That, of course, can be very manipulative. The third is the Christian value of *agape*, loving others (or God) for their sake. *Agape* is frequently portrayed as the ideal kind of sacrificial love, drawn and told in a modern story form by Shel Silverstein in his illustrated book *The Giving Tree*.[8] But St. Bernard does not stop there. Beyond, or deeper yet, is the call to love oneself for the sake of others (or God)—if I do not care for myself, I will not be able to care for others (or God) over the long haul. That theological admonition is one way of helping both family and professional caregivers recognize that it is more than permissible to ask for help because we need one another and God. Asking for help is also sanctioned and blessed by God so that one may continue to love, serve, and care.[9]

Asking for help is still hard to do even if it is a sign of strength and a need blessed by God, sometimes especially for people of faith. According to Carol Levine, the most disliked euphemism spoken to those who are hurting is, "The Lord does not give you more than you can bear."[10] Add in the biblical injunction that "it is more blessed to give than to receive" (Ats 20:35), and the result is that many of us believe we are to be givers, not receivers. To be honest, for many of us, asking and receiving is harder than giving because it means an honest acknowledgment of limitation and the need for support. That deeply ingrained habit can become a shell, one that leaves caregivers with the complex mix of issues: "I really am exhausted. I need some help. I don't know how to ask or if I should, and I don't want to be a burden." It is sometimes interpreted in religious terms that symbolize the sense of loneliness, burden, and anger: "It is just my lot in life" or "the cross I have to bear." That shell can be cracked by friends and loved ones who both offer support in concrete ways and mean what they say. As I have heard friends say, "Don't tell me, 'Let me know what I can do.' Ask me and tell me something concrete, for example, 'I would like to come watch your kids [wife, husband, etc.] on Tuesday afternoon. Would that be okay?'"

Friends, relatives, neighbors, and others may know that the caregivers need support and do not like to ask, but those same friends and potential sources of caregiving support can get blocked by their own internal sense of uncertainty or incapacity—"We would like to do something but don't know how to ask. And we don't want to intrude." When those dynamics are operating at the same time on both sides, there is a real loss of opportunity to receive respite and support on the one hand along with the loss of a concrete way to give and help on the other. It is often hard for anyone who needs help to believe that another person may truly want to do so simply for the sake of the relationship or for the joy and meaning it provides them. That is where another form of obligation, duty, and responsibility can be utilized in a very positive way to address someone's reluctance to ask: "I do this because I want to." Or "That's what we do as friends (neighbors, community, congregation, etc.)."

In addition to the "ask and tell me something concrete" approach of addressing that gap, another is to find a person whom the family trusts to do the asking for them, so they are not always put in that position. In the world of professional services, case managers and care coordinators play that role. In the world of communities and congregations, it is those people who are "the askers"—people who know a lot of people and are not hesitant to ask or recruit others for a project or a task. If families could call a designated asker, for example, in a congregation, then they would not have to feel that reluctance to call a list of people. That role is another reason why faith communities have so much potential as sources of respite, relief, and renewal.

FAITH COMMUNITIES AND RESPITE CARE: SABBATHS EVERYWHERE AND ANYTIME

Think of many of the words in this chapter associated with faith communities: Sabbath, family, need, sanctuary, rest, renewal, support, care, relationships, community, responsibility, call, and opportunity. The list could go on. Thankfully, respite care is no longer a foreign word in many faith communities as congregations become more aware of its need and are themselves composed of people who have multiple caregiving roles. That awareness has also grown as many faith communities have become more intentional in including and supporting families with disabled members. My colleague, researcher Erik Carter, frequently illustrates the statistic that one in four families is impacted by some form of disability by using Google Maps to zoom in on the neighborhood surrounding a congregation and put an X on every fourth house.[11] Statistically, if these families are not involved in congregations, where are they?

Families and individuals who are ongoing caregivers of someone with a disability or chronic illness and who are also members of faith communities have sometimes said, "We would love to come, but who is going to watch our son or daughter?" Husbands and wives might say, "We just have to take turns coming"; "It just ends up being too much work to get someone ready to participate in congregational activities so it defeats the purpose of going. It is more restful to stay at home"; or, "We can't, because there is nothing at the church for them." More than one family has told me that a religious education program leader says, "We would be glad to have your child come, but we would need you to be there as well," a requirement that defeats the possibility that a caregiver could use that time to be with other adults in other concurrent activities just like most of the other parents. Having your parent in your class may also be the last thing a child or teenager wants. In the Protestant, Christian world in which I grew up, family members who were not able to come for one reason or another got assigned the label of "shut-in." There has been a growing awareness in faith communities that people can be shut out by barriers of architecture, attitude, and inclusive programming as much as they are shut in.

Diverse forms of respite care ministries are sprouting across North America that demonstrate the creative potential of a caring community that is committed to supporting one another in concrete ways. Respite care does not have to begin with a "program" but simply an awareness that respite may be needed, a willingness to ask, and the capacity of faith communities to respond to needs in their midst. For example, several individuals in a congregation, or other families, might be willing to get to know the family needing respite care, spend some time with them so the parents can teach them tasks related to special needs of their family member, and then provide respite for an evening, a day, a few hours, a weekend, or the like. The same thing could work for a relative caring for an elderly parent with dementia or other health conditions. Exploratory discussions with caregivers may indicate simply a need for someone to help do chores, provide occasional transportation, or perform maintenance around the home.

A "respite circle" or "support team" of several people or families means that people can take turns and caregivers have more than one option, thus helping them to feel like they are not burdening someone else. That kind of circle of support can be intentional about developing the kinds of opportunities that others take for granted, such as just inviting a child with a disability over to another child's home to play or having a respite volunteer help someone participate in community-based activities. One congregation asked a family what they needed, and it turned out having someone come on Sunday morning to help get their child with a disability ready to go to church while the parents dealt with the other children made a huge difference in relieving a stressful time. Increasing numbers of congregations are using peer/

buddy models to facilitate inclusion in religious education programs. Some of those same buddies or teenagers could become sitters whom a family would trust.

Other congregations have begun more formally organized programs, such as Mother's Morning Out or fun Saturdays so parents can spend time with their other children or do chores while their child with a disability has fun and participates in activities at the church. Highland Park United Methodist Church in Dallas has a very popular Night Owls respite program on Friday evenings staffed by volunteers from the congregation and some paid staff so they can include children or adults with more complex health-care needs. The parents can drop them off early in the evening, come back late, and in between there are a variety of activities for everyone involved. Congregation volunteers have brought other congregational members who were unsure at first but then became both dedicated volunteers as well as friends with the people they got to know. The church also provides a gift certificate so the parents can go out to dinner. Some congregations have evenings like these when the parents or caregivers can participate in a support group in another part of the building. Other congregations, such as McLean Bible Church in the metro Washington, D.C., area, have had the resources to build a respite facility on their grounds called Jill's House, with a mission specifically focused on overnight respites for families with children with multiple and complex disabilities. Other congregations around the country have begun respite programs that developed into collaborative, community-based programs that involve both respite facilities and home-based respite service.

The variety of respite supports that can be provided through communities of faith depends both on the specific (i.e., person- or family-centered) needs of individual caregivers and families and the willingness of a congregation to make a commitment to find ways to respond. There is no "one model fits all" approach to faith-based respite care, nor should there be. A period off for respite or renewal will depend on what is most important for individual caregivers. It could be at any time of the week. One new and creative form of respite care has been provided by a congregation who had several members who rented out rooms through Airbnb hosts. With some training by the families involved, those hosts were willing to have the family member with a disability as their guest for an overnight stay or longer, and in this case, the congregation paid the bill.

Some of the most important resources that faith communities have for respite care already exist but are not called by that name, nor are they created for that purpose. When typical families bring children to religious education, the parents can then participate in other activities that are meaningful to them. It also then enables children to know and experience the care of other adults and a community of peers. The respite, as it were, goes both ways. When someone walks the halls with a restless youngster on the autism spectrum and enables the parents to stay in the worship service, that's a break. When teenagers go to youth group or on overnight/weekend retreats, parents also get a break. Even better, a faith-based camp week or two in the summer can be life-changing times for children or teenagers while also providing immense support to families. When faith communities make the commitment to include children, teenagers, or adults with disabilities in those kinds of programs with everyone else, their primary caregivers get the kind of break that all others take for granted. It also gives children, teenagers, or adults with a disability time to do something they love, meet others, and develop new relationships. Those kinds of programs also give teenagers and adults without disabilities the opportunity to be volunteers, buddies, or camp counselors, roles that help them live out their own faith and that can lead to ongoing friendships with individuals with disabilities. In addition, for teenagers and young people who are serving in the counselor or buddy roles, this may be the place where their vocational direction is born.

Thus, one of the key strategies for both faith-based and community-based respite services is to help all kinds of programs and activities for specific age ranges to expand their mission to include children or adults with disabilities. The additional value in this approach is that it is focused on the interests of, and benefits to, the person with a disability. Caregivers who are reluctant to ask for respite because they feel guilty or selfish about asking for something for themselves can then feel that they are doing something that is primarily for the benefit of their son or daughter. These kinds of programs then grow organically, benefit everyone involved, and provide opportunities for the development of long-term relationships characterized by trust and friendship. Those outcomes may be as valuable as the respite care itself. They highlight the fact that it is not only the primary caregivers who may need respite care. Children and adults with disabilities in family homes also need *respite from* the usual routines, opportunities to try new things as well as do things they love, be with friends they want to be with, meet new people, and experience care from others besides their parents or family.

These kinds of stories, models, and possibilities may sound relatively easy because they sound so "typical," but that is rarely the case, especially when relationships need to be developed or when it is a new venture for a congregation. This is new territory, so to speak, so careful planning is called for because people will have many questions as they work through what it means to be volunteer caregivers with children, adults, and families. If the caregiving involves children or adults with complex needs, planning needs to include ways to help volunteers trust in their own ability, such as spending time with the family and being trained by them. That is also a way for the family to gain trust. The development of backup plans will also ease anxiety by preparing for unexpected challenges. The anxiety about new ventures into caregiving or helping relationships often comes out in the form of questions about liability for a congregation, its ministries, and the people involved. Those fears will often subside much more quickly with care-full planning about how to handle any challenges, special care needs, or potential emergencies involved. Anxiety can also be addressed by starting small in more natural, person- or family-centered forms of respite care as well as by expanding current activities to include people as participants rather than as "receivers of care." There are liability questions in any form of congregational activity, programming, and caregiving (e.g., picking someone up to take them somewhere), so they need to be addressed in the same way that those questions are addressed for anyone else. Otherwise, the anxiety around newness, disability, or "specialness" magnifies the concerns about liability and "special training requirements" into questions larger than they need to be.

CONCLUSION: STRENGTHENING THE CAPACITY TO CARE FOR AND WITH ONE ANOTHER

Respite caregiving might be likened in our times to the concrete "cup of water given in my name" (Matt 10:42; Mark 9:41) or the hospitality offered to strangers that included water, food, and shelter on their journey. In a world full of hurry, worry, work, and responsibilities that tax most of us at different times, respite and rest is a need magnified by its frequent absence, especially for people who have ongoing responsibilities to care for others with atypical needs. Respite care can happen in many creative ways, but it also calls for attention, intention, and habit. Keeping a Sabbath, on a regular basis, "for it is holy" (Exod 20:8; Deut 5:12), is perhaps the most profound way of recognizing and honoring those universal human needs.

Hospitality and respite are also enormous businesses. Think of the ways that hotels sell themselves and vacation destinations are marketed. That can also be the case in human services, when and where respite care and other forms of long-term supports grow as a way of supporting primary caregivers. Human service agencies often face a dual challenge: (1) inadequate funding levels to be able to provide respite care at reasonable costs and (2) the growing difficulty of recruiting and keeping staff for those roles. For most of us, respite happens in more individualized ways and through relationships characterized by mutuality, shared responsibilities or resources used for an evening out, a day off, regular time for one's self, or a weekend away.

The potential of various forms of respite care as components of faith communities brings with it the opportunity for both congregations and communities to become more intentional about caring for one another, whether it is through the gift of time, companionship, planned activities, or other more typical exchanges of support and care in community settings. Thus, respite care can be part of a vision for the kind of caring congregation or community we want to be or feel called to be. It is also a way of "remembering forward"[12] the kinds of neighborhoods, communities, and congregations where people just watch out for one another. Disability, like other unexpected life events, can happen anyplace, anytime. So might our own need for respite care. We can all "pay it forward" by thinking intentionally about how to support those in our midst who need that break in the here and now.

IV

SPIRITUALITY AND PROFESSIONALS

10

Integrating Spirituality in Professional Services and Roles

Questions about how to integrate spirituality in professional roles and services raise a prior question: "What does it mean to be a professional?" "Professional" as a noun means one "engaged or qualified in a particular profession," engaged in an activity as an occupation, not just a pastime, and "competent, or skilled, in a particular activity."[1] That definition fits most common usage and modern understandings. The surprise is that the origin of the word "professional" is from the word "profess," which in the Middle Ages, in Latin, meant originally "the declaration made on entering into membership of a church or religious order."[2] A more secular meaning evolved in "to make one's profession" around the beginning of the sixteenth century and was first used with the "-al" at the end of 1747 to mean "pertaining to, proper to, or connected with one's profession or calling."[3] In more recent times, "professional" has come to mean a level of skill that assumes corresponding levels of focus and commitment. Before its primary meaning evolved to this acquisition of a certain level of knowledge and skill (along with adherence to professional standards and expectations), the training to become a "professional" involved long periods of apprenticeship and mentoring. For centuries, spiritual communities and religious orders have called that process "formation."

The challenges posed by changing professional roles and identity in services with people with disabilities and their families lead us back to a need to recover parts of the original definition, especially when one looks at the assumptions and barriers that have separated "professional" from "spirituality." Since the 1970s, research interest in the importance of spirituality in health care and human services has exploded in quantity and quality, along with corresponding strategies for addressing spirituality in care and treatment. Assessing and utilizing spirituality brings its own cautions for the appropriate roles by professional caregivers. Professionals' understanding of their own spirituality can be a key part of enhancing their professional role as well as of enhancing their capacity to work with the spiritual dimensions of care for their patients (or clients) and families.

BARRIERS TO ADDRESSING SPIRITUALITY IN
SERVICES WITH PEOPLE WITH DISABILITIES AND
THEIR FAMILIES AND REASONS TO ADDRESS THEM

Some of the barriers to addressing spiritual needs and interests in assessments and professional services have already been mentioned briefly. The current models of diagnosing and assessing intellectual and developmental disabilities do not include spirituality as a dimension of assessment. Neither the Supports Intensity Scale of the AAIDD nor the major American model for assessing quality of life explicitly address spirituality. Both can lead to questions that explore spiritual interests, needs, and participation. However, as with most assessment and intake processes, questions and conversations about spirituality rarely go past basic information about someone's faith tradition. Person-centered planning processes can go more in depth as a planning team of professionals, caregivers, friends, and family explores what is *important to* someone and the supports he or she needs to address that area of importance, which could easily include interests and dreams related to spiritual expression, growth, and participation. Doing that well depends on the capacity of the facilitators to ask questions that go deeper than "going to church." The Council on Quality and Leadership, one of the American accrediting organizations that is focused on person-centered services, does in fact have some excellent guidelines for exploring spirituality in the context of person-centered planning and supports.[4]

A second issue is that there are not many good models for assessing and tapping spirituality in the context of inclusive, community-based services and supports. One of the impediments has been what one might call the "oral tradition" of so many negative stories about the responses of people of faith and faith communities to individuals with disabilities and their families. Professionals hear those stories from people with disabilities and their families, or from other professionals, usually around injunctions about "what not to do" or passed on as a rationale for not addressing spirituality. The stories are shared among networks of individuals with disabilities and family members. Until the past twenty to thirty years, those negative stories have not had many positive ones to balance the scales,[5] so to speak, and to thus serve as examples of the many ways that spirituality and faith communities have been important to both individuals and families.

That oral tradition in human services forms a backdrop on which other barriers easily get magnified. A major example is the professional injunction against proselytizing. Professional ethics guidelines simply or directly state that professionals are not to let their values or beliefs get in the way of their professional role. As the more secular definition of "professional" gained way from the eighteenth century onward, and as the sciences made rapid progress in health and human services, there was a corresponding development, with good reason, that professionals should avoid "proselytizing" at all costs, that is, trying to change a person's religious beliefs or making that change a condition for service. The pendulum swung to such an extreme that many professionals became afraid (and still are) of even talking about spirituality or faith as a component of someone's life or treatment. A recent example was some critique leveled at missionary doctors in West Africa in the 2014–2015 Ebola outbreak by the Western press for even mentioning that they were there because of their vocation and calling as missionaries.

With the birth of psychiatry and the impact of Freud, religious beliefs were often seen as a symptom of mental illness rather than as a form of meaning making and source of support. Delusions about being God or another religious figure can certainly be symptoms of some mental illnesses. Assessing religion as the cause of those delusions, rather than as a metaphor of other meanings, meant religion and spirituality were at fault and thus needed to be eradicated. That conclusion both fails to understand the ways that symbols and beliefs may express deeper emotional or spiritual issues while also failing to see that the injunction was its own form of proselytizing. A former colleague, now a chaplain, worked for years to overcome her own struggle with multiple personalities. She once defined her dilemma poignantly: "In my treatment, my faith was a symptom, and in my congregation, my mental illness made me an outcast." That tradition has changed radically in the past fifty years as more and more research has been done into the ways that spirituality and faith can be a force for both good as well as harm in the lives of persons with mental illness. As with other forms of disability, the major forms of harm are the equations of mental illness with sin, the demonic, or lack of faith.

Another barrier is that most public services receive government funding. The professional injunction to avoid proselytizing has sometimes been interpreted to mean that religion or spirituality cannot be discussed at all for fear of losing funding. The separation of church and state clause clearly and rightly states that government and government services should not seek to impose religious beliefs or a specific tradition, but it does not mean that beliefs and areas of life important to someone cannot be explored for the sake of more holistic person- and family-centered treatment.

That fear grows because of very public and contentious battles over issues like prayer in schools and other controversies such as gay marriage, abortion, and religion in the public square. Laying those public issues against the contextual background of negative stories about religion and disability, seeing religious beliefs as symptoms, and the professional ethic of avoiding proselytizing, it is no wonder that providers of professional services and supports have been leery and hesitant to address spirituality and faith. With those issues come a fear of the power of spirituality to hurt, which runs right into the fact that "Do no harm" is a foundation of many codes of ethics. However, that hesitancy contradicts other values such as holistic treatment, person-centered care, use of generic and natural supports, and the evidence of ways that spirituality, spiritual practices, and spiritual supports can play very positive, powerful roles in care, support, and healing. Think back to the example of the Whitt family and try to imagine where else they could have received the emotional, psychological, and spiritual supports that have been so important to them.

Finally, even with a professional desire to address spiritual needs and supports, the confusion amid the diversity of beliefs, traditions, and practices is quite daunting, just as the language and systems of health care and human services can be indecipherable to the average person (or religious person) who lacks familiarity with those worlds. That variety and diversity extends within different traditions as well as across them. Until recently, most professionals have not had any training in the ways that spirituality can be addressed in supports and services or the chance to develop skills in collaborating effectively with spiritual leaders and communities. Again, the growing interest in spirituality and research into its impact in medicine, psychology, social work, nursing, occupational therapy, and other professional services is opening the doors to awareness, skill development, and opportunities to collaborate with clergy and other spiritual leaders and communities.

Thus, the rationale for addressing those barriers of professional culture, practice, and training lies *both* within the power of spirituality as a helpful resource to individuals and families *as well as* within the core values that shape services and supports. The core values that drive disability services—independence, productivity, inclusion, self-determination, and cultural competence—all have barely explored and untapped spiritual foundations and dimensions. Given the barriers and cautions, how might spirituality be responsibly and effectively integrated into professional practices, services, and supports? As with disability, one can start with assessments.

ASSESSING OR CLASSIFYING SPIRITUALITY

As the recognition of spirituality has grown in the light of individual and family stories and supports, tools have been developed for describing spirituality that try to crystallize story, experience, and belief into more objective information. The result has been models of assessing someone's spirituality as a functional way of determining what needs and gifts should be addressed. For example, spirituality, cultural beliefs and traditions, and communication issues (from either language or disability) are three of the major areas discussed by the Joint Commission on the accreditation of hospitals and organizations in a "Roadmap" for good patient- and family-centered care.[6] Spiritual assessments have also arisen as one way to integrate chaplaincy, pastoral care, and other forms of spiritual supports into treatment and service plans. Some of them are simple, others very complex.

Before describing several of those models, what is the process and meaning of "assessment"? Assessment leads professionals in divergent directions. The concepts of assessment and classification described in the first chapter on disability usually involve a process that produces an *objective* description of a disability or the kinds of supports needed. The implication is one of "standing back" or "apart" from the person, leading, understandably, to how the "detachment" of professionals can be both a strength and a liability. Diagnosis and assessment can lead to intense disagreement about the ways labels are used and how they function as self-fulfilling prophecies of lowered expectations as well as devalued public stereotypes. When a disability or deficit become the only word used to describe the person, the unintended consequence is to build walls to relationships. Diagnoses and assessments may lead to helpful "answers" to many "unknowns" for individuals and their families as well as to ways of framing supports. But they can also lead to avoidance. For example, when people have multiple or complex disabilities, especially involving behavioral issues that have frustrated treatment plans over and over again, their assessments can carry a more generic meaning as people with "severe reputations."[7]

The key questions are how the assessment *functions* and what are its results: Does it help bring people and supports toward someone or push them away? Quality of life measures attempt to address areas that are often subjective domains, but "measuring" already limits the kind of results to objective categories. Pastoral theologian Gordon Hilsman notes a far different understanding of "assessment" by recovering the meaning of its Latin root as "to sit by" or "next to."[8] That implies a closeness that can be both objective and subjective, as well as pointing to the importance of a trusted, long-term presence and relationship when areas of vulnerability, deep personal values, and beliefs are being explored. Nothing illustrates that more than the Hebrew verb *yada*, meaning "to know" in the Bible, a verb also used for an intimate, personal, and sexual encounter. There, one sees the reasons for reams of ethical boundaries and of cases involving that violation of professional intimacy. Professional care needs to be a balancing act between those two meanings of assessment, or, if you will, a dance and art form.

MODELS OF SPIRITUAL ASSESSMENTS

With the cautions thus noted, assessments can be an important aid to supports and services. For examples, let us begin with the two authors and helping professionals whose definitions of spirituality were cited earlier: Dr. Cristina Puchalski and Rev. George Fitchett. At the George Washington Institute for Spirituality and Health, Dr. Puchalski developed the FICA spiritual history tool, an acronym easy to remember in the United States because FICA is also used to describe the Social Security Administration tax withdrawal from individual paychecks.

The FICA tool has four areas of questions that can be explored either quickly or in depth:

- *Faith*: Preference, choice, tradition, identity. Do you consider yourself a person of faith, or are you religious?
- *Influence and Importance*: How important is it to you? How does it influence your daily life?
- *Communal Expression*: What form does it take, if any? Would you like it to?
- *Assistance*: How can I/we assist you to address this part of your identity as part of your treatment or supports?[9]

The last question points to the kind of role a professional may be able to play. It is not a proselytizing question because it gives the power to the persons being served to define how they wish a professional team to honor and address their spiritual needs and interests.

George Fitchett and colleagues developed what they have called the 7×7 model, in which spirituality is seen as one of seven key domains in a holistic assessment.[10] This kind of model is one that could easily be adapted into frameworks for assessing any form of disability or quality of life in ways that include multiple dimensions of human life. There are seven kinds of assessments within their holistic framework, including spirituality, and seven areas to explore within the domain of what is considered "spiritual."

Holistic Assessment	Spiritual Assessment
Biological (Medical) Dimension	Belief and Meaning
Psychological Dimension	Vocation and Obligations
Family Systems Dimension	Experience and Emotion
Psychosocial Dimension	Courage and Growth
Ethnic/Racial/Cultural Dimension	Ritual and Practice
Social Issues Dimension	Community
Spiritual Dimension	Authority and Guidance

In the seven domains under spirituality, belief and meaning refers to someone's major beliefs, sense of purpose, core values, symbols of meaning, and affiliation, which is like the question of core identity: "Who am I?" Vocation and obligations explore one's sense of calling and duty—"Why am I?" Experience and emotion refers to the ways in which one experiences what one considers to be divine, sacred, or demonic, and one's feelings and interpretations associated with those experiences. Courage and growth includes sources of hope and what helps someone be open to changes in beliefs based on experience. Ritual and practice may be very personal ways of acting out meaning or, more typically, communal practices associated with their beliefs and meaning systems. Community is the "Whose am I?" question—where and what are the formal or informal networks of shared belief, meaning, ritual, and practice? What is someone's style of participation in those communal expressions? Finally, authority and guidance, Where does one find a sense of authority for their beliefs and practices? To whom does one turn for guidance? Are those sources within or without, in others, including systems of belief and institutions?

Both the FICA and 7×7 models are very functional. The 7×7 model addresses the complexity and possible depths of spirituality more thoroughly—it is a "thicker" definition. Some other models attempt to be more substantial by determining how one images God, the core spiritual experiences or questions that one is experiencing, and what kind of spiritual "diagnosis" one might assign. An example is a spiritual assessment format developed by Chaplain Lex Tartaglia and colleagues at the University of Rochester Medical Center.

Spiritual Diagnosis	Image of God	Experience	Existential Question	Experience	Image of God	Spiritual Diagnosis
Fear	Unpredictable Capricious Chaotic	Mistrust Victimization Helplessness Passivity	"Am I safe?" "Is my world a threat or an opportunity?"	Hope Courage Active agency Opportunity	Trustworthy Reliable	Faith
Alienation	Vengeful Divisive	Social stigma External judgment Rejection Estrangement	"Do I belong?"	Social acceptance Communion Embracement	Loving Inclusive	Community
Guilt	Punishing Judgmental	Internal-ized stigma Personal respon-sibility for illness	"Am I worthy?"	Grace Repentance	Merciful Compassionate	Reconciliation
Despair	Withholding Silent Absent	Meaninglessness Death anxiety Nonbeing	"Am I valued?" "Do I leave a legacy?" "Did my life make a difference?" "Am I content?" "Regretful?"	Vocation Purpose Creativity Meaning	Blessing Affirming Revealing	Providence

Their model is particularly thought provoking for the ways it combines both the experience of fundamental spiritual questions with possible interpretations of that experience. Starting in the middle of the chart, their "existential questions" are very similar to the core spiritual questions of identity/meaning, connection/belonging, and purpose. One value of this model is that it can be used to describe the ways that spirituality is expressed through both positive and negative or wounding experiences related to core existential questions.[11]

Any of these spiritual assessments could be used in any setting with people with most forms of disabilities. In more recent years, several other models for spiritual assessments have come from people working with individuals with intellectual and developmental disabilities. Simple assessments ask questions about people's faith background and preference, their interest in participation in spiritual activities or communities, their choices about doing so, whether they would like to do more or less, and the supports they might need to make that happen. Some are more sophisticated and complex by using pictures and symbols as ways of communicating with people whose verbal skills are limited.[12] Other provider agencies have utilized the Council on Quality and Leadership Spiritual Practice Guidelines.[13]

One model for assessing spirituality and developing guidelines for supporting spiritual interests and needs for people with intellectual and developmental disabilities came from a research project in the United Kingdom called A Space to Listen, led by John Swinton, one of the premier pastoral theologians exploring disability, theology, and spirituality. A product from this study is a short booklet entitled *No Box to Tick*—no place on the assessment forms or records of activities to enter spiritual preferences or experiences. The booklet describes areas of friendship, loss, mourning, loneliness, celebration, solitude, and participation in faith communities as examples of spiritual activities. Both titles point to the lack of ways to assess and describe spirituality in everyday services: the absence of questions about spirituality in typical assessments, and the simple fact that it takes time and space to listen deeply to what is most important to people, their sense of identity, their connections, and that which motivates their own hopes and desire.[14]

GOING SLOW: SOME CAUTION SIGNS

Having enough time and space to listen deeply to someone or to their caregivers, given a person's level of communication skills, means that assessing spirituality is not a quick process, unless one utilizes a model like FICA to determine whether patients or individuals would like someone representing their spiritual community to be called in and to work with others on the caregiving team. So it is slow and usually takes time to feel and know someone's "spirit." Going slow is a challenge for professionals, especially in most acute care settings, but if services and supports are provided over a longer time, or over someone's lifetime, there is time for spirituality to be explored and integrated into care.

A trusting relationship is crucial to exploring some of the beliefs, feelings, and experiences related to spiritual life. In one participatory action research study on the role of spirituality and religion in quality of life for families, the researchers found that spirituality was very important to families in shaping their own resilience in several ways: having faith in God, using prayer, attributing meaning to disability, and participating in religious communities. The authors suggested that families were looking for three things: acceptance of their child, spiritual and emotional support for themselves as parents, and supports within the congregation for their child to participate in worship and other activities. But they also noted:

> Due to the importance of spirituality and religion to families, as evidenced by the number and intensity of comments, spiritual well-being was originally a separate domain [in the 10 domains of family quality of life]. However, based on input from our PAR committee, spirituality was encompassed into emotional well-being. PAR committee members felt that the presence of and specific form of spiritual and religious beliefs of family members should be private and that any family quality of life model should recognize spirituality, and provide spiritually appropriate supports, but not get into specific belief systems. Although we did not intend to advance a specific spiritual belief system, the presence of spirituality as a domain seemed to indicate that we were advocating for a specifically spiritual component to family quality of life. It was thought that this might be a concern or be off-putting to some families who did not have a spiritual belief system.[15]

Their findings are a key reminder of the power of the spiritual dimensions of life and the need to address them sensitively and slowly. The limitations of defining spirituality solely as a "belief system" harkens back to the same issue in the quality of life model from the World Health Organization. The FICA process could be the kind of introductory exploration that gives families the power to determine how much they want to reveal and, potentially, to whom. As planning increasingly seeks to be more person centered and family centered, other methods will evolve for professionals to recognize ways that individuals, families, and professionals can together address spiritual needs and interests while also giving the individuals and families the control over how to do so.

THE SPIRITUALITY OF PROFESSIONALS

Health and human service professionals are also holistic human beings. Being professionals means being aware of the ways our own spirituality can impact our professional role and our skills. Trust in professionals by individuals and families does not come simply from respecting a professional's knowledge. If one asks a group of individuals with disabilities or family members a similar question to the open-ended question about religious experience—"Tell me your stories with professionals"—one will also get a huge range of experiences and value judgments. For example, in a conversation over coffee with the parent of a son with autism, I asked about their experience with professionals. She briefly described some of them and then noted about one they had first worked with, "He's the only one who has not deserted us." Trust comes from experiencing both skill in care and treatment as well as compassion and commitment. It comes from sensing a professional's core identity, sense of purpose, and capacity for relationship. Or, one might say, it comes from a professional's spirituality.

Professional awareness of one's own spirituality is even more important in a changing system of services and supports where care is given in the community rather than in institutional settings. In institutional settings, it was and is easier to separate professional life from community life. Professionals of many disciplines may now also know individuals with disabilities and their families in roles other than "person served," such as neighbor, fellow congregant, member of clubs and associations, shared advocacy, and more. The list could go on and on. Meeting one another will not always be in the context of a clinic, school, program, or facility.

In his presidential address to the American Association on Intellectual and Developmental Disabilities in 2013, Jim Thompson succinctly articulated the changing role of professionals in a time when the social model of disability increasingly comes to the fore:

> *To be useful* professionals must strive to: (1) Understand each person holistically, with particular sensitivity to the fact that all people have relative strengths to go along with relative impairments; (2) Focus professional efforts on arranging personalized supports that bridge the gap between any limitations in personal competency and the demands of settings and activities; and (3) Recognize that empowering people with disabilities to live full lives in their communities not only enhances the quality of life of people with disabilities but also enables the general population to experience the contributions and richness that people with disabilities provide to their communities.[16]

Professionals thus become much more than assessors, prescribers, and persons who deliver specific services. They also become partners who get to know and understand people holistically, interpreters of the complex worlds of disability supports to many others, occasional negotiators between individuals and families with public and private service systems (e.g., eligibility for services), and allies in the long-term journeys of individuals and families toward inclusive community supports. They take on the spiritual roles of being present, listening deeply, and being a guide to understanding systems and meaning, an advocates and an ally in building a community that supports people with disabilities and their families in natural, generic ways in addition to professionalized services.

That is just the beginning. There are multiple other reasons for exploring and integrating one's own spirituality into a professional's identity and role. The first is professional honesty. A professional image that mandates separation between one's personal values or beliefs and professional role while also asserting that the first does not impact the other is at heart a denial that they are connected. Another way of saying this is that professionals are not called to be "value-free" but rather "value-clear." People being served and supported want to know the core values of people supporting them. They will feel them implicitly. That does not mean that a professional always needs to be explicit with those spiritual dimensions, but it may mean being able and willing to talk more about them if asked. That honesty is essential in a process of building a trusting relationship. Professionals work in contexts that all have mission and value statements, as well as individual professional codes of ethics. Those values and beliefs come alive only through the actions of individual caregivers. "Practicing what we preach" covers all forms of professionals.

Second, enhanced professional ability calls for skills to deal with spiritual interests and need. The very willingness to develop those skills may be dependent on one's own beliefs and feelings. More succinctly, the way any professional skills are demonstrated says something about the spirituality of the professional(s) involved.

For example, the process of assessment and diagnosis carries inherent ethical and moral values. A diagnostic and assessment process does not happen in a vacuum. First, the process carries significant social power by virtue of its role in determining eligibility for publicly funded services and supports. On a more personal level, professionals in that role may say that their role is to determine, scientifically, the cause of a child's disability or failure to develop in typically expected ways. An assessment or diagnosis may be fairly technical, but it carries great power. The parents have come for both understanding and help. Professionals have the responsibility to share the results of an assessment but to do so in ways that honor the deep parental desire for both clarity and hope. A diagnosis can be devastating, a possibility that heightens the professional responsibility to know the sources of support for a family and to be clear about how professional services and support can be of help in the future. Parents want and need to know what to do and to try.

In other words, a diagnosis can be used to help someone find hope, energize care, and express the innate parental love and responsibility that are already there. Thus, the way a professional uses his or her knowledge and technologies is crucial. Professionals usually refer to ethical principles and procedures, but even those beg for the kind of knowing that involves character. Dan Hall, a surgeon and clergyman, in a guest medical humanities program lecture at Baylor in 2014, talked about the ways that professional ethical discussions lead to deep complexity:

> In short order, they produce the "four principles": autonomy, beneficence, non-maleficence and justice. We spend time defining these words in simple terms: do good, avoid bad, be fair, and respect others' choices. But when we start trying to use those principles to guide a clinical decision, things often start to fall apart. Doing the good thing may not always be fair; what is fair may not correspond to the patient's choice; and what the patient chooses may lead to significant harm to self or others. We come to realize that difficult ethical decisions are difficult precisely because one or more of these principles come into conflict with each other, and when that happens, there isn't an easy way to resolve the tension.

The problem, he noted, is that the focus on procedural ethics is a fairly modern one, but, for ages before, ethicists like Aristotle "did not try to fence off the content of our character, but rather strived to develop character according to theories of virtue." Wisdom did not simply mean knowledge but "phronesis," practical wisdom or prudence—"the capacity to choose the best from among multiple imperfect options." The goal of that wisdom is "flourishing," similar to having a "thick" description and knowledge of someone's life. One acquires practical wisdom through experience and mentoring, but that wisdom cannot "be exercised without first eliciting from the patient her particular, thickly described goals and hopes." Procedural ethics, he noted, "promises consensus and fears passionate disagreement" while virtue ethics "seeks wise, contextual action even at the risk of passionate disagreement."[17]

To understand others "thickly" means professionals need to understand themselves that way as well. To learn and exercise practical wisdom means knowing when to do something as well as how, knowing who it is being done to as well as who is doing it, so that a caring and empowering partnership evolves. It also means being able to talk about the "whys" of a suggested treatment in terms of the core meanings in someone's life.[18] Stated another way, good professional care is an art form, one that is not just about the skilled application of paint on the surface but also about the depth of shared symbols, meaning, and story between the artist and the viewer, the professional and the people being served—the spirituality of that relationship.

Third, an increased awareness of one's spirituality as a professional is one way of recovering and strengthening professional vocation and calling. In a talk following his reception of the COMISS Award (Congress on Ministries in Specialized Settings) in 1994, Henri Nouwen silenced the crowd by stating that in his multiple accomplishments through the roles of teaching, writing, and leading, "my career was doing fine but I had forgotten my vocation."[19] Core to one's professional identity is an understanding of purpose, meaning, calling, and community. That community now includes the communities in which they live with the people they serve as well as the communities of practice in their own professions. As noted in the origins of the word "profession," it meant a statement of commitment and allegiance to a particular set of values and beliefs. That professional could then be trusted by someone seeking help because in a world of conflicting powers and shifting allegiances, people needed to trust the core values that shaped a professional's motivation and practice. Today, a person with a disability or their family may come for help with multiple questions about how a professional sees disability, his or her own professional role in a complex, often highly politicized system, and the power dynamics in those systems that constantly move toward depersonalization and disempowerment despite the ideologies of person and family centeredness.

Another reason for recovering a sense of vocation and calling is to develop language and opportunities to talk about it not only with people being served but also with other professionals. Talking about what drew us to a particular vocation and calling can be a time for learning from others, shared support, and renewed commitment to both personal and professional visions. In that possibility of renewal is also the injunction for "physicians to heal themselves," that is, to practice self-care that goes beyond continuing education that imparts more knowledge or technique to strategies for renewing compassion and commitment.

Renewing vocation and calling is the subject of Parker Palmer's well-known book *The Courage to Teach: Recovering the Inner Landscape of a Teacher's Life*.[20] Palmer calls us back to the simple fact that the best teachers in our lives are the ones who not only knew their material but whose heart and passion also showed through in their relationships with students. Another way to talk about professional recovery of "practical wisdom" and its focus on virtues, character, and flourishing might use an older term associated with both "spirituality" and "profession": "formation." Formation is a process of shaping identity and character that involves multiple kinds of intelligence and learning, most of which defy objectivity and depend upon relationship.[21]

Fourth, another implication of professional honesty and of recognizing what drew us to our calling is recognizing the ways that our work as professionals gives us meaning. One cannot live or work in the arenas of disability without being touched, deeply, by powerful experiences that may embody questions about, or revelations of, profound human values and truths. Those experiences can involve despair and horror that lead to "we can never let that happen again," but those moments also can be ones of amazement, wonder, discovery, joy, and the experience of deep connections in places of vulnerability and strength. In other words, in giving, professionals also receive.

Thus, we professionals need the opportunity, language, and sanction to share and talk about those stories and what we have learned from our experiences and reflection on them. Our passions for specific types of care or research come from those experiences and stories, yet they are mostly hidden in professional scientific discourse that has no language to talk about them, with the exception of being occasionally used as "examples." Those experiences can be key origin stories, stories from which our identity arose and that continue to drive a commitment to more effective practice. Alternatively, the stories could be new ones that both feed our calling and potentially call us in new directions.

One strategy for doing this reflection in private and in community is through various processes of "action/reflection" learning. In clinical pastoral education, for example, students are required to write verbatims of experiences that impact them with questions or new understandings. Those are discussed in supervision but also in a learning group with peers (i.e., a community of practice) with the dual purpose of learning better skills and exploring personal identity, issues, and history that may have been a gift or impediment in that experience, and the spiritual, theological, and sociological issues at the heart of the experience. It is a way of integrating the personal with the professional.

In the CPE program I ran through the Boggs Center on Developmental Disabilities in New Jersey, all the students "practiced" in agencies serving people with disabilities. Once during each training year, we would invite the professional mentors from the sites in which the students did their pastoral practice to come and be part of that discussion. Those mentors were professionals from a variety of helping disciplines. Almost every time, those professionals commented at the end about how rarely they could do that kind of reflecting and learning in their own work, the kind of self-critique that explores how and why they do what they do, and who they are, in the context of a supportive peer group.

Finally, the questions in my own journey that have shaped my conviction of the importance of integrating spirituality in our professional roles first started from relationships with people with intellectual and developmental disabilities toward the end of their lives. One of the usual implications of "professional caregiver" is that we should not be "friends" with the people we support. We sometimes say that our role is to help people develop friendships, especially in community-based supports where we know that a core indicator of quality of life is the number of friends in someone's life.

However, to say to people with disabilities that we support that we cannot be a friend is an illusion or delusion based on the fact that professionals are very uncertain about how to describe intense, long-term relationships with people who have been their patients or clients. Those relationships also give professionals meaning, purpose, and connection. To say we cannot be someone's friend is first a statement about who holds most of the power in the context of long-term relationships. Thus, it flies in the face of all we say about empowerment of others through helping them find their own voice. If we ask people with disabilities to name their friends, our names may be included. If we say then that we cannot be considered their friends, we are claiming the sole power to define the relationship. Remember the title question of Robert Chambers' book is *Whose Reality Counts?* The fact of the matter is that huge parts of someone's life may have been in the "services" world, especially for those who never grew up in communities. As they move into the latter stages of their lives, who is going to be with them? Who is going to tell them how their lives have made a difference in the world if not the professionals who have long been a part of their lives and with whom they have had long, trusted relationships?

Might not professionals help give others meaning and purpose by sharing our expressions of gratitude for what we have learned from them and how their lives have blessed our own? Those individuals might see us well within their circle of friends, and we, in return, need to be able to let them know how we celebrate their lives and the gifts they have given us. For a system newly focused on the importance of recognizing gifts, how do people know they have gifts that have made a difference unless someone tells them? This is certainly not the case with every professional relationship, but professionals need to take precautions so that their identity does not get in the way of their humanity. Part of professional capacity should be the capability to negotiate boundaries flexibly and artfully as well as to say "Thank you" to those on whom our "profession" has depended.

CONCLUSION

The gratitude that can come from integrating spirituality and recovering its role in professional identity and training is thus also a matter of justice. There has been a huge imbalance of power in the roles of professional, and persons being served. One is seen as giver and helper, the other as receiver and consumer. That dynamic has to change if professionals claim to live up to the values of self-determination, empowerment, and inclusive communities. There is a lot of inertia in professionally run human services systems; that imbalance will probably be here for a long time to come.

As evidence of their professional commitment, early religious "professions" into a religious order or role usually called for the "giving up" of culturally normative sources of motivation by making vows of poverty, chastity, and humility. Those are obviously not vows required of any modern professional guilds except some Western and Eastern religious orders. However, the one thing that professionals in the worlds of disability can give up is power. To do so means acute and sensitive awareness of how it is used. To do so is not just to hand it over but also to assist people unaccustomed to developing their own voice and agency to learn how to use it effectively. To do so means also to share our gratitude for how they have impacted us so they know how we have heard them, as well as how they have made a difference and impacted the world around them. Again, whose reality counts? And how do the "first" learn how put themselves "last" as a way of practicing the core values at the very heart of current services and supports?

To do so calls for a professional willingness to examine our own attitudes about disability and the way we see and understand ourselves in relationship to others.[22] A role is ultimately a relationship. There are echoes here of earlier discussions, such as the question of who is doing the diagnosing and why. What personal, professional, and cultural assumptions underlie those attitudes and perspectives? Using the construct of spirituality, what are a professional's core values and sources of meaning, sense of purpose and calling, and the kinds of connections he or she has with others? Being willing to closely examine the attitudes and power in the professional roles such as diagnostician, researcher, caregiver, and observer may indeed be a spiritual as well as an ethical exercise. It means beginning to deal with paradoxes of support—"the giver is also receiver" and "the first becomes last." Being aware of paradox and, indeed, embracing it, has long been a mark of spiritual learning and wisdom. That awareness and embrace is also critical in the art of building and empowering inclusive and supportive communities, but it starts in one-to-one relationships.

11

Spirituality, Care, and Commitment

The past fifty years have brought significant changes in laws, policies, and practices for people with disabilities and their families. What has driven those changes? At first, the advocacy of families with children with intellectual and developmental disabilities aligned with that of veterans with disabilities after the Second World War. Then, following the civil rights era of the 1960s and the initial efforts of the Kennedy administration, the disability rights movement grew and began to effect changes in law and policy, leading to the passage of several major laws, culminating with the Americans with Disabilities Act of 1990. Just as with many social justice and cultural movements, the changes were driven not so much by people in power but by people without power and position who changed their own understanding of disability and identity from stigma to strength, and went on to claim the rights and opportunities available to any other citizen.

Those changes in identity and advocacy took amazing acts of dedication and commitment. Joseph Shapiro was one of the first to trace the history with his book *No Pity: People with Disabilities Forging a New Civil Rights Movement*.[1] In 2015, initiatives related to the twenty-fifth anniversary of the ADA began to collect the history and stories of the initial leaders and the movements that they led. Individuals, families, and professionals have also spearheaded long and determined struggles to change educational and service systems and supports from segregated to inclusive community-based settings. A core theme of the twenty-fifth anniversary was that many things have changed but the promise of full participation in the lives of communities still remains unfulfilled, especially in the arena of opportunities for people with disabilities to be productive, contributing members—employment.

What fueled this determination and commitment? Personal stories, exposés of terrible treatment, visions of civil rights, dreams of better lives for people with disabilities and their families, powerful leaders: all of these and more. Additional research is needed on the "spirit" of these movements and what has kept them alive and going. The spirituality of those movements is reflected in (1) the shifts in personal identity that reframed disability from negative stigma to "disability pride," embracing gifts and strengths; (2) the passions that built connections among individuals, families, and allies in many sectors of the society; and (3) the sense of purpose, mainly framed around the rights of children and adults as citizens. All helped shape the sense of mission, calling, and vocation embodied in so many leaders and organizations. While "spiritual" at one or more levels, the disability rights and inclusion movements have not had the same religious foundations as the civil rights movement, in which clergy were key leaders and where faith and congregation served as ongoing sources of renewal and commitment. The religious community, in fact, lobbied for core exemptions from the Americans with Disabilities Act, thereby adding to the negative images around religion and disability while also abdicating, until recently, what could have been a source for moral leadership, support, and renewal.

The question now is what will help renew, expand, and sustain the commitment needed to foster and maintain changes in attitudes, laws, policies, and practices so that people with disabilities are respected and welcomed in all parts of community life. That question has a "macro" level that needs to be addressed by leaders, policy makers, community organizers, media, employers, disability studies researchers and teachers, and other shapers of public opinion, including clergy.[2] My focus is more on the "micro" level, on the relationships among people with disabilities, their allies and friends, and the professionals who support them in one or more ways through paid services. Here, the questions revolve around how we sustain the kinds of caring relationships that truly support and empower everyone: the person with a disability, family members, and professionals alike. The problem is that many of the caring systems that have evolved end up impeding or choking off the very kind of commitment and care that is needed to help everyone flourish.

COMPLIANCE, COMMITMENT, AND UNINTENDED OUTCOMES

More than twenty years ago at an American Association on Mental Retardation[3] conference in Los Angeles, I was talking to a former chaplain at a state institution in California who had moved into a new role in the quality assurance department. Those were the heydays of active treatment, long and very specific interdisciplinary developmental plans for individuals for their programs and staff. There were also growing numbers of regulations and standards whose purpose was to protect the health and safety of individuals with intellectual disabilities being served, including protection from the kinds of abuse and neglect (and subsequent bad publicity) that still happened too frequently in either institutional or community-based services. My colleague made a statement that I have never forgotten: "In a system that does not know how to enhance commitment, it relies instead on compliance."[4]

What are the pressures in the systems of care that push toward compliance? Certainly, the impetus to change inhumane systems leads to new laws, then to policies, new programs, training, and more, but it also leads to increased pressure to conform to standards and policies that define good care. The result may be what Ivan Illich called "paradoxical counter-productivity"—a system designed to provide supportive and safer care actually becomes less so.[5] Steve Taylor, former director of the Center for Human Policy at Syracuse and longtime editor of the journal *Mental Retardation*, defined the paradox of compliance in a journal issue containing the papers of a symposium on compliance and quality in residential life: "Herein lies the paradox: In order to meet the regulations, a setting or a home must become more impersonal, hierarchical, and bureaucratic, and these are some of the features that made institutions dehumanizing and abusive in the first place."[6]

If anything, that dichotomy and paradox has grown over the past twenty years. Our systems of services and supports call for professionals and direct care staff to have a broader array of skills and a deeper commitment to the vision and ideals of the systems in which we work.[7] Professionals are not only to assess and treat from their chosen professional disciplines but also to provide direct and person-centered care in ways that fulfill dreams and goals. They are to provide specific kinds of daily living skills and care, keep people safe and well, teach skill development, empower *consumer participation and choice*, help connect and include people in inclusive community settings, and serve as effective advocates for the families and systems with whom they work. Quality of life, person-centered care and outcomes, and self-directed supports are all mantras in the values and visions that drive our systems of care and support. Formal supports based on good person-centered plans call for creative, caring, and committed support providers, and ones with skills in all those areas just listed.

Along with those values, visions, and skills, however, there comes an increasingly complex web of regulations and legal requirements. It is very difficult to avoid both the standardization and codification of creative processes when bringing them to scale from creative pockets of innovative care to system-wide change. Our service systems also import the language of customer service from the business world, yet the real customers that drive the system are realistically the funding streams from public sources on which they depend. Funding then depends implicitly and explicitly on meeting certain licensing standards or policies, or, more recently, upon delivering a promised level of observable, measureable outcomes as if caregiving and development were an exact science or a production process. When problems do occur, they can result in attempts at system-wide fixes for individual problems, leading to more complexity or, when abuse or accidents continue to happen, increasingly specific laws that criminalize poor professional judgment or behavior.[8]

The paradoxical result is service systems and care that are based more on law rather than commitment, with fear being more prominent than a positive vision of growth, development, and participation. There is fear of abuse, fear of risk, fear of discipline, fear of bad publicity, fear of making a mistake, fear of failure—all compounded by a fear of losing funding. The additional pressure to produce outcomes drives the collection of more and more data to prove that something successful happened, which then increases the paperwork. Fear does not enhance commitment; rather, it feeds compliance.[9] Accountability is to the regulators, inspectors, or to the outcomes in an individual's plan, not to the relationships with the people one supports or to fellow staff and families. Add to this the fact that many service agencies are large, top-down, bureaucratic organizations where the ones doing the most direct care are the ones with the lowest pay and least training, the ones expected to follow the plans but usually without a lot of voice in their development, and the ones often directly supervised by people who have recently been promoted without any training in management or good supervisory skills, then you have a recipe for disaster.[10] That disaster is evident in the huge turnover rate of direct care staff in many service organizations throughout the United States, often a vicious cycle in itself where turnover and vacancies lead to frenetic and sometimes frantic (i.e., fearful) attempts to hire enough people to provide basic care but whose lack of training, longevity, and commitment create more mistakes; more attempts to control or prevent them by rules, regulation, and punishment; and then more turnover.[11]

The impact is not hard to see or imagine. An agency where I have done some training and consultation shared one story from its agency-wide self-evaluation of turnover. It had taken one of its "consumers," a woman with physical and intellectual disabilities in her fifties who needed direct and hands-on care, and went through her records to figure out the number of direct caregivers who had been in her life. They stopped counting at five hundred.[12] That discovery led them to a new priority of focusing on the care and training of direct support staff.

As I worked on a statewide career path project for direct support professionals during the first decade of this century in New Jersey, one agency's associate director laid out the rationale succinctly:

> Turnover and vacancies have a significant impact on the quality of lives of the individuals we support. All the services and supports we provide are anchored in relationships, relationships between the individuals and the people who support them. You cannot effectively support someone unless you know them and they you and they trust you and you them. Direct support professionals are involved in the most intimate aspects of people's lives. They know their hopes and dreams, comfort them through disappointments and tragedy, celebrate the good times, and provide reassurance when sick or even dying. How can this be done if the individual does not have a relationship with the staff person? How can

a relationship be built when there is a different person every few weeks or months or worse when a position is vacant, a substitute or a different temp every day? If a person does not feel supported, then are we really providing support?[13]

Despite these barriers and trends, there are also *many* caring and committed professional caregivers, at many different levels. At least two questions follow: "What sustains them?" and "How can commitment and compliance be rebalanced?" There are clear factors such as a livable wage, more effective training, and managing or treating staff in the same ways that you want them to support the people being served. But professional commitment is also impacted by an individual's spirituality and by the "spirituality" of an organization.

FOCUSING ON COMMITMENT AS WELL AS COMPLIANCE

Given the reliance on public funding for services and supports, compliance with regulations and markers of quality care and assurance are not going away. Evaluation through objective tools and compliance with objective measures are an important part of any system of caregiving and relationships. But how do we pay direct attention to the importance of commitment and provide the resources and educational opportunities that bring the classic polarities of law and spirit back into a little more balance? To phrase it differently, how do we find the balance between meeting the letter of the law and the spirit of the law or, in biblical terms, remember that doing justice, loving mercy, and walking humbly (Mic 6:8 NIV) are more important than rules, commandments, and quantifiable numbers?

This is not just an issue in services for and with people with disabilities. It has been a major factor in the development of the Green Houses, led by Dr. Bill Thomas, in services with people who are elderly and frail. A PBS interview summarized the issue succinctly:

JOYCE EBMEIER (Green House Administrator): Death gets harder in a Green House because, when you are smaller and when you are engaged in the way that the shahbazim [their name for quality direct care staff] are engaged in the lives of the elders they love so much, it is like losing your dearest family member.

SUSAN DENTZER (correspondent): All this reminded us of something else Thomas had said back in 2001 about the central problem with nursing homes.

DR. BILL THOMAS: In long-term care, love matters. And the heart of the problem is institutions can't love.

SUSAN DENTZER: Do you think you've finally helped create a place that can love?

DR. BILL THOMAS: Yes. In fact, I think it's the signal achievement of the Green House: making a place where love matters.[14]

How do we create places where love matters and where commitment can be deepened? To be incredibly simplistic, we do not cause it or control it, but we can create the kinds of necessary and sufficient conditions and structures where it can be fostered, nurtured, and encouraged. Most of our services focus on where the services take place, what people do to and for others, how it should be done (via the plan), and how often or when. What gets disregarded is the "Who?" of the caregivers and the "Why?" those people are doing what they are doing in the first place, what they learn from it, and hence the nature of the relationship and commitment between staff and "consumer."[15]

Many care providers would say they are doing what they are doing by reflecting on the mission and values of their organization and its services, or simply because they like to help people. Creative management strategies are imported from other kinds of businesses and organizations, such as customer service and satisfaction, the importance of vision and purpose, and structures that allow for flexibility and imagination. Flattening the organization; empowering the front lines; soliciting input; focusing on creative recruitment, training, and retention are all markers of these initiatives. The two focal points are the "consumer" and the "bottom line." Both of those may also lead to paying more attention to the regulatory and funding agencies than to the staff.

One of the areas of research and practice in business organizations that has not been imported is a significant amount of attention and research on workplace spirituality. Core elements of workforce spirituality, as noted by researchers and writers in organizational sciences, include the fact that many employees create meaningful identities through their work, seek connections with others, and desire to do work that has a meaningful purpose and impact on their community.[16] One of the dimensions studied through both empirical and qualitative studies has been the relationship between workplace spirituality and organizational commitment. Two researchers sum up their exploration of the literature and their own study:

> Spirituality is a deeply personal experience. People live it in very different ways, and nourish it from different sources. But, no charges of heresy can be made if we argue that most human beings like to perform meaningful work in the context of a community, hope that others respect their inner life, have a desire to work in an organization whose values are congruent with their own, and want to experience joy at work. If organizations allow them to get these "spiritual resources" and satisfy their "spiritual needs" it is likely that they bring their entire self (physical, mental, emotional and spiritual) to the organization, assume work as a mission more than a job, feel that they are developing their full potential, and become more affectively and normatively attached to their organizations.[17]

The second major resource for a renewed focus on commitment is our understanding of who we are as professional caregivers, our sense of calling and vocation, and that which develops and sustains us in caregiving roles that beg for long-term commitment as well as skilled care—for love as well as good outcomes. To take "professional" and "caregiving" education further, it is an ongoing educational process that focuses on character, commitment, and community. It is education as formation, shaping identity and calling in addition to the acquisition of knowledge, skills, and techniques.

Parker Palmer's *Courage to Teach* project focused on education that enabled reflection, honesty, sharing from the heart, openness to a sense of call and vocation, and the willingness to act on what is learned. Training opportunities then focused on identity rather than skills, working from the inside out rather than the outside in, and remembering the powerful role of the teacher, his or her integrity, and the quality of relationships with students.

What gets in the way of our doing more of this? Palmer comes back to the pervasive and primary barrier of fear, a fear not unlike the one we find in a system of care focused on compliance. He notes three dimensions of fear:

1. Fear in our way of knowing. Valuing objective knowledge above all else is, in his perspective, at one level a fear of relationship, a fear of being challenged and changed by what we know, and a focus on power over things.
2. Fear in our students, who are often people on the margins (certainly the case of direct care workers), whose fear is of failure, not "making it," not being valued, or being denied opportunity.
3. Fear in our teachers, the fear that we cannot impart to others the knowledge we have, or the commitment we feel, or, like with the students, fear of failure and not being valued.[18]

That work with teachers led to work with other professions, including medical education. In an article written about medical education, Palmer defines "the new professional" as "a person who is not only competent in his or her own discipline but has the skill and the will to deal with the institutional pathologies that threaten the profession's highest standards. . . . We need professionals who are 'in but not of' their institutions, whose allegiance to the core values of their fields makes them resist the institutional diminishment of those values." That professional needs to have emotional as well as a rational intelligence— the capacity to translate feelings into knowledge and social change. To do so, Parker suggests, one needs a trusted community of discernment where experiences, feelings, and issues can be shared and explored in ways that lead to deeper understandings of one's self and values and enhanced capacity to live an "undivided life," close to one's core passions and commitments.[19]

Let me suggest, similarly, that there are at least three strategies for rebalancing caregiving relationships in compliance/outcome-focused systems toward enhancing the quality of care by focusing on commit-ment. They involve a focus on the "Who?" and "Why?" questions of caregiving and the times "When?" those questions can be shared and explored. All involve a reframing or expansion of that considered to be true, right, and important.

The "Who?" of the Caregiver

Service agencies typically ask prospective employees about education and experience and negotiate wages or salaries. They do not often ask an applicant who is going to be working in direct relationships with people with disabilities about who they are as an individual. The ques-tions in that area might explore the nature of someone's spirituality:

- Why are you interested in this job? (Is there a sense of call or vocation?)
- What kinds of relationships have you had with people with disabilities in the past?
- What kinds of gifts do you feel you bring to your work?
- What are some of your core passions or values?
- What is your understanding of diversity? What are your experiences in relationships with people from a variety of backgrounds? (Many staff will be working with immigrants, ethnic minorities, and people from widely different cultural and religious backgrounds.)
- If one of the people we serve asks you, "Who are you, real-ly?" how would you answer?
- What kinds of connections and relationships are most im-portant to you?
- How does this position relate to your own sense of pur-pose? What kind of difference do you want to make in the lives of others?

These kind of questions, along with a realistic explanation of the caregiving job and the kinds of situations or questions that may come up, not only provide an employer and potential team members a sense of who this person is but also what kind of commitment they bring to the position. Is he or she truly willing to engage in relationships with the people he or she supports while also handling the kinds of personal questions that might arise? Those questions also signal to an applicant that this organization is one in which relationships are valued as well as the expectation that a key role is helping the people being served to nourish their own relationships and connections.

The "Why?" of Commitment: Rediscovering the Languages

Professional caregivers of all levels of skill and responsibility need the opportunity to reflect on why they do what they do. Decades ago, Wolf Wolfensberger noted the phenomenon that one of the prophetic voices and roles of people with mental retardation (to use the terms of the time) was that they were providing a sense of vocation and calling for many, many others.[20] Staff may get asked when they apply for a job why they are interested, but that exploration often stops there.

There are at least two major reasons why it does not happen more often: finding the language and finding the time or, stated otherwise, building in the opportunity. Finding the language for relationships and commitment is not a question of there being no language, but there is not a language that has been welcomed, recognized, or utilized in any extensive way within modalities of care based either on scientific or manager/customer frameworks of care. The language of science is the language of objective measurement, outcomes, and "evidence-based practices." Remember John Swinton's observations: in the "world" of scientific caregiving, the "good" becomes that which is observable, the "true" that which is measurable, and the "beautiful" that which is replicable.[21] Hans Reinders has also noted that a major paradox in a system of care based on liberal philosophic principles (choice, freedom, equality) is that the system will not be able to understand the reasons that motivate many people to care for, live with, and relate to (i.e., be committed to) people with limited intellectual ability.[22]

Finding the language in a system based on liberal public philosophy and scientific principles then means finding a way to reintegrate the languages of relationships: poetry, spirituality, emotions, symbols, art, stories, and song. These are the ways that people talk about their relationships, share the depths of their experiences, and find meaning in the depths of what they discover. These are the languages of community. There are indeed growing examples and indications of this reintegration in the work being done in community building:

literature and self-story by people with disabilities, poetry, art in many different forms, dramatic photography, plays, movies, recognition of spirituality, theological exploration, cartoons, slogans, symbols, and songs.[23]

One of the most powerful examples for me is a poem written by a direct care worker, Nick Hadju, at an interfaith summit related to disability services, reflecting on his relationship with his friend Charlie (a young man, nonverbal, wheelchair user):

"MY FRIEND CHARLIE"

He is my friend: I am his friend
I help him out: He helps me to learn
I help him to learn: He helps me to grow
I help him to grow: He teaches me to accept

His struggle: Is my struggle
His vulnerability: Leads to my respect
My respect: Leads him to trust
His trust: Leads to my devotion

His availability: Feeds my desire to be needed
I keep his secrets: He keeps mine
   We have an arrangement
His lack of self-consciousness: Leads to my tolerance
His constant need for stimulation: Leads to my patience
His discomfort: Sharpens my sensitivity
His unhappiness: Is my challenge
His presence: Eases my isolation
His loyalty: Leads to my loyalty
   Which leads to mutual appreciation

His brokenness: Makes me accept my own brokenness
   Which leads to healing
His humanity: Leads to personal connection
His steadfastness: Centers me

His smile: Is my reward
His joy: Lifts my spirits
His happiness: Gives me a sense of purpose
His struggles: Expose my anxieties
   Which tests me

Then strengthens me
And in turn bolsters my faith

In guiding: I am guided
In helping: I am helped
In teaching: I am taught

In his laughter: There is joy
In that joy: There is energy
In that energy: There is spirit
In that spirit: There is grace

In his eyes: There is a glow
In that glow: Is his soul
In his soul: There is God
And in God: There is peace.[24]

Thus, the question is how people involved in direct caregiving relationships can be encouraged to reflect on their experiences in ways other than progress notes, data sheets, and "unusual incident reports." Those alternative ways of expression can be ways of both sharing and enhancing valued relationships as well as talking about people with disabilities in languages that the wider community can understand. Basically, a social model of disability needs languages beyond those coming from a medical or behavioral model. That has been part of the mission of disability studies programs, but the languages there are often profoundly academic.

Enhancing Commitment: Making the Opportunity

"My Friend Charlie" is an example of the language of relationship, friendship, mutuality, and commitment. At whatever level of caregiving, professionals all have their favorite stories about the people with whom they work and the relationships and experiences that invited and called them into the work they are now doing. What they do not have is the time and opportunity to reflect on those dimensions of caregiving in the context of their work, an invitation to share them with one another, and the ways to find new insights and renewed spirits from each other's stories. The agendas of team meetings, staff retreats, and conferences could be changed to include times of reflecting on the

"Whys?"; times for sharing the powerful stories; times for talking about what people in our care do for us while we do for and with them; and times for finding out how others deal with the inevitable periods of dismay, hopelessness, and struggle.[25]

Doing so thus would be one way of talking about the spiritual dimensions of professional work and care. The core values of independence, productivity, integration, and self-determination at the heart of our Western systems of care involve the core questions of identity, purpose, and community: "Who am I?" "Why am I?" and "Whose am I?"[26] Those apply to staff as well. One cannot do direct, hands-on care in relationships in this arena without encountering profound spiritual, philosophical, and theological questions. There are any number of action-reflection strategies for exploring caregiving experiences that enable people to talk about the personal and professional issues raised in those powerful experiences. Reflection can also focus on why people did what they did and what could help frame a different response or understanding.[27] The major challenge is making the time to share those kinds of questions and experiences; learn from them; learn more about each other; and together build personal, professional, and communal commitment in our relationships with the people we serve and support.

CONCLUSION: RECLAIMING THE SOUL OF OUR WORK

Building in that kind of training and opportunities for reflection and renewal in a system of institutions focused on objective and data-driven outcomes and compliance will not be easy. It means reframing the very image of what it means to be "professional," moving away from the expert with the knowledge, power, and control to the "professional" being called for by people with disabilities and their families, the one who walks and journeys with people, assisting them through skills and through mutual relationships of shared responsibility and care. It means recognizing that our role is to be value-clear, not value-free, and that what others need and value from us as professionals goes beyond assessment, technique, program, and procedure to a relationship over the long haul in which trust is built, relationships formed, and commitments and communities nourished.

Bill Ebenstein, one of the pioneers in workforce development issues in direct care, names the challenge as rediscovering the soul of our field, a soul that acknowledges "the complex web and texture of relationships that exist between folks with disabilities and direct service workers," and that also rediscovers the souls of the workers, the souls of the people served, and the souls of trainers and managers.[28] That entails building the capacity for self-reflection, vulnerability, and self-critique, such as exploring ways for helping agencies to be hospitable to the community, just as our agencies are asking the community to be hospitable to people with disabilities.[29] Or, stated slightly differently, it means exploring who we are as organizations as well as individuals, why we do what we do, and how we can connect more deeply with our selves, each other, and the communities in which we work.[30] As we do so, perhaps we will then be able to enhance commitment and rely less on compliance.

V

ALL OF US
Friendships, Relationships, and Community

12

Gift and Call
Recovering the Spiritual Dimensions of Friendship

One constant theme in discussions on spirituality and disability is the importance of friendships.[1] Respite care through natural relationships and activities, peer supports and relationships in transition, finding employment through friends, growing up in a caring and loving community, and helping to build community: these areas of practice and policy all point to the key importance of natural supports. Natural supports, in turn, reflect the hope and belief that friendship will be one critical form of the relationships that connect and bind people with disabilities in the webs of community life and participation.

In his classic book *The Four Loves*, theologian C. S. Lewis notes that friendship to the ancient world was the most human of loves, yet it is by and large ignored in the modern world. If, however, the ancients were right, he says, one "can hardly write a chapter on it except as rehabilitation."[2] That is true in the world of intellectual and developmental disabilities as well. Friendship was long ignored in both theory and practice until recently. Friends, even in form of volunteers, have been seen as nice but not necessary, more unusual than usual. Individual growth and development meant a movement up a client-development ladder, one that depended on the acquisition of skills rather than the acquisition of friends. As in a modern, mobile society, personal success in growth and development has been more important than ongoing relationships, ties, and bonds with friends and family.

As the phenomena of friendship has emerged as a key component of helping people with developmental disabilities become part of
community life, both caregivers and advocates cannot begin to explore
the meaning of friendship without a fundamental "rehabilitation" of the
way we view people with disabilities, our systems of care, and our roles
as professionals and caregivers in the context of community life. Our
professional struggle in that "rehabilitation" is in part caused by the fact
that as friendship is validated by its importance in community living, we
are pushed to recognize that the power of friendship has been evident
all along, either in its presence or absence. We are also compelled to
look at the ways that even the best of services and supports may not
only fail to develop new friendships but also get in the way of ones that
people already have.

I expect that my experience is not much different from that of many
other professionals who have been in this area of service for thirty to
forty years. Many of us have had the experience of working in segregated
caregiving facilities where the greatest tragedy was not the disabilities of
the persons served but their separation from any opportunities for ongoing friendships with others in the community. Limited numbers of staff,
even with skills and commitment, could not fulfill the needs for friendship. I have been with people we call "consumers" or "clients" whose
demeanor changed when they received a visit or a phone call. Lives
changed when a friendship developed where there had been none. Long
ago I marveled at the ways in which institutional "residents" continually
requested and enjoyed songs and music that spoke of friendship and
love, such as "God Is My Friend," or "Jesus Loves Me." I have witnessed
people who began as volunteers become genuine friends, establishing
bonds that were not easily explained other than by saying the relationship
had been a gift to them and that it answered a deep call within them.
I have personally struggled with a professional role in which I knew
I was the only friend for many people. Other staff and caregivers also
formed deep friendships with "clients," yet we worked in a system where
the "program" rather than the "person" was paramount. More recently,
while "talking the talk" on the importance of friendships, even in good
person-centered planning strategies, putting those plans into action is
much more difficult. Building and maintaining friendships challenges
caregiver skills and organizational policies—"the usual way of doing

things." One sometimes feels that service and support systems struggle to believe that unpaid persons would actually want to be friends[3] with the people we serve, while we also fail to look at the ways policies and practices impede those kinds of relationships.

Rehabilitating friendship compels us to reexamine personal assumptions, beliefs, and experiences of friendship. It calls us to search for those past and present voices that can help to explain the transforming power of friendships which we have witnessed in the lives of people whom we call "clients" and "consumers," people whom we have seldom been permitted (or allowed ourselves) to call "friends." In short, it pushes us to examine what we believe about friendship in general, the reasons for its relative absence in professional literature and practice, and the challenge to change. No wonder it has been avoided. The concept and experience of friendship lays claim to understandings of person, policy, and practice in ways like no other.

HISTORICAL FOUNDATIONS OF FRIENDSHIP

Practitioners in the field of intellectual developmental disabilities have increasingly become more aware of the importance of friends and friendship, even if it is by first noting their absence. The focus has been on the importance of friendship as a relationship characterized by mutual enjoyment, reciprocity, and acceptance *in contrast to* relationships in which a person is continually a "client" or "consumer," where one is continually being treated, programmed, or fixed.[4] There is, thus, an unintentional understanding of two of the three basic elements of friendship in the classic philosophical and Judeo-Christian traditions: (1) Friends enjoy each other's company through an acceptance and appreciation of gifts, and (2) friends are useful to each other—reciprocity.

The third component in those traditions is the moral or spiritual dimension of friendship, a shared common commitment to the values that form the foundation of a good life or a good society.[5] The current theoretical and practical work in the system of care with persons with disabilities to clarify what is a "quality of life," especially in the context of a caregiving, inclusive community, leads us directly into a renewed dialogue with these classic understandings of the moral and spiritual dimensions of friendship.

The Classical Tradition

In classic essays on friendship by Plato, Aristotle, Cicero, Augustine, Bacon, Montaigne, and others, friendship, or, in Greek, *philos*, was viewed as the most important of all human forms of love[6] and the most "instinctual natural basis for all positive social relationships."[7] Friendship was associated not only with mutual love and usefulness but also with the development of a virtuous life. Friends were needed to help understand the purpose for which life had been given.[8]

Friendship differed from other forms of love while at the same time retaining some of their elements. Its mutuality made it different from altruism or charity, which implies a giving to others that was not necessarily reciprocal. Friendship had some possible sexual dimensions, but it was neither the same as sexual love (*eros*) nor affection, such as the love of a parent for a child. Because friendship was by definition a relationship with specific others and indicates a preference, it was not *agape*, an understanding of love that is universal, inclusive, and sacrificial. That understanding of *agape* forms part of the historical uneasiness of professional caregiving with the concept and experience of friendship.

In classic Greek philosophy, the dilemmas of friendship focused not on sexuality but on the relationship between teacher and student. The question was whether "good" men needed friends. The answer was that friendship was necessary to understand and participate in universal values.[9] Its characteristics of mutuality, acceptance, and reciprocity did not mean an unconditional acceptance that led to an abandonment of moral standards.[10] Specific friendships, rather, led one beyond oneself to the nature of that which was universally good. Thus, Aristotle would say, "No one would choose to live without friends, even if he had all other goods."[11]

In classic traditions, then, friendship was a great gift and treasure but also an imperative. It was not simply a source of mutual pleasure that differed from other more "natural" pleasures. While a key dimension was reciprocity, or mutual usefulness, Bellah points out that it was not solely a utilitarian tool for developing economic success and power (e.g., *How to Win Friends and Influence People*) or individual well-being and health (modern therapy).[12] It was, rather, a pathway to understanding of truth and knowledge about oneself, one's community, and the meaning and purpose of life. In C. S. Lewis' words, friendships are "about something," a seeing or caring about a common truth.[13]

The Biblical Tradition

At the risk of being too simplistic, one could summarize the classical philosophical view of the friendship by stating that friendships were necessary for an understanding of universal values and truth. In the biblical tradition, friendship reveals the grace, love, and call of a caring God. In the classical view, friendship was a human pathway to the universal or divine. In the biblical tradition, it is a pathway of the divine to humankind, a gift of grace that calls for human response, one that receives but then also shares, gives, or, as Hans Reinders says, "pays forward" to others.[14]

Like the classical tradition, there is no single understanding of friendship in the Judeo-Christian tradition but rather a rich weaving of stories, traditions, and themes that relate to friendship.[15] Friendship is rarely used in the Bible as a description of the divine human relationship. God is not often called a "friend," but friendships reveal many of the characteristics of God's love for humankind. The more common metaphors used for the relationship of God and humans are those of creator, lord, and parent (usually images of father, but sometimes of mother). Humans are called not to be God's friends but rather to love and befriend others as a way of responding to the gift of God's creation and love. Thus, friendships are one of the expressions of God's grace, a grace that compels the receiving of unconditional love and a giving of thanks through loving others.

There are at least five biblical themes related to this, and, like the classic understanding, they involve both gift and call. However, the primary biblical emphasis is on friendship as gift.

First, we are created in God's image for relationship, with God and with others. In Genesis God creates humankind because God was lonely. The two great commandments in the biblical tradition are to love God and to love your neighbor as yourself.[16] Not only is the act of creation an act of God's love and grace, but also, in the biblical tradition, God reaches out, over and over again, to redeem humankind because of that promise of relationship: "But now thus says the Lord, he who created you, O Jacob, he who formed you, O Israel: Fear not, for I have redeemed you; I have called you by name and you are mine. . . . Because you are precious in my eyes, and honored, and I will love you" (Isa 43:1, 4 RSV).

The first biblical answer to the "Why?" of friendship and love is that we have been given value by virtue of our creation, not our abilities or accomplishments, and are thus called to see that value in every person. As John Landgraf talks about love and friendship:

> I love you. This means, "I perceive you to be precious," infinitely worthy and priceless. No matter what kind of body you may have, no matter what kind of mind you may have, no matter what kind of talent you may have, no matter what kind of performance you put on. None of these has anything to do with the fact—and it is a fact—that you are precious. You are precious simply because you *are*, whatever your equipment and however you may use it. You were born that way—created in the image of God and given life by the breath of God. To see that is to be grasped by the reality of what it is to love.[17]

Second, true friendship is a mirror of God's love and acceptance. Much of the human importance of friendship simply comes from the gift of acceptance that comes from a friend. A friend is someone who accepts and loves me as I am. In the face of feeling unworthy, unloved, lonely, or, words used more in the world of developmental disabilities, "devalued," "stigmatized," "labeled," or "isolated," the gift of friendship is first of all its acceptance of the other, and indeed, on the basis of being created in God's image, its celebration of the other. In the biblical story, we are simply called to love with that kind of acceptance because God first loved us. The choosing and acceptance of another as friend, or receiving that acceptance by a friend, is a gift not of our control and doing but an expression or evidence of God's acceptance of us. We cannot say that we love God and then hate our neighbor.[18] In both the Old and New Testaments, God's choosing, freeing, and saving of the people are evidence of God's acceptance and commitment not because of, but usually in spite of, human accomplishments or abilities. We are saved by grace, not by our works (Eph 2:8-9).

Third, in the Bible friends can be both faithful and unfaithful.[19] In contrast, God's faithfulness is evidence of commitment to a relationship, a covenant, a promise of continual and ongoing presence in which God yearns for reception of that love and response to it. The choosing and faithfulness both implies and builds the kind of bond that is at the heart of an everlasting friendship. In true friendship, as in covenant, there is a sense of choosing and being chosen. The few times that individual people are called "God's friend" in the Bible are used to point to the eternal nature of God's covenant.[20]

Fourth, we are called to love others as God loves us. In the Old Testament, God refuses to give up on God's people in spite of the anguish they may have caused. In the New Testament, the call to love others in ways that risks one's own well-being (*agape*) is a call to love others in the same radical, impartial, universal, and inclusive way that God has loved. "When you give a feast, don't invite friends and neighbors, lest they invite you, and you be repaid. But when you give a feast, invite the poor, the maimed, the lame, the blind, and you will be blessed" (Luke 14:12 RSV). It is sometimes a call to paradox, that in giving one receives, and in losing one's life it is found. It is a call beyond the usual boundaries to love one's neighbor, as in the parable of the good Samaritan, wherever or whoever that turns out to be. It is the call to love in the way that one loves willingly for a friend at a cost to oneself.

Fifth, we are called to be hospitable to strangers, which is not so much loving "universally" as it is "particularly"—attributed to Menachem Begin, at the Camp David peace talks, although the actual text of his toast at the conclusion is "In the Jewish teachings, there is a tradition that the greatest achievement of a human being is to turn his enemy into a friend, and this we do in reciprocity."[21] At the heart of all three major Western religions (Christianity, Judaism, and Islam) is an injunction to welcome the stranger in the act of hospitality. It is through the act of hospitality that the host creates a space where a stranger is welcomed and accepted in a way that gives to others the same kind of sanctuary that the host has received. The paradox in these traditions is that the gift is not just from the host to the stranger, for in welcoming the stranger, the host is often the one who receives. The stranger turns out to be a messenger or revelation from God. The angels appear to Abraham and Sarah as strangers with the ridiculous gift of proclaiming that she will bear a child at her age (Gen 18). The disciples welcome the stranger on the road to Emmaus (Luke 24:13-35). "As you did it to the least of these, so you did it unto me" (Matt 25:40 RSV). "Do not neglect to show hospitality to strangers, for thereby some have entertained angels unaware" (Heb 13:2 RSV). The stranger can be the leper, the child, the blind man, the woman at the well . . . anyone unknown or thought to be beyond the scope of God's people and love. The call to hospitality to the stranger turns out to be gift to everyone involved.

As stated earlier, the call to hospitality in the scriptural tradition also brings one back full circle to being prepared to see and welcome God's spirit or image in every person. Part of the importance of hospitality as one of the dimensions of friendship and love in the Bible is that it balances the challenge of universal love with the specificity of individual people known under the label of "stranger." To love equally, fairly, justly, and universally, as God loves everyone, is a challenge that can overwhelm and lead, paradoxically, to a disengagement and distance from others. But humans are not God, and it is particular "others" we are called to love or to "befriend."

The Classical and Biblical Foundations: Dilemma or Paradox

On one level, there are profound differences between classical understandings of friendship (*philos*) and biblical understandings of love and friendship (*agape*). In the classical philosophical traditions, particular friendships were formed by mutual attraction and reciprocal relationships. They were seen as necessary for development, growth, change, and for understanding the true values of the society and universe. Friends "called" each other to be better people.

In biblical understandings, good friendships were an expression of the gift of God's grace and love. The major difference from the classical traditions was in the biblical call to love your neighbor, the call to universal, sacrificial love, *agape*, a way of expressing and showing God's universal, self-giving love for every person. Understandings of *agape* historically form part of the understanding of what constitutes good "professional care": caring and loving others must be done impartially and, at best, demonstrate a sacrificial service to others.[22] One who "professed to serve" was to love others equally, as God loves all, and was to give without thought of mutuality and reciprocity, since that was a demonstration of the gift of grace in God's first and ongoing love of humankind.

In the call to *agape*, one can then see the seeds of a kind of caring that detaches from relationships that appear to be preferential. That theological theory matched, first, the historical reality that "profession" originally meant to separate oneself from family and friends to serve God and, second, the practical reality that to love everyone equally with the same kind of self-giving love demonstrated by God is a human impossibility. One can also see the historical seeds of understanding caregiving as charity, for one was to give to others without thought of reciprocity or mutuality. A calling to service meant being called to benefit others. That also makes it hard to see the others as friends— relationships characterized by mutuality and reciprocity.

These two historical strands of understanding the spiritual foundations of friendship would thus appear to lead in opposite directions, one that celebrates specific, preferential friendships and one in which the call to love was not preferential or necessarily mutual. As seen in the earlier discussion of biblical dimensions of friendship, the dilemma is more paradox than contradiction. The call to universal love or friendship is to be acted out in the context of hospitality to specific neighbors or strangers. Gift and giving become reciprocal; the bond that recognizes, accepts, and celebrates inherent value in one another as part of God's creation and covenant is profoundly mutual. Thus, in the biblical tradition, specific friendships both demonstrate the valuing, choosing, accepting, and welcoming qualities of God's steadfast relationship with humankind as well as challenge or call us to share that gift with others.

Thus, the similarity between classical and biblical understandings of the spiritual qualities of friendship is more important than the dilemma or the paradox. While using different words and concepts, both focus on the importance of friendship as gift and grace, a celebration of mutual enjoyment, acceptance, usefulness, reciprocity, and caring that is different from other human relationships. There is always, as Amado says in the *Friends manual*,[23] a sense of magic or a feeling that something in the friendship is greater than the sum of its parts. In addition to being felt as gift, grace, or magic, the second fundamental spiritual dimension of friendship in both the classical and biblical traditions is that it calls us beyond and out of ourselves to new understandings of ourselves, others, community, and God.

LIVING OUT OF GIFT AND CALL: THE CHALLENGE
OF FRIENDSHIP FOR PROFESSIONAL CAREGIVERS

If the preceding summary of the historical understandings of the spiritual foundations of friendship is accurate, it is no wonder that friendship is both a concept and experience that challenges current systems of care and understandings of the role of caregivers. First and foremost, if friendship is as fundamental and important a human need as proposed by both philosophical and scriptural traditions, it has been a need that has certainly been overlooked, unappreciated, and devalued. At one level, segregated facilities and services have too often made friendships improbable, impossible, or unacknowledged. As friendship has received growing attention because of its importance as a key to integration or inclusion in community life, it also challenges our understandings of caregiving roles.

If, for example, one asked about friendship in current practice in light of classical understandings, the question begins with, "Where do people we call 'consumers' have that experience?" "Where are the places and relationships characterized by mutual appreciation and enjoyment?" "Where are there opportunities for a sense of reciprocity and usefulness to others?" The question confronting us as professionals, families, advocates, and consumers is, "What constitutes community, or a 'real' or 'good' experience of community?" It first of all means having friends.

In light of the biblical dimensions of friendship, the indictment of a current system perhaps is even stronger. As stated at the beginning of the chapter, we have just begun to talk about the inherent value and giftedness of each person, what the Bible symbolizes in the "image of God." But we continue to struggle with our ability to see and affirm the uniqueness and value of each person whose label or category of "client" or "consumer" precedes his or her name given at birth. Professionals struggle with the label or name to call people whom we serve. Can that name be "friend"? Who gets to decide?

Second, we have also been part of a system of care in which there has been very little focus on the grace and gift of mutual acceptance at the heart of friendship, which is captured in the old gospel song "Just as I Am." Acceptance, celebration, and reward, in fact, too often come in a behavioral system after an accomplishment and achieving a goal. That is, in biblical terms, a system based on being "saved," or "made whole," by "works," not by grace. The underlying message

One is that "professional" has come to mean "expert" and "detached problem solver." "To profess" meant originally to make a commitment or to take vows for a religious order. As "profession" widened to include other kinds of service to the community or humankind, it became more attached to science, medicine, and other forms of knowledge connected with a university. There, "professional" evolved into knowing how to "fix" or "cure." As understandings of knowledge became more objective, rather than focused on faith and a vow of commitment, "profession" came to mean mastery of a body of knowledge, including facts, theories, and methodologies.[27] The core of the pursuit of new knowledge through scientific research implied a detachment between the knower and the known, or, as caregiving professions became more scientific, between the professional and the patient and client. When the impetus toward that detachment is combined with the understanding of the spiritual call to service as universal, impartial, and sacrificial love, it is not difficult to see how religion and science combined forces to shape an understanding of a professional caregiver who was an impartial, dedicated, knowledgeable dispenser of care and help in relationships that were neither mutual nor reciprocal.

Along with those historical strands went the understanding that reciprocity comes by being paid, only subsistence at first, but more highly as "profession" disconnected from vows of faith and poverty. "Profession" came to mean a career path that offered honor and advancement.[28] "Professional" also became a social class of distinction, with rights, privileges, and, not least of all, power and position.[29] To guard against overzealous or inappropriate expressions of religion or commitment in caregiving relationships, "professionals" were cautioned not to let their values or beliefs get in the way of their professional care. Friendships thus become suspect because of their implications of exclusivity, preferential treatment, or challenge to objectivity in care. In any social order where there is concern for maintaining power and control, friendships have also been suspect because of the very way they empower (a mutual recognition of gifts) and lead to (call for) a questioning of long-held assumptions in light of new understandings of the common good.

This discussion is not meant to dismiss the importance of recognizing and utilizing boundaries in human caregiving relationships. Appropriate boundaries are first and foremost an awareness of limits, something in which we as "professional experts" often have little expertise. Neither is it a call for professionals to be "friends" with everyone whom they serve. But it is an affirmation that reframing professional roles in light of changing understandings of community and care does mean the call to recover what it means to be "professional." To profess was to make a declaration of one's faith and values. "What motivates you?" "What are your intentions?" One "professed" in both response to a sense of the gifts of God and the call. That may mean being more honest about what we as professionals receive from the people we serve. The question is not just what gifts they have for families and communities. "What gifts do they bring to us?" "What do 'they' do for 'us,'?" or, even more pointedly, "What does he or she do for me, in the course of my relationship with him or her?" Or, as Hans Reinders states very compellingly in his book on friendship and persons with profound disabilities, one of their possible gifts to us is teaching us about our brokenness and our need to receive.[30]

"To profess" was also "to follow," to recognize and respond to the call to use one's gifts in service to God and community. It was, at least in early religious and caregiving professions, also a sense that one was giving up something (*agape*'s call to sacrificial love) in order to serve. It was a commitment of permanence, a covenant of new bonds other than family or civic status, a willingness to "stand with" others in a shared community. As "professionals," we may be called to give up some of the detachment, status, or boundaries we have maintained between work and community in response to the call inherent in friendship. It pushes us to ask, "What kind of commitment are we making to people whom we serve over the long haul?" To facilitate the experience of belonging inherent in friendship and community means to share, and perhaps give up, ownership. Can we learn how to give our knowledge away to others in the community? Can we also learn to be careful about the ways that professional systems place unexamined barriers in the way of community friendships? Learning how to empower others means a reversal of the age-old stance of empowering special services by asking others for adequate funding. Responding to the call certainly pushes us to give up some of the temptation to overmanage or control. It also asks the question, "What really provides safety over the long haul: ever more complex safeguards and regulations or a network of relationships that includes a significant number of real friends?"

The challenge of helping people find, develop, and maintain friend-ships is also more about a messy, emotion-filled art than it is about scientific knowledge. It calls for different skills, but it also calls for lots of people to be involved, not just one strata or job description in a world of services and supports. Thus, part of our call is to believe that others may discover gifts in relationships with people with intellectual and developmental disabilities and that they do not have to become "experts" to do so but rather an acquaintance who might become a friend, and a good one at that.

HOLDING ON TO GIFT AND CALL

Reframed in the context of my defining framework of spirituality, friendship is the essence of connection and mutuality. Friendships shape our identities and understandings of who we are, what we believe, and what is most important to us. True to the classical meaning of friend-ships, they may call us forth to discover and live a life of purpose. Its call is just that, a call to respond, perhaps on the reciprocal level of an I.O.U. but also more deeply through sharing an unearned, uncondi-tional gift with others. One form of the Golden Rule is a reciprocal "Do unto others as you would have them do unto you." Another moves more deeply, in "doing unto others (in love or friendship) what has been done unto you," or "giving what you have received."

Holding on to "gift" and "call" in the realm of friendship also means that, as we (families, professionals, friends) walk alongside people with intellectual and developmental disabilities into the dreams of new relationships in community life, we must also believe in the gifts of others and the possibility of friendships. Hans Reinders notes we are pressed to do so even in a culture whose values may question the very heart of our belief that those relationships can be ones of immense value. It means we must believe in the gifts and call that others might bring and find in those relationships, ones that are not defined by professional contract but by covenant. None of us become friends with every person we meet. We are not in control. But we can help people "choose" and make a commitment to get to know a single person and help that person see his or her own gifts and capacity for doing so.

Holding on to "call" more sharply focuses the need to approach the art of making introductions[31] and the gift of hospitality, a belief that people respond in love to others most genuinely when they act in response to their own sense of call and commitment. It means believing that others may in fact commit themselves to a relationship and friendship in ways that defy explanation. It means operating from the framework that friendship is a covenant relationship, not one characterized by a giver-receiver relationship or by service systems' reliance on "compliance with code." A covenant means space for individual choice, an awareness that relationships and friendships often grow slowly and fluctuate in intensity. It is awareness that friendships are neither controlled nor fixed. Helping friendships begin and develop is more like planting seeds and nurturing, but all the while being aware you do not control the growth.[32]

The challenge also means rediscovering that truth in relationships is different from truth in science. Science operates on objective facts, relationships on seeing truth as "troth." Through seeking truth in the context of relationships, we become "betrothed" in trust and commitment.[33] For those of us in service systems who are so easily tempted to use relationships as tools for growth, development, or inclusion, perhaps the best injunction is to remember that the art of befriending is characterized much more by "courtship" than it is "control."[34]

Almost any community space or organization can be a place where new relationships may start and friendships may evolve. Much of my work has been based on a belief that faith communities are treasure chests of possibilities, but the same attitudes and strategies apply in most other settings, perhaps with some changes in the language used.[35] Expressed theologically, some of those core strategies are:

1. Start with a theology of creation. People with developmental disabilities are first of all people, created, like others, in the image of God. Each is, as all of us, one of God's children and thereby part of God's family. Thus they belong, whether it has been their experience or not. If their gifts have not been seen and used in the context of the people of God, it is our call, as with everyone, to discover them.

2. Articulate the importance of acceptance in everyone's lives, but particularly in the lives of people with developmental disabilities. Become able to talk about that in biblical, psychological, social, and very personal terms.

3. See the importance of congregational involvement as a way of enhancing spiritual identity and journey over time, as well as developing relationships that can be friendships characterized by steadfastness, long-term commitment, and covenant. "Typical" people often talk of their faith or congregation being an "anchor" in seas of transition and change. Can both service providers and congregations see the importance of honoring and nurturing those long-term relationships with people who have often been given little choice or opportunity to be in those kinds of relationships?

4. Help interpret the risk or fear that others may have in relationships with people with disabilities as an expression of the call to love in ways that are inclusive, risk taking (sacrificial), and part of the second great commandment, "to love thy neighbor as thyself." The irony is that most typical people feel "disabled" in their capacity to relate to people with developmental disabilities. It means helping others to see that God has promised to be with them as they reach out in service to others in ways that feel risky. Such service lives out God's love for humankind and can lead to new discoveries of grace, gift, and presence in oneself and others. It also means being prepared to support others who make that commitment as well as to learn from, and celebrate, both the difficulties and the joys.

5. Balance the spiritual call to universal love with the specific gift of hospitality that welcomes specific individuals. Help congregations to envision inclusive ministries with people with disabilities not as "special ministries" that require "special people with special gifts and call"[36] but as part of the biblical injunction to welcome the stranger. Thus, the call is to common tradition and strengths, rather than becoming another form of social service agency or human service program. Practicing the gift of hospitality may mean doing things differently, but it is an attitude of "doing what it takes" to welcome and include, with a vision that what may happen is that the stranger becomes the giver and the friend. Friendships, in spiritual traditions, can be transforming. So can the call to welcome and befriend.

CONCLUSION: CALLED TO BE FRIENDS

As service providers, advocates, families, clergy, laypeople, individuals with developmental disabilities, and others rediscover the power of the gift of friendship, the challenge for everyone is to reaffirm, in the best of both the classical and spiritual traditions, friendship's inherent call to new forms of relationship, profession, and community. Friendship means being able to operate with a high tolerance for paradox, for friendship as gift is not a tool but it is a resource. A specific and special friendship is celebrated for its mutual enjoyment and usefulness to one another, but also for the way it calls both parties beyond themselves to universal values or to God. People respond to the call and need for friendship through choice, but it is not controlled. We are challenged to love fairly and equally, yet in each stranger and neighbor there is the possibility of a new friend. Developing friendships takes intentional work and commitment, on the one hand, and a celebration of gift and discovery, on the other.

The ultimate paradox, of course, is that people with intellectual and developmental disabilities may be more skilled in the art of friendship than "typical" people and thus can be our teachers and experts. If cultivating friendships means doing things like giving priority to relationships; being open with feelings, thoughts, and affections; practicing acceptance; learning the gestures and touches of warmth, listening, and seeing in every stranger a potential friend, then "we" are the learners.[37]

If we want others to become their friends, we have to be willing to tell stories about, or give witness to, the ways their friendships have brought value to us. "Let me tell you about my friend." It means that reframing a role as "professional" reaffirms the ancient spiritual role of guide and companion. It is not a "fix-it" guide or a "how-to" guide, but a guide that walks with others in their mutual response to gift and call, and helps introduce, facilitate, accommodate, and interpret. "I will no longer all you servants (consumers, clients, patients, or providers) but friends" (John 15:15). It is indeed difficult to write about friendship except as an act of rehabilitation.

13

Relationships Are Not Easy
Challenging Behaviors, Positive Behavior Supports, and Spirituality

Relationships are sometimes very hard. Even the task of maintaining friendships is often a challenge when either party acts in a way that belies the positive feelings of connection, the history of a friendship, or the underlying personal, social, and cultural understandings of those relationships. This is no less true for and with people with intellectual and developmental disabilities and their relationships with others, or, alternatively, our relationships with them. People with intellectual and developmental disabilities often communicate a hunger for relationship and friendship. That does not mean relationships with others are always easily established or maintained. The reasons abound: stereotypes, fears, lack of experience, assumptions about capacity to learn, assumptions about responsibility, and the lack of opportunity to be in "typical" human relationships and contexts where relationships and social mores can be observed and practiced from childhood.

Many people with intellectual and developmental disabilities also live in situations and structures where their behavior is highly monitored because of their need for care and support. That monitoring can be a by-product of the need for ongoing observation and supervision in the most loving of settings. It can also take the form of explicit or implicit pressure for them to "behave" in "appropriate ways," that is, according to norms that may vary from setting to setting. Observation and supervision are also a central part of caregiving systems and services where planning often leads to detailed schedules, pressures to document progress, policies to keep people safe, and practices to prevent what are called "unexpected or unusual incidents" that usually involve copious documentation.

The shadow side of that close and careful support is that it limits the times, spaces, and places where one can simply be one's self. Thus, at one level, a friend, advocate, or caregiver is tempted to say, "Wait a minute! People with intellectual and developmental disabilities have their own idiosyncrasies, just like anyone else. They are not the only ones who can act in strange, weird, threatening, and sometimes harmful ways." Those advocates and friends would be right, but they would also need to remember that challenging, unexplainable, and uncontrollable behaviors by people with various forms of disabilities have historically been the social impetus behind fear, seclusion, exclusion, or even punishment. The realm of the "spiritual" has often been blamed—those behaviors are the result of evil spirits or demons that have taken over a person's mind or soul. Or, conversely, the "spiritual," in the form of saints, healers, wise men, and others, has gotten the credit for healing or casting out the demons by powers that seem to be just as inexplicable as the cause, except for the fact that those truly known as healers were also known for their kindness and willingness to enter relationships with those whom society had shunned.[1]

Some of the behaviors called "challenging" in our times are some of the same ones seen in ancient times: inexplicable outbursts, unexplained aggression toward others, self-injurious behavior, ritualistic behaviors like beating one's head on the wall, and behaviors that violate sexual mores, among others. They are even more challenging when done by people whose communication skills are very limited, thus compounding the inability to explain and understand by both the person with the behaviors and others in the community who are present when the behaviors occur.

As multiple scientific disciplines have sought to deal with these and other forms of challenging behaviors, there has been a remarkable convergence of what the human sciences call the field of positive behavioral supports (PBS) with what I have discussed as the essence of spirituality and the best of spiritual supports. There is, in my opinion, an unexplored similarity between some of the best practices and foundations of positive behavior supports and the philosophy and practices of Jean Vanier and the L'Arche communities. Positive behavior supports are based on intense and detailed multidisciplinary scientific principles and a solid but less explicit moral foundation. The L'Arche communities are founded on deep interpersonal and spiritual relationships between individuals with intellectual and developmental disabilities (core members) and their caregivers (assistants). It seems somewhat ironic that the former is based on very detailed observation and specific methods of support while the latter is rooted in love, the accepting of another, and the creation of space and relationships for a deep sense of acceptance, affirmation, and belonging. The paradox of this contrast and convergence can even be more sharply illustrated in some methods that use the best of scientifically based positive behavior supports (PBS), principles, and practices to enable children and teenagers on the autism spectrum to learn how to attend and participate in religious services and rites of passage. That is yet another illustration that the "worlds" of disability and spirituality are intricately part of the same whole.

CHALLENGING BEHAVIOR: WHAT IS IT?

Challenging behavior is one of those names and labels that can cast a very wide net. A challenging behavior is certainly dependent on the point of view of the one doing the labeling and classification. To reverse roles, many families and people with disabilities could talk, for example, about "challenging behaviors" in professionals with whom they have not had good relationships. During the years when I was working as a chaplain in direct service and ministry, I was often both troubled and bemused when staff at all levels would label the behavior of a person with intellectual and developmental disabilities as "noncompliant" or "manipulative." Noncompliant means not following the rules and expected behavioral norms, which vary greatly by context and by who has the power. "Manipulative" was an even more ironic descriptor, since most of the programs and services were geared toward teaching and training (or manipulating) people to learn and follow those norms. Both are ways of exercising power by the people being served through resisting or attempting to change the structures in which they lived.

With that caveat, "challenging behavior" has some very specific definitions in the behavioral and educational sciences. A succinct example is that challenging behavior is (1) any repeated pattern of behavior that interferes with learning or engagement in prosocial interactions with peers and adults and (2) behaviors that are not responsive to the use of developmentally appropriate guidance procedures. Examples include prolonged tantrums, physical and verbal aggression, disruptive vocal and motor behavior (e.g., screaming and repeated stereotyped behaviors), property destruction, self-injury, withdrawal, and other forms of noncompliance.[2] Michael Smull notes that people with challenging behaviors who tend to get moved from one service system to another often become "people with severe reputations."[3] I have heard it put more bluntly in some settings with the phrase, "he or she is a behavior." In other words, an individual's identity is reduced to a single characteristic. Nigerian-born novelist Chimamanda Ngozi Adichie, not referring to disability at all, calls this "the danger of a single story."[4]

These are behaviors that can happen in any context yet sometimes are context specific. A congregational leader in inclusive ministries told me about a young boy with autism whose nonverbal behavior became the major issue at his IEP meeting to which she had been invited. In the discussion about his unwilllingness to talk, she noted that the boy had sung in a church pageant the week before. The question became one about the differences in the contexts: Why was he verbal in one setting but not another? Whatever the type of behavior and wherever they happen, challenging behaviors are often ones that confound, frustrate, and anger family members, caregivers, and peers. Far too often, the end results are that the person with the behavior first gets blamed without taking the context into account, and, second, the power dynamics of trying to gain control ratchets up on both sides, often leading to punishment, isolation, or exclusion (or worse), with no one pleased about the outcome.

There are other frameworks or constructs for interpreting these kinds of behavior.[5] Jean Vanier talks about the woundedness of many people with intellectual and developmental disabilities, wounds from psychological or physical abuse that leads to mistrust and acting out at many levels. Psychologist David Pitonyak notes that the lives of many people with challenging behaviors have been devoid of meaning, full of loneliness, lack of power, and sometimes undiagnosed physical or psychiatric issues.[6] Paying attention to those needs often lessens forms of challenging behaviors.

For example, challenging behaviors can sometimes be a way of acting out grief that has not been recognized or supported in appropriate ways. One of my clinical pastoral education students in New Jersey started a pastoral relationship with a man who was a recent resident of a group home run by the agency at which she was placed. The man was exhibiting increasingly severe behavioral outbursts, which included hitting others and punching a hole in a wall. This was in October. As she got to know him and his history, it turned out that he had been moved out of his family home when his mother died around the previous Thanksgiving. He had passed through several emergency placements and then to this agency, which was beginning to believe it could no longer support him and that he would have to be admitted to a psychiatric facility. In her conversations with him, the chaplain discovered that he had not been able to go to his mother's funeral and, in fact, did not know the location of her grave. Thanksgiving, a favorite holiday for the family, was coming up. Together, the chaplain and the man planned a memorial service for his mother in the group home, made a memory box, and prepared a meal with macaroni and cheese for after the service, one of his favorite meals made by his mother. The reduction in his outbursts was immediate. The anniversary had been remembered, and, with the memory box, he had an ongoing way of remembering his mother and talking about her with others.

One key contribution of positive behavior supports is the understanding that a problem behavior is "challenging" to others and, for people with a problem behavior, an ineffective way of acting to get something they want or avoiding something they do not want. That behavior has a function for that individual and needs to be understood as such. Or, in other words, it serves a purpose and needs to be understood as a form of communication about a pressing need in the absence of socially appropriate alternatives.[7] That understanding necessitates a profound commitment to listening in new ways as well as to helping individuals learn to communicate in new ways, both of which are hallmarks of effective positive behavior supports.

FROM SKINNER TO POSITIVE BEHAVIOR
SUPPORTS: A BRIEF HISTORY

In the 1950s B. F. Skinner became famous for his theory that all behavior could be explained by understanding its antecedents and its consequences.[8] With associates and students, that work led to the foundations for applied behavioral analysis, which assumes that if one understands the functional relationship of behavior through its antecedents and consequences, it is then possible to predict and control human behavior. At heart it was an affirmation that living beings could learn, but ABA also ruled out matters of the heart as having any influence on behavior, including internal mental and emotional phenomena, culture, spirituality, and other factors that might relate to the meaning or social construction of behavior.

I was just beginning my first position as a chaplain at Newark State School when ABA began to be implemented. The positive side was indeed the hope that challenging behaviors by people with severe intellectual and developmental disabilities could be changed. People could learn, rather than being seen as "vegetables" or "untrainable." ABA developed tools (or what are sometimes called "technologies") called functional behavioral assessments, which are very careful and specific documented observations of a specific behavior. Those functional behavioral assessments seek to capture what comes before and after a specific behavior. Thus, those assessments are essentially structured forms of listening to behavior, albeit only to its observable dimensions. ABA is grounded in the belief that, in a controlled environment, you could target discrete behaviors for modification through positive rewards, ignoring, or negative consequences, including punishment. Indeed, there were successes, for example, with people who had become very self-abusive or aggressive.

At the American Association on Mental Deficiency (as the AAIDD was called then) in 1975, I heard Jean Vanier speak for his first and only time at this national professional association. L'Arche was about ten years old. He talked about the vision of L'Arche as creating "communities of celebration that reawakened desire" for people with severe disabilities who had also been deeply wounded emotionally. He noted how they also relied on consulting psychiatrists and psychologists, saying, "You Americans are very good with those little units of growth."

But the talk mostly focused on creation of a loving community. Right after he finished, I overheard two behavioral psychologists behind me complain, "He did not leave any room for us."

The irony of that statement is twofold. First, they missed his point about their crucial contributions and, second, the reverse had much more truth. ABA and behavior modification did not leave any room for the kind of relationships and community that L'Arche embodied. Along with successes, there were soon glaring problems in the ABA model, especially as it ended up being applied in systematic ways. I remember a woman who was in a wheelchair, also blind, but someone who could talk and understand relatively well. The unit on which she lived was devoid of much positive stimulation or relationships. She essentially had nothing to do. She was known for outbursts of frustration and anger. But she loved my coming to the unit to lead a simple religious service. She liked to sing and to engage with me. Sometimes she was not present, and when I asked, it was clear that she was being prevented from coming as a punishment, or, in other words, being able to come was also a reward. In that gray area between those two poles, I remember her coming a couple of times with both of her arms strapped down to the wooden lap table of her chair and staff warnings about getting too close.

Thus, the shadow side of ABA was (and still can be) that negative consequences and punishments get increased—the power of the powerful misused, to the point it was justified under the terminology of "aversive treatments." It was a form of "do whatever it takes" to change the person, without seriously looking at the morality of doing so, much less questioning the theory that behavior could be predicted and controlled. I remember numbers of occasions when my role became one of stepping in to diffuse an escalating altercation between a person with a disability and his or her direct support staff, each trying to exercise more power and control than the other. Diffusing that crisis meant trying to give everyone the space to listen more carefully to what was going on.

Two significant trends in services began to create significant cognitive and moral dissonance about a singular focus on ABA and thus impetus for change. First, people began to move out of isolated and regimented institutions under the banner of normalization, with the hope of creating ways of life that were more typical to the general community. As they did so, psychologists, professionals, and policy leaders realized that aversive treatments could not be justified in community settings.[9] Nor could someone's life be controlled in the same ways that were possible in institutions. The new focus was on participation in community living, work, recreation, faith, and social environments. By statute, education and care had to be provided in the "least restrictive environment." Behavioral therapies needed to be ones that helped people fit into a variety of social contexts. Inflicting pain or harm without a moral foundation was, by its own definition of reason and truth, irrational.

The second impetus for shifting the focus of functional assessments and ABA was the emergence of concepts like positive role and identity development, self-determination, and person-centered planning that take into account a person's preferences, beliefs, and culture. All of those were very difficult to reconcile with the ABA rejection of mental and cultural phenomena as a potential causes of behavior.[10] Positive behavior supports began as a system of exploring ways to change behavior by identifying and changing environmental stimuli that might cause problem behaviors, focusing intently on the function and purpose of a learned behavior, and then trying to figure out ways that an individual might learn "positive" ways to reach those same goals or meet their needs. As Singer and Wang so eloquently phrase it, "PBS cut its teeth by providing positive alternatives for the treatment of people who may not be moral agents[11] but who are all the more vulnerable to mistreatment in the name of social control."[12]

PBS then shifted the primary focus from controlling negative behaviors by unnecessary restrictions or consequences to teaching "positive" behaviors that helped enhance both inclusion and quality of life. In its functional behavioral analyses, PBS utilizes insights from multiple disciplines about how behavior can be influenced by multiple sources, including the context in which it occurs. A tool may also be only as good as the relationships between the analyst or therapist and the one being analyzed. Enhancing positive choices and preferences means a more mutual, trusting relationship between both parties. That can mean helping people with limited communication skills to learn and use alternative forms of assisted communication, such as through pictures, symbols, and signs. PBS also recognizes that undiagnosed physical or psychological issues may be the cause of challenging behaviors. A specific behavior may also be problematic or "inappropriate" in one cultural context but not in another. As PBS developed and spread from beyond particular clinical or classroom environments, it has also been used (1) to enhance the skills of parents working with their child at home and (2) as a system for organizing whole learning environments, such as school-wide positive behavior programs that stress positive reinforcement of learning for all children, explicit teaching of social and emotional skills for some, and intensive, individualized interventions using PBS for those who have the more challenging behaviors.[13]

Thus, PBS has developed into a set of strategies whose origin is in the world of intellectual and developmental disabilities but whose applicability is much wider. Once again, learning that developed in the crucible of issues raised by disability turns out to be at the heart of creative ways of addressing the needs of "normal" children and adults. PBS, in contrast to behavior modification and the more narrowly defined applied behavioral analysis, embodies current values such as person-centered planning and supports, the highlighting of strengths and gifts rather than a singular focus on deficits or pathologies, the teaching of skills that enhance both communication and competence (i.e., connection and achievement), and the respecting of an individual's preferences as well as the culture and context in which he or she lives. Singer and Wang summarize this by observing:

> Culture, as an indispensable ecological context of human development, has a profound impact on human cultural identities defined by ethnicity, language, religion, or other specific social identity in which people determine behavior as appropriate, inappropriate, or problematic on the basis of specific cultural values and beliefs as well as the certain circumstances in which the behavior occurs.[14]

SPIRITUALITY AND POSITIVE BEHAVIOR SUPPORTS: DIFFERENT PATHS TO THE SAME DESTINATION?

Based on those values in the ongoing development of positive behavior supports, my question is whether spirituality and PBS could be considered different paths to the vision of more inclusive participation in community for people with behavioral challenges or, alternatively, very similar paths, traveled with different guidebooks that effectively complement each other for the sake of those travelers, friends, and caregivers. As noted, there was a moral impetus to the development of positive behavior supports that came from both from an aversion to aversive treatments (so to speak) as well as a commitment to find ways of shaping and teaching behavior that did not depend on pain, punishment, or harm. There was a recognition that behavioral therapies focused purely on ABA principles but delivered without careful training had the potential for professionals to misuse the power that they had in those relationships. That argument and debate is not over, as evidenced by the past decade of attempts to stop the aversive therapies, including electric shock, used by the Judge Rotenberg Center in Massachusetts.[15] In simple form, the Golden Rule was one of the foundations as well as the rights that protected people from harm and from overly restrictive environments.

In addition, if the tools of functional behavioral analyses and positive behavioral supports are used with care and attention to personal-centered approaches as well as for building skills to enhance communication and learning, one can describe them as very careful forms of listening to others to discover the reasons why people do what they do, including contexts, antecedents, needs, goals, and preferences. The teaching of more effective communication skills and behavioral skills then becomes a process of building personal and cultural identity, connections with others, and much more effective ways to "act out" inner desires, hopes, needs, and feelings.

Stated in other words, those are forms of enhancing and supporting dimensions of spirituality. First, with its focus on the meaning of behavior, positive behavior supports include values and methods that seek to find out what motivates an individual, to understand the multiple dimensions of the meaning of a behavior and what matters most to that person. PBS then assists him or her in creating positive identities through more effective interaction with others in multiple environments, and enabling others to see and appreciate that individual's strengths as well as needs. PBS is based on faith in the *capacity* of everyone to learn.

Second, PBS focuses on the importance of relationships as well as rewards, knowing that trust and rapport is crucial in interactions that seek to shape behavior. More effective communication leads to better connections and then to better relationships. The entry of positive relationships often dispels the original behaviors that came from attention seeking or loneliness. Those connections and relationships can be with families, friends, peers, places, religious and cultural events, and more. David Pitonyak notes that many people with challenging behaviors may have had little experience both with unconditional love and care as well as with people who are doing things *with* them, not *to* them.[16]

One of the related frameworks for exhibiting this kind of foundational care for positive behavior supports is John McGee's "gentle teaching." McGee believed that most problematic behaviors came from an absence of bonding in loving ways with others. To break cycles of domineering behavior based on teaching obedience and compliance, McGee urged caregivers to look within themselves first:

> When in doubt about what to do, a gentle caregiver looks at any question or situation from this perspective—what will help the person feel safe and loved at this very moment? Instead of worrying about issues like compliance, independence, or self-determination, the gentle caregiver is concerned with teaching children and adults to feel safe and loved. Rather than fixed answers, we need to examine ourselves and our values, especially nonviolence and the ability to express unconditional love in the face of violence and rejection.[17]

The similarities between McGee's theory and practice and Jean Vanier's "community of celebration that embraces the wounds of people with severe disabilities and reawakens desire" are striking.[18] Both strive toward creating an environment in which people feel loved, an environment committed to individual growth, relationships, and hope. Attitudes of the heart, as it were, are just as important as the technologies and tools of the mind in shaping behavior.

Third, positive behavior supports are built on importance of purpose: (1) understanding the purpose and meaning of problematic behavior and what is being communicated; (2) helping individuals to learn more positive, purposeful behaviors that enable them to meet their own goals and needs with hope and effective action; and (3) enabling people to use their own gifts in ways that contribute purposefully to others. PBS stresses choices (i.e., free will) rather than command or control. Many attempts to control behavior end up creating environments where fear is pervasive and compliance is the focus of interventions. In contrast, PBS and its strategies are geared toward "catching" a person doing something well rather than what's wrong and by rewarding behavior rather than punishing.

COLLABORATIVE PRACTICE: MOVING AHEAD OF THEORY

The dearth of theoretical or, indeed, theological explorations of spirituality and positive behavior supports was both evident and surprising when my simple Internet search using those keywords together turned up almost nothing in the process of my own research. But there are practitioners on both "sides" working together by tapping principles and tools of positive behavior supports to facilitate participation by individuals and families in spiritual communities. Let us look at three examples.

First, Barbara Newman and others connected to the CLC Network in Michigan have utilized an inclusive Christian school setting to develop strategies to help congregations include children and adults whose behavior has often overwhelmed religious education teachers and worship leaders. Many of those involve careful attention to the meaning of behavior, multisensory ways of communication, individualized supports understood and used by a whole team, the use of peers as mentors, creative adaptations of established routines, and other strategies.[19]

Second, I have been privileged to work with and learn from several people in the Archdiocese of Newark, New Jersey, including Ann Masters, the director of the Office of Pastoral Ministries with People with Disabilities, and Mary Beth Walsh, the parent of a son with autism, a professional with a statewide parent support network called Mom2Mom and a professor of theology at Caldwell University. They have worked with members of the Applied Behavioral Analysis section of the Caldwell Psychology Department, families, and the lay staff or volunteers of individual parishes to shape individualized positive behavioral support plans to help children and teenagers with challenging behaviors participate in meaningful, inclusive ways in religious education programs, worship, and rites of passage such as first communion and confirmation. They have used strategies from PBS such as storyboarding and other visual ways of prompting the steps in any community ritual, practicing individual components at home and in other settings, backward chaining to help a child experience a successful ending of a religious service rather than starting at the beginning and having to leave, and then coming a bit earlier as skills for participation are learned, and, finally, finding ways for a child or teenager to contribute.[20] That careful and caring work takes time and patience but also allows the community to learn and join in the collective work of accommodation and inclusion. To cite three examples:

1. Members of the consulting team helped a synagogue, a young girl with autism, and her family prepare for her bat mitzvah. There was a united commitment to help her learn and demonstrate her capacity for learning. They broke the usual roles for a young girl in her bat mitzvah service down to 170+ steps and addressed each one in their preparation for a successful and extremely meaningful service that the family, originally, had not thought possible.

2. In Dr. Walsh's parish, a young adult on the autism spectrum who was aging out of school usually sat with great enjoyment in the right front next to the choir. He began to hit himself and then pinch others, leading to a serious incident of doing so on a Palm Sunday. They pulled everyone together to figure out what was going on. Finally, they realized that the routine of participation in the Eucharist had been changed recently, so that instead of lines receiving communion at the front of three aisles, everyone was now supposed to move to the center aisle and come up together. The young man had been used to being at the front of the right line. As in most churches, separate servers bring communion to the choir so they can participate and then, often, sing during the distribution of the Eucharist. With the blessing of the priest, ushers, and choir, they then made it possible for the young man to receive communion as the first person when the servers came to the choir. That stopped the behavioral issues because everyone had learned their meaning.

3. Third, in her book *Dancing with Max*, Emily Colson tells the story of how her autistic son made church participation very difficult for several years. In fact, they stayed away. Finally, she

made the decision that they really needed to go, for both of their sakes. She started with the backward chaining technique, coming to the church the first time just as it was ending and a group of guys, nicknamed the Grunt Crew, were starting to put away the chairs. They invited Max to help them, which he did immediately. Thereby began his relationship with a bunch of guys and the opportunity to contribute, which became major factors in his development of a positive relationship with that faith community.[21]

CONCLUSION: MORE ALIKE THAN NOT?

In a modern context of human services, both applied behavioral analysis and positive behavioral supports stress that they are behavioral *sciences*. From my perspective and experience, both with the theory of positive behavior supports and the people who have developed and learned to practice it effectively, it is also a profoundly spiritual enterprise. Its respect for the "spirit" of each person, and the spirit of care, attention to detail, patience, and optimism exhibited by many of its practitioners, can be both felt and observed. Most human service professionals would not say that PBS is based on any form of religious foundations. As Singer and Wang note, PBS is much more comfortable with a moral foundation built on the work of people like Bernard Gert for whom reason is primary and theories about the foundations of values and morals are very suspect. In a fascinating sentence, they write, "It is an alternative to ethics based on religion at a time when morality has been distorted in the name of religious fundamentalism."[22]

The discomfort is no doubt felt in the other direction as well, with people of faith or deep spiritual commitments somewhat suspicious of approaches that are called purely "scientific" and that utilize languages that seem very esoteric. One of the real ironies is that the two frameworks of science and spirituality/religion often judge one another by the fundamentalists on each side. Both frameworks have grown and developed in critical and creative response to the "fundamentalists" in their own ranks, whether the pure behaviorists on one side or a moral/religious fundamentalism on the other. Both can be known for their insularity and strict adherence to their respective doctrines (or theories). There is some obvious similarity between both scientific *and* religious perspectives built almost exclusively on the power of reward and punishment as the sole ways to shape human behavior. It is somewhat akin to two antagonistic families judging the other family solely on the "black sheep" in the other's members.

The belief, passion, and commitment of any theoretical or theological system faces the real danger of losing its heart when people become certain of their own certainty and resistant to anything that challenges the ways they have determined truth is known. That becomes another irony because it belies the ways its founders and proponents criticized other systems certain of their own truths as, for example, when behavioral analysis initially grew in the face of critique from more psychodynamic understandings of human behavior. Positive behavior supports, like any emerging, effective body of knowledge and practice, face the dangers of being misused, especially as a source of power in and over people's lives. My own faith in its potential is based, first, on the willingness of PBS to include multiple perspectives and partners in its theory and practice and, second, on the importance of trusting relationships in its effective practice. Human beings, at all levels of ability, have the capacity to sense when they are being misused for the sake of other people's gains and the power to figure out ways to confound any singular version of the truth by new ways of thinking or acting, which in themselves may become a new form of "challenging behaviors."

14

Spirituality, Diversity, and Community
Moving toward Belonging

Being a part of a welcoming and inclusive community is a fundamental part of the vision and dreams of most people with disabilities and their families. Community inclusion and participation is a core value and mission of professional human service organizations, caregiving and support networks, advocacy groups, and, indeed, public policies. But living and being in a community setting does not mean one is a part of a community or the "communities" within that community. Securing rights to equal treatment, accommodations, and services does not mean that lasting relationships are formed and nurtured, nor does it mean that people have a sense that they belong.

Equal treatment under the law, respect for the rights of every citizen, and the experiences of welcoming, inclusion, and belonging are not just issues for people with disabilities and their families. They are perhaps the central issues of our time as communities, societies, and the global community all struggle with equality and respect in a world where distance is all but eliminated by instantaneous communication but community itself seems to get harder. Fostering connections that lead to understanding and respect is not easy in the face of differences and diversity expressed in ethnicity, culture, sexuality, ability, age, and religion. Difference is far too often experienced with anxiety and fear rather than curiosity and a desire to learn. Identities harden in reaction to the "other," however defined, and lead to assumptions and judgments that block the awareness of connection, common values, and shared purpose on which any sense of community depends.

Identity, meaning, shared purpose, and connection: those are the fundamental dimensions of spirituality as well as an indication of its value and importance in finding and building community amid difference. Spirituality's power can be experienced in the negative, as when religious and spiritual identities and values are used to justify uniqueness and discrimination while also demonizing difference. But, rightly addressed, spirituality is a crucial resource for building a community where the usual forces of rights and laws have their own kinds of limitations.

The goal of including people with disabilities and their families faces an arena with broad forces at play. As a Christian, I might even call them the "principalities and powers" (Rom 8:37-39; Eph 6:12) that seem to work for evil rather than good in the world. That goal calls us to explore what we mean by community. Inclusion and belonging put disability within the wider arena of respecting and valuing cultural diversity. That vision calls for all caregivers and service systems to be "culturally competent." The promise is that the skills learned in facilitating community building with people with disabilities through spiritual resources can also be used in building connections across many other areas of difference.[1]

COMMUNITY: WHAT ARE WE TALKING ABOUT?

The foundational question in community building is, of course: What does it mean to be "community" or "in community?" The meanings may be varied, along with the visions and dreams for the kind of community to which people are willing to commit their time, energy, and spirit. If we say we are welcoming or inclusive communities, what does that mean? In the past thirty years, as people have worked with people with disabilities and their families on community inclusion, that vision, or answer, begs the question over and over again.

Lynn Seagle, executive director of the Hope House in Virginia, describes the radical transformation in the agency after all the people in its twelve group homes were asked to dream about the place they wanted to live. None of them opted for the group homes. All the people they support are now living in a variety of smaller living arrangements, their own apartments and houses, with supports. Lynn noted that after all the assessments and planning and everything else is done with people with a variety of disability labels, their hopes and dreams come down to the same as most others: "I would like a place to live that is my home, something to do that makes a contribution, and someone(s) to love and who love me."[2] Community building, she notes, is an art.

John O'Brien and Connie Lyle O'Brien have been two of the leaders in person-centered planning approaches to assist community supports and inclusion. Their "Five Accomplishments" have provided a guide for understanding caregiving that leads to person-centered development and community inclusion.[3]

Moving Away from a Past Characterized by	Toward Daily Experiences That Include
Isolation, seclusion, separation	Community presence (i.e., living there)
Rejection, loneliness, always on the outside, ignored	Community participation (working, playing, worshipping, shopping, etc.)
Old stories, bad reputations, labels	Dignity by encouraging valued social roles (i.e., identities broader than the label that makes them an "other")
Limited voice, restriction, lack of representation, no power	Promoting choice (and now self-determination)
Unproductive, severely ignored, undeveloped, no resources	Supporting contribution (sense of purpose, making a difference)

Thus, being part of community means much more than being a client, consumer, patient, or stranger. It means that identities are much broader (or thicker), that strengths and gifts are seen and used, and that people give as well as receive. It means being a member of any number of organizations and networks based on interests, choices, and abilities. It means moving beyond tolerance toward inclusion and then, finally, to a real sense of belonging.

Inclusion and belonging with people with disabilities and their families are important not only within the community at large but also within the multiple "communities" of which they are a part. For example, people with disabilities and their families who are members of minority communities are often on the margins of those communities as well. No single cultural, ethnic, religious, or sexual minority group does an exemplary job of including people with disabilities and their families within their own organizations and activities. More harshly, when individuals with disabilities and their families are marginalized within a marginalized group, complicated issues can get even more complex.

For instance, one example is that families with members with disabilities from ethnic minorities may not know about the supports and services available in the wider culture because they come from cultures or countries where nothing similar exists, especially as an entitlement. They may bring cultural values that say a person with a disability is a shame on the family or, if not a shame, totally the family's responsibility. They may also be very frightened to apply for services, especially if their immigration status is undocumented. Thus, public and private services and supports that seek to reach out to people with disabilities and their families then must have skills in two overlapping areas: (1) cultural sensitivity/competence in working between cultures and (2) skills in working within that culture on the inclusion of people with disabilities and their families.

The broader "disability community" (or "communities") is not immune to the same double challenge—needing to be culturally sensitive but also needing, at times, to deal with the "pecking order" within and among people with various forms of disability and their families. Value judgments about intellectual capacity most often mean that people with intellectual and developmental disabilities can come out at the low end of the totem pole. Or, in a broader example, one might hear people who are aging say, "Well, I may be old, but I am not disabled."

Both community building and cultural competency must thus deal with projections, stereotypes, and value judgments. They both deal with fears of the "other" and the human tendency and need to make a "difference" into "an other." Being in community by definition means learning to live with people who are different. In a paradoxical turn of phrase, Parker Palmer notes two axioms of community life that came out of a study of intentional religious communities: (1) the first rule of community is that it is the place where the person we would rather not be around is already there and (2) the second is that, as soon as that person leaves, someone else will automatically take his or her place.[4]

Those observations are another way of noting the human need, in the contexts of groups and organizations, to find others to blame for feelings or issues that may be felt by everyone.

Thus, community builders and cultural brokers (a name often used for a person skilled in bridging two or more cultural groups) must address spiritual and religious beliefs, mores, and practices because of the ways they are directly connected to cultural values. Faith communities are often key organizations in the social and cultural life of a given community. Faith communities have been a critical part of every wave of immigration from different countries that has come to North America as organizations that preserved cultural values, assisted one another in the face of hostility and prejudice, and served as a foundation for building bridges with the wider community. As people with disabilities move out of segregated services in this country back into "the community," those same spiritual and faith communities can serve as "ports of entry."[5]

Dealing with cultural mores, values, and "ways of doing things" is also a part of working with any community organization, whether or not they are faith communities. Civic organizations, governmental organizations, clubs, businesses, neighborhoods—they all have their own unique cultures within the wider culture of which they are a part. One of the clearest examples is what the autism community calls the "hidden curriculum" in any social setting. Every congregation, for example, has its own culture and its own expectations about behaviors, if not beliefs. Most of those cultural traditions and rules are not written down and only become apparent when someone is breaking them, usually unconsciously. Expectations need to be more explicit than implicit for individuals with autism and other forms of disability. For them, just as for many other people without disabilities, if you have not grown up within a given faith community or had extensive opportunities to participate and "practice" the expected norms of behavior, knowing how to act "appropriately" can become an issue. Otherwise, an unusual behavior that is problematic to others can get blamed on a person's disability rather than on the lack of opportunity to participate and to learn.

Thus, professionals, advocates, individuals, families, and allies who work in community-building roles need to think through the ways that introductions are made and connections are built. Community building and cultural brokering are both arts, sometimes a form of dance rather than a treatment process built upon policy and procedure or a legal system based on laws and rights. They require professionals and service providers to become aware of our own habits and roles as well as to learn skills in connecting people with disabilities with others. That involves at least four areas of learning: (1) moving beyond some cultural polarities impacting this dance; (2) developing skills not usually within the "professional" skill set; (3) learning how to tap the spiritual dimensions that are often at the heart of helping "different" people move past the barriers of anxiety, fear, and uncertainly about capacity; and (4) learning to deal with and even embrace paradox, one of the historical skills in spiritual wisdom, even when it comes in new ways.

MOVING BEYOND POLARITIES

Initiatives in community building that come from supporting and including the other must help move us beyond polarities, the human tendency to turn issues and questions into "us" versus "them." There are multiple examples of this in the worlds of disability.

First, people get separated into "disabled" or "different" on the one hand versus "normal" or "typical" on the other. Our labels about the "other" often say a great deal about the assumptions of the labeler and ignore the ways that all of us may be vulnerable, limited, or have other characteristics that would turn us into an "other" in someone else's eyes. It is another version of an almost universal need to set up an "us" versus "them." Stated in another way by a person with a developmental disability at a national conference on self-determination, "I am not a case and I don't want to be managed." Jessica Mathis, a young African American woman with cerebral palsy said it perfectly with a comment at a 2015 Georgia conference on community building: "I am not a special need."

Second, realms of inquiry, theory, and services get separated into spiritual/religious on the one hand and scientific/secular on the other.

Scientific and public initiatives to care for people with a variety of differences and labels have indeed been responsible for great gains in care and service in community settings. But barriers to community-based supports and holistic care get put up when an agency says to someone, "Sorry, we can't address your spiritual needs" (because our assessments and planning are based on scientific premises) or "We can't even talk about it, since we are funded by the state."

Third, options for services and support get polarized in to "segregated" services on the one hand versus "inclusive" on the other. A variety of educational and service systems in communities are the scenes of pitched theoretical and ideological battles about whether supports are best provided in segregated or inclusive settings. The either/or often prevents people from working on the both/and model. For example, in a congregation, a segregated special religious education class may have long been the norm. Even if for some reason that is necessary, the members should be included in other activities of the whole faith community as often as is possible. The polarization also fails to recognize the default option should be inclusion, with exclusion or segregated services the ones that need to be justified.

Fourth, people with disabilities and their caregivers too often are caught between an identity of "victim" on the one hand and "hero" on the other. You may be called a wheelchair victim, a victim of abuse or mental illness, or a poor disabled person, or, alternatively, an overcomer, a super-crip, or a heroic achiever. Caregiving families often face the same polarity, being stigmatized and isolated as that "poor family" on the one hand or as "saints" on the other. The polarity also keeps everyone from having appropriately high expectations for children and people with disabilities rather than the low expectations that are often presumed. One of the tragic ways this gets played out is when a "heroic" or "saintly" parent or caregiver snaps under the demands of caregiving and lack of community supports. In the extreme, those stories involve a parent killing his or her child (or adult child) and, sometimes, him- or herself. The media often can interpret the former as a caring or merciful act, rather than as a moral wrong partly occasioned by the desperate lack of support.[6]

Polarities are danger signs as we move into new roles and new (or perhaps old) forms of community. That is true for the wider society as well. Parker Palmer's most recent work is a book called *Healing the Heart of Democracy*. He summarizes five "Habits of the Heart" that make democracy possible: (1) an understanding we are all in this together, (2) an appreciation of the value of "otherness," (3) an ability to hold tension in life-giving ways, (4) a sense of personal voice and agency, and (5) a capacity to create community.[7] Every one of those are part of the "spiritual" skills in moving from seeing people with disabilities as "apart from" the community to a vital "part of it." Let us look at some of the skills and roles that can embody those habits of the heart.

ROLES IN CREATING AND ENERGIZING CARING COMMUNITIES

The task facing professional caregivers to assist in the creation and energizing of caring communities is sometimes one that gets assigned to a specific professional—the social worker, the chaplain, a "community bridge builder," case manager, or others. That may be a first step, but that is not going to work unless a whole service system, and all the staff, sees its mission within community inclusion and contribution and everyone's role (with their own community connections) as a possible resource for the task. Community building involves several key gifts and abilities, any one of which can be demonstrated by laypersons, family members, professionals, and friends. In my own experience, there are at least four.[8]

First, consultation is the ability to ask, rather than prescribe or tell. In his book *Who Cares? Rediscovering Community*, David Schwartz describes the power of "askers," people in community organizations, such as congregations, who know everyone and do not mind asking others to get involved in something.[9] Professionals in the world of disability can begin with asking individuals and their families about connections they already have in the community beyond extended family. What relationships can be supported, rather than replaced, by professional caregivers and professional services?

For many professionals "consultation" has often meant contacting another even more knowledgeable or specialized professional. But it also means acknowledging, "I don't know, so let me help you ask." Consulting means others may know better. It means involving those people in planning supports early on, not calling them with a plan of care already figured out and trying to dictate roles. The key preposition is "with," not "for." Who is around that table where the plans are made? Consultation is even more effective when the asking is done in a way that requests someone else's expertise or capacity to help figure something out; for example, "I am working with someone who really wants to go back to a Methodist church, because that is where she grew up. I don't know much about Methodists. You do. Would you be willing to help us figure this out?" Or "You are Methodist. Do you know some Methodists who would be willing to sit with us and figure this out?" Given the space, the person who is asked might more readily say, "Oh, interesting. I'll help you."

Second, good consultation then calls for ongoing cooperation and collaboration. If the basic attitude and assumption in consultation is sharing knowledge, because we do not know it all, the root of good collaboration is sharing power, responsibility, and control. Collaboration calls for new alliances between "formal" and "informal" organizations in communities to support caregiving families and the "natural supports" within their communities. There are very real differences between the ways that systems work and communities work. As John McKnight is famous for describing, a system is a hierarchy with a chain of command. A community is not.[10] Caregiving cultures are very different, even more so when a system is trying to work with a community culture it does not understand. Power and authority must be shared with the sources of power and authority within that other cultural community to foster true engagement and shared responsibility.

Third, how might the Western default position of "competition" be used as a good community-building skill? It is by recognizing that communities and organizations of all sorts can be mobilized by hearing someone say, for example, "Well, you know, in that community, the town has organized a new respite care for families with parents with Alzheimer's that involves all kinds of community groups." Or it might be, "You know, in the Catholic Church in another community, people with disabilities of all kinds are encouraged to take leadership and service roles in the church if they want to. If they can do it, can't we do that here?" In sports, competition gets used to help individuals, or a team, do something they never thought they could.

Competition, then, can be friendly and inspiring. In professional services, we often call it "state of the art" or "model" services. But it means knowing enough of the kinds of creative community initiatives around the country to be able to say, "They did it there. We can do it here. Maybe even better."

Fourth, also from the world of sports, the metaphor of a "coach" is perhaps the most significant for professionals who want to develop new roles and skills in creating and energizing caring communities. Think of what it means. A coach is also an artist. A coach is not the one playing the game but the one on the sidelines, teaching, encouraging, demonstrating, supporting, motivating, and celebrating. A good coach is always finding and supporting the gifts and skills of individual team members or the team, and knowing how and when to give away what he or she knows as coach in ways and at times that others learn best. Why not expand that role to think of "coaching" potential caregivers and sources of support? A good coach has several crucial roles, including a poet, a storyteller, a motivator, a guide, and a celebrant, each important in its own ways.

As a poet, a coach is an artist, philosopher, theologian, or musician. Common to all those roles is the capacity to listen to a community and the groups within it to discover the images, symbols, and values that define and illuminate the heart of a community, its beliefs, and its vision of its own identity or dreams of what it could be. For professionals that means listening to feeling, belief, and other sources of commitment and imagination. It means being able to set aside the jargon of various professional disciplines and service systems as well as to translate care-giving issues into words that people use and understand. This is one of the reasons that the symbols, drawings, and colors of graphic recording are so important for a variety of person-centered planning processes.[11]

For example, if a professional working in disability services is working with any community organization around inclusion and participation with people with disabilities, the first goal should be finding out how that organization—for example, a congregation—sees itself and its mission. Then a good coach can work from within its framework of mission and values to indicate how a specific form of inclusion or support meets its image and vision of who its members want to be, not that of the latest jargon from a service system.

Second, a coach bears witness and tells stories. A coach not only knows the theories and facts but also is able to tell stories and to share personal experiences in ways that reveal something of his or her own value system. That is crucial to understanding and motivation. Communities are energized not through professional theory and ideology as much as through story and examples of strategies that work. That means when professional service providers talk with community members, leaders, and organizations, they must be willing to tell stories rather than cite cases and to talk about individuals and families in ways that reveal the depths of their understanding and appreciation of them as people. We are inviting community members into a relationship as support giver or possible friend that builds on the depths and foundations of human friendships and relationships, not on a set of professional skills. To help people overcome fear of the new, a coach can tell stories that illustrate values and, perhaps, some of his or her own stories. Better yet, a coach can also help set up opportunities in which people with disabilities or family members can tell their own story, rather than it being defined by others.

Third, a coach motivates, teaches, and then guides. But it is a different kind of guidance than is present in most "formal" human service systems. There, the role may be to guide people through the complicated and confusing maze of the (paid) services that system offers. We hire patient advocates and social workers to help guide people through strange jargon, mazes where the entryways are hard to find, and then on to other referral systems when we are stymied. Professional caregivers are also, often, the fix-it guides, the ones with the answers, the techniques, the algorithms of care, the ones who write the "how to" books that fix relationships, health problems, and human needs in the same way others fix that old house or landscape your yard.

The guide in community building is more like a "spiritual guide" or a guide on an Outward Bound expedition. The coach as guide invites people into a new, sometimes scary world, models and demonstrates new abilities and skills, and also works from where people are, listening to all questions and helping them learn their own skills, gifts, and capacity to meet the challenges in front of them. Professional providers may "guide" others into a world of illness and disability and support their caregiving skills, but they also need to let others guide them into the dynamics of a particular association, congregation, organization, or community. In other words, a guide is also an asker and a receiver.

Finally, coaching involves celebrating gifts, skills, strengths, effort, and accomplishments. A good coach helps a player or team find things to celebrate when they have tried hard, even in a loss, even when progress is slow, even when we cannot find the "fix" or "cure." Celebration has many dimensions. It means seeing gifts and strengths in others where others may not see them, including the gifts and strengths of people who need support or care. It means seeing capacity where others see deficit. For professional caregivers, so often focused on assessing needs, limitations, or illness, that means another set of eyes and a new vision. It means assuming there is abundance in community rather than scarcity.[12]

Celebration in formal systems often takes the form of "volunteer recognition," which is important. A deeper foundation of celebration is one based on mutuality and shared story. We are celebrating not just what you or we have done for others who need supports, but what they have done for us. What have we learned? In a Bill Moyers series on PBS, *On Our Own Terms*, one of the moving scenes took place in a volunteer hospice in San Francisco. One of its "ritual celebrations" was gathering the volunteers in the room of a person who had just died, after the initial preparation of the body, and sharing stories and feelings about the strengths and gifts of that person.[13] Thus, a celebrant helps others to find and celebrate individual and shared gifts and recognizes the importance of finding traditional rituals or creating new ones that give community caregiving initiatives a way to celebrate commitment, vision, relationships, and accomplishments.

FROM ROLES INTO PRACTICE: FINDING THE THIRD THING IN THIRD PLACES

One way to visualize the process of community building that is based on personal gifts, strengths, and dreams is to look for the connections that do not depend on the deficit or need. So often we look for people in a community to help the "other" in need, but that also sets up a giver/receiver relationship that fails to recognize the sense of mutuality and friendship that often develops. The labels, projections, anxieties, uncertainties, fears, or patronizing that can so often be embedded in the space between "person in community" and "person considered other" in the drawing below can be addressed directly, but it can take very hard work because of the sense of "deficit" on both sides. Someone asks a community member to volunteer with or help someone else with a particular kind of deficit or limitation, which can then give rise to the community member feeling his or her own lack of capacity or knowledge about how to do so. In other words, the community member might feel "disabled" about helping someone with a "disability."

There's often a simpler way through a "third" thing that might connect people in "side-by-side" relationships, not top down, a third that involves questions of "Who?" "What?" "Where?" "When?" "How?" and "Why?"[14]

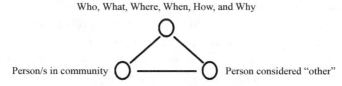

Who, What, Where, When, How, and Why

Person/s in community   Person considered "other"

FIGURE 14-1. *The "Third Way" of Community Building*

The "Who?" is the bridge builder, the introducer, and the facilitator of a circle, the networker, the asker, or community builder. A newer term is the "gapper." It can be a professional working in new ways; it can be a friend. It is usually not a "case manager" because his or her usual role is accessing or coordinating formal supports. It can be a support broker or support coordinator. There are varieties of new roles here emerging in these processes of community building.

"What?" are the passions, interests, and dreams that might connect people with one another over and around the barriers of stigma and difference, beyond the polarities of roles. What are the gifts that people have in those areas? For example, as an asker, I might discover that a person with a disability has a passionate interest in a particular musical genre with which I am not familiar at all and may not even like. My role, then, with others, is to figure out who shares that musical interest and invite that person to help us find people who have the same gifts and passion. Thus, the asker appeals to the strengths and gifts of others and asks them to respond and help out of that ability, rather than asking them to help someone with a disability or specific need about which they may feel they have little skill. The intermediary can offer to help with anything needed about the disability, but that asker is asking another precisely because the asker does not have that interest or talent.

Rick Thompson, an inclusion facilitator in Australia, told me a classic story that illustrates this process. He was working with a man with severe cerebral palsy who lived in a nursing home and who had no community connections. As he got to know him, it was clear what his interests were. His walls were covered with pictures of Harley Davidsons and naked women. Rick, the asker, did not tell me if he did anything around the second interest, but he got him connected to a Harley Davidson biker group, who, of course, were dismayed that a Harley lover did not have the opportunity to act on that love. After getting to know him, they changed their bylaws to make him an honorary member (you were supposed to own and drive a bike). After several years, he died. At his funeral, a procession of bikers appeared and not only participated but led the way, took over the procession, and carried him to his grave. That would have never happened had the initial "What?" focus been on the cerebral palsy.

When interests and gifts are identified, the question then becomes "Where?" What clubs, groups, or "third places" (neither home nor work) exist where people with those interests and gifts gather?[15] It could be a congregation, a sports bar, a hobby group, a service organization, a music store . . . it goes on and on. How can the facilitator find someone who knows someone there to whom an introduction can be made and a discussion begun so that an individual can be included because of the shared interest rather than being helped because of a disability?

Once those places are found, "When?" are the daily, weekly, and annual times, celebrations, rituals, or events where people with shared interests and passions gather. When will others be there, with the opportunity to join in, when the "stranger" can work, enjoy, serve, play, eat, celebrate, or worship along with others who share that interest and need?

Finally, "How?" The strategies here are where all the skills of consultation, collaboration, competition, and coaching come into play.

In the literature of person-centered planning, circles of support, and social capital, there are excellent discussions of strategies for exploring, inviting, connecting, and facilitating relationships and community inclusion. As a way of combining some of the best of those with my own interests in community in spirituality and faith traditions, the following "lessons learned" blend images and ideas from all of those "worlds."

1. Who is around the table? As we plan and work with others on community inclusion, who gets included in the planning? The person considered "other" should be at the center, along with everyone potentially involved—family, friends, direct support staff, and community members. That table is much wider than an interdisciplinary professional process. Or, as the unofficial motto of the self-advocacy movement reminds us, "Nothing about me without me." The same injunction, said with a little more bite and sarcasm: "If you are not around the table, you may be on the menu."

2. Reverse the questions. When we ask how someone with this difference or condition can be included in a community activity, make sure that the questions about "him or her" are asked about everyone. How do we do it? Do we get it right all the time? For example, what do "we" do when others misbehave or act out? In Christian communities, the question may be about communion or the Eucharist: "How do we know they understand?" Reversing the question asks, "How do we know anyone understands?"

3. A second version of reversal is to "reverse the tragedy." As the Australian story earlier illustrated, the "tragedy" was not the man's cerebral palsy. The "tragedy" was that he never had the opportunity to live out his passion for Harley Davidsons. For anyone deeply committed to a community of shared interests and passions—for example, being a Green Bay Packer fan—it is a tragedy when someone else does not get to go to games or watch with others.

4. Reverse the answers. The skills and strategies that are successful in helping kids with disabilities, for example, to be included in an educational or recreation program may also be good for lots of other "typical" kids. Good person-centered planning

can be adapted into an inclusion plan in religious education or the congregation. The skills in positive behavior supports and helping children learn the "hidden curriculum" might help teachers in any congregation with all the kids, not just the one with a behavioral issue.

5. "Who do you say that I am?" Be careful with words and language. In community building, we need to be very careful with the overuse of professional jargon and language that comes from diagnosis, assessments, and therapies. Help people name and claim their identity beyond the disability, and let the relationship build from there. Most basically, begin with someone's name.

6. Build a Joshua committee, the name of the first circle of support for Judith Snow—a circle of friends and professionals who helped her get out of a medical institution when all the professional systems could not; a group, in other words, who helped her get from personal wilderness into her own land of promise and dream.[16] It may not happen quickly, for it is an ongoing process of learning from what is tried and figuring out what is needed next by a group not locked into formal processes and systems.

7. Develop a Jericho strategy—getting into a community or city or organization by the power of persistent celebration. That image is based on the biblical story of the walls coming down after the Israelites processed and paraded, in great celebration, around the walls of Jericho over and over. Positive vision, hope, and joy all draw others out and people in, and barriers, walls, or boxes we put people in get overcome.

8. Use a fish-and-loaves approach to community planning. There were five thousand people to be fed. The disciples first response was, "Send them somewhere"—in other words, "Refer them." "No, it's your/our responsibility," they were told. Their second response, "Give us some money and we will buy food"—a grant or more public funding. They were told the same thing. And then the crowd was gathered in smaller groups, a small boy offered his gifts of loaves and fishes, and they were transformed. One of the miracles in the story is believing that there is abundance of spirit and desire to help in any community that can

be tapped, especially when the crowds are broken down into smaller groups, truly face and see one another, and begin to offer out of their own strengths or capacity.

9. Believe in the call, giving voice to the values, spirituality, and vision that compels and motivates others. Give people time and place to reflect on that call and their sense of vocation, what they are learning and who they want to be. One reason "professionals" and "volunteers" burn out is that there is neither time nor place for this way of renewing the spirit of compassion and care.[17] This is for the long haul, not the short fix, and renewal and other ways to rekindle the spirit are crucial.

10. "What is most critical is invisible to the eye," said the fox to the Little Prince in Antoine de Saint-Exupéry's classic story.[18] Relationships, friendships, connections, and belonging are not as visible as care centers, workshops, and programs of any kind. But they are the bedrock for good quality of life.

11. Watch out for the idolatry of ideology. Professional service systems and advocates of many kinds get caught up in dogmatism about values and techniques in the same ways that religious communities do. Then nothing gets done, and the barriers may even grow stronger. Small concrete, incarnate steps that move in the right direction are better than a perfect response that never gets off the ground. As stated in the corporate and planning world, "The perfect can be the enemy of the good."

12. When building partnerships, work from within the mission and vision of the other individual, group, organization, or community toward a shared one. One might call it the Tom Sawyer skill: helping others get interested in, get excited about, and want to take over the task to which you are also committed—in his case, painting a fence. Including and supporting people with disabilities and their families is not just about fulfilling your goals as a leader in inclusive supports; it is also about fulfilling their image of who they think they are and want to be.

"Why?" is the first and final question for community-building initiatives. It starts with what kind of life someone wants and dreams about having and what kind of community (church, club, organization, town, state, country) we want to be. There are values and visions that drive our commitment. They can come from civic, spiritual, and scientific sources. There are ancient understandings of community and the singular importance of hospitality to those considered to be strangers. There is the call of vocation, the why we do what we do individually and communally, the sense of direction and purpose for ourselves as a people. There are the core values of how we see ourselves as a culture or nation. Exploring the "Why?" is where personal and communal values infuse professional roles and call us together, beyond whatever role or label or difference we wear. The "Whys?" are there throughout and at the end. They can broaden, deepen, change, and evolve as we connect our "Whys?" and our answers with those of others.

EMBRACING AND ENJOYING THE PARADOXES

Finding the third thing, in the third places, is a paradox unto itself. The most direct route to a relationship or goal may not be the straightest. That is only one of the paradoxes in building community and relationships across what appear to be major gaps. Another is that we build service systems based on human needs, but we build communities based on gifts and strengths. Nothing would happen in any organization or community if we focused only on the needs or deficits of its members. A building would not get built, a church would not grow, and a business would not thrive. The question is whether we have "capacity vision": "Is the glass half empty or half full?" The critical theory and wisdom of this is explored most thoroughly in asset-based community development literature and practice.[19]

Caregiving also involves both "being with" and "doing for." One problem with many service systems is that they work on a paradigm of "fixing" and "curing." It is not by definition a bad impulse, but many "others" do not want "fixing." Rather, "Be with me. Hear my story. Don't try to fix or save me. Listen. Know me as more than my problem or deficit. And let me be with you." Nancy Eiesland calls this the time of "just listening," listening with an ear to justice as well as empathy, recognizing that there are often real imbalances of power and privilege between caregivers and those whose need and seek support.[20]

We also build caregiving systems and services by developing specialized skills; we build communities by finding out what others know and working from their gifts as well as giving away what we know. Specialized systems of care have been built by community and public advocacy that lead to new funding sources or public/private programs. One unintentional consequence is that communities then sometimes believe that special skills, degrees, or credentials are needed to provide any care at all.[21] For example, "I can't include that child with autism in my Sunday school; I don't have any special education training." The schoolteacher could then say, or lead by saying, "I don't know Sunday school or how you all do it. But I do know autism and I know this child. I can help you with that, but you are the experts in Sunday school."

Another paradox, stated earlier, is that a complementary skill for professionals related to community building is to know what they don't know—to acknowledge the boundaries of their knowledge and the limits of their roles. If we want to help others become parts of communities, then there are other "experts" out there, experts without titles or degrees, people who are natural askers and connectors who know how to become a member of this or that organization, people who know everyone else in the community.

Finally, we are all the same, but we are all different. Or, as Thomas Merton said it in reverse, there is a "hidden wholeness" under all the differences and diversity.[22] We are challenged to think universally but act locally. There may be similarities in gifts and strategies for working with civic groups, congregations, and neighborhoods, but the task is working with an individual person in a specific part of a community. In faith terms, one might say, "Think on an ecumenical, or multifaith basis, but act parochially." In health and human sciences, it is treating an individual person, not the class of people who have the same label or disease.

These paradoxes and others were combined in a reflection written at the end of a cultural competence conference in New Jersey:

"THE JOURNEY TOWARD CULTURAL COMPETENCE"

> To heal, assess what helps people to stay well.
> To have people come to you, go to them.
> To help others grow, start with yourself.
> To learn, listen.
> To teach, let yourself be taught.
> To help, empower others to do it.

To lead, hand over the reins.
To accomplish your mission, help others accomplish theirs.
To get somewhere with others, walk beside them.
To collaborate, ask for help.
To give, be willing to receive.
To be an expert, know what you don't know.
And to be competent, practice humility.[23]

CONCLUSION

Each of those paradoxes, strategies, and roles can enlighten the paths
of community builders no matter whether they are individuals, family
members, professionals, community members, or friends. They are
true in dealing with any form of diversity and difference. In the face
of assumed difference, the skills are about respecting unique gifts as
well as discovering shared interests and passions, and then acting on
personal and communal purpose and call.

In the process of recognizing and including those assumed to be
different or deficient, the greatest paradox is that the *whole* community grows. Or, one might say, real community may get created and
appreciated. The art of building community relationships between
community members and people with disabilities is sometimes not
so much an act of including people in a community as it is creating a
sense of community that was not there to begin with. Bishop Lesslie
Newbigin of India once said this about the Christian community by
rephrasing the words of Paul about the "body of Christ": "We cannot
say we are including people with disabilities in the whole body of Christ.
We are not whole unless they are present."[24]

Conclusion

Restoring Wholeness—It Is about All of Us

Recognizing, respecting, and supporting the spirituality of people with disabilities and everyone connected with them—in other words, everybody—is a vision and journey long overdue. So many of the lenses we use to understand human life and one another lead to assessing and judging differences rather than to an appreciation of the diversity of humankind and the diverse ways for exploring and explaining who we are and what is fundamental to all of us. If that vision is to be realized, even partially, it will take an increased willingness to recognize limitations and gifts in all kinds of people and perspectives as well as a fundamental commitment to change attitudes and practices that keep people dissected into separate boxes of knowledge, distinguished more by their differences and limits than by their gifts. If this is true, then it is a truth that calls for faith, the capacity to keep acting, hoping, and loving on the basis of that vision in the face of all kinds of obstacles and resistance.

One of my seminary professors at Union Theological Seminary, ethicist Paul Lehmann, described faith as the process of "hoping backward and remembering forward," a paradox that essentially means, first of all, we have to build our hopes not just on future vision but also on a solid recognition of how we got here. Second, when we are all tempted to return to the "good old days," we need to bring the visions and values of past individuals, cultures, and times back to the present, and see how we can make them come alive anew.

Faith leading to action is also, in the wonderful Jewish image *tikkum olam*, repairing the breach (or breaches)—in this case, the breaches between the "worlds" of disability and spirituality. I am convinced that there is a real aching for the profound connections between the two to be recognized, restored, and integrated into relationships and care or, more to the point, approached with a vision that they are part of one whole. Exploring a brief history of disability and the ways that theorists now seek to find adequate, functionally helpful definitions leads us to psychological/social/biological realities that include both personal and social constructs about the ways people understand and value themselves. Those constructs are inseparably entwined with the attitudes, values, and practices of others in their respective cultures. Understandings of one's self and the attitudes and beliefs of others take one directly into the world of spirituality, or, alternatively, to a recognition that it has been there all along.

Starting from a different direction, the understandings of spirituality in both religious and cultural contexts (including secular contexts) lead into those times and places in human life where the core questions are raised and experienced. The "Who am I?" "Why am I?" and "Whose am I?" questions are asked in myriads of ways, but especially when and where things inevitably happen in life that bring one face to face with the vulnerability and fragility of human life as well as with the ways that people in the past and present have responded to them. In a world that worships both physical and intellectual images of power and perfection, disability is a major tempest in that fragile teapot. Power and perfection both lead to assumptions of invulnerability and control, both of which are ultimately illusions about our omnipotence and omniscience. The historical irony is that disability has not received a lot of attention in the rich history of spirituality in religious traditions and other frameworks of identity, meaning, and purpose. The reasons lie partly in the minority status of people with disabilities and, in relation to intellectual and developmental disabilities in particular, the continued assumptions that spirituality depends on reason and understanding.

If disability and spirituality each lead to the other, then neither the image nor the frequently experienced reality of two separate worlds is accurate. We must acknowledge that there have been powerful forces and experiences that have kept them apart or, so to speak, dis-membered them.[1] The scientific and social models of disability have been reluctant to include spirituality and religion because of their assumptions about ways of knowing, and vice versa. One of the biggest barriers has been the lived experiences of blame, rejection, or abuse at the hands of spiritual traditions, including religious interpretations and responses to disability that have sanctified ignorance and fear, justified separation, and too often blamed the person or the divine for their lack of power to change. But there are now serious efforts attempting to change that tradition, in both theology and practice.

The many disciplines involved in disability studies have begun the process of interpreting the experience of disability and telling its stories through multiple lenses. Our ways of thinking and talking about disability and spirituality can each be enriched and deepened by broadening the conceptual boundaries to include the other, a move that would recognize the inseparable connections and the common bonds they share in the experience of real lives. Each, as it were, has gifts to bring to the limits of the other. Inclusion for these two dimensions of human life begins at home, perhaps with a first acknowledgment that each has belonged to the other all along.

I have explored a variety of ways in which spirituality can be seen, felt, described, and experienced in the lives of people with disabilities and their families. There are multiple ways in which its power can be explored and tapped to enrich and empower rather than to judge and harm. Services and supports increasingly focus on the power of natural and community-based supports, social capital, and the importance of multiple interpretive stories of the lives of people with disabilities, especially coming in their own voice. The spiritual and religious dimensions of life have much to offer the definitions and descriptions of both disability and supports by recognizing the depth and breadth of the lived experience. To borrow from the sociologists, we then begin to develop "thick" rather than "thin" narratives of disability that can more truthfully represent the richness of people's lives. As Atul Gawande fondly recalled a conversation with Oliver Sacks, Sacks said the same thing: "To restore the human subject at the centre—the suffering, afflicted, fighting, human subject—we must deepen a case history to a narrative or tale."[2]

Conversely, there are so many resources from the various worlds of disability that have much to offer the worlds of spirituality, especially to faith communities and others for whom spirituality is a major factor in their lives. The negative spiritual experiences that many have had related to disability often come from old stereotypes and assumptions, fear, and one's own powerlessness. More accurate facts about disability, its origins, effective therapies and supports, and its connections to so many dimensions of human life would be both helpful and liberating. They can empower people who want to help but are unsure how. The social, cultural, and legal stories and resources about disability have much in common with the ways that faith communities have addressed diversity and inequality, and thus could help people of faith to recognize that disability is not that different. Particular strategies for supporting individuals and families—such as person-centered planning, family supports, respite care, positive behavior supports, and community building—have so much to offer people in faith communities who face similar needs but do not even know that those tools exist, much less how they could be utilized to empower their care and support for many families or congregational members who are caring for children, elderly family members, or others at home or in the context of their community whom they would not see as "disabled" at all.

WITH THE POSSIBILITIES, PRECAUTIONS

Those possibilities for enriching the lives of people with disabilities and their families, while also enriching the lives of others in caregiving systems and in the community, depend first on expanding the ways we bring spirituality and faith to the disability table, and vice versa. Then it is a matter of listening to people's stories and respecting the ways that people coming from different perspectives seek to understand and describe them. It means learning to be very careful with oversimplified prescriptions and judgments. Even more important is recognizing that we are at the same human table as everyone else.

That sounds easy. It obviously is not. There are so many questions, starting perhaps with agreement followed by, "But. . . ." I have a few of my own "buts."

First, there is a real temptation to think that spirituality and spiritual supports can be commoditized as means to an end. Religious traditions sometimes have long histories in doing that: "Believe this, and you will be saved!" "Do this, and you will be blessed!" "If you had more faith, you would be healed." Or too often, the public image of faith is a more negative version: "Don't do this, otherwise. . . ." To put it simply, both versions drive people of deep faith and spirituality up the proverbial walls because they represent far too simplistic understandings of spirituality and faith. The somewhat dubious consolation is that hucksters, bigots, and purveyors of false promises come from many other dimensions of human discourse as well, including, at times, the sciences.

The point of caution is more subtle in the arena of services and supports with people with disabilities. Addressing spirituality in supporting the lives of persons with disabilities needs to be done for its own sake, not because it *will* lead to a better self-image, less social prejudice, stronger personalities, more friendships, or ways of being productive members of the community, to name a few. It may indeed lead to those kinds of outcomes, and those correlations need to be researched and studied, but one of the real dangers in any kind of support or service is that we think it will necessarily lead to a specific, predetermined outcome. When we do so, we are yielding to the temptation to believe that the process is under our control—it becomes a "technology."

Second, and closely related, there are numerous studies about spirituality and faith in the realms of physical and psychological health, substance abuse, and organizations in which the practice implications sometimes justify spiritual assessments and interventions because they lead to faster healing times, better patient satisfaction, better recovery, or other outcomes deemed more important than simply respecting or honoring someone's spirituality or faith. In other words, spirituality is a means to other ends that can then be used to justify paying attention to spirituality in the first place because those culturally accepted ends have more perceived value. Respecting and honoring the spirituality and faith of people with disabilities and their families is a means to understanding them better, listening more carefully, helping people feel heard at the depth of their identities and values, building deeper connections and relationships, and understanding what gives people hope and purpose. As such, spirituality can be an area of profound

meaning and deep feelings, both positively and negatively—it is powerful. It means a deeper and more respectful knowledge of someone
who is being supported. That may be expressed, in a phrase such as
"to live and serve my God more faithfully," which resists observable,
measurable, and replicable outcomes as we typically understand them
in human services.

A third precaution about facile understanding and use of spirituality in human services is that spiritual exploration can indeed question
the very foundations of our assumptions and values in human services.
That is a good outcome, in my opinion, because it also works the other
way around—the values of more secular, scientific human services can
help us question how we define and describe spirituality. Spirituality helps us recognize the limitations and complexity of core cultural
values and interpretations of human life and the ways that they have
become idolized and then followed without critique. For example, the
spiritual questions under the core policy values of independence (Who
am I?), productivity (Why am I?), and inclusion (Whose am I?) can
lead to profound philosophical and theological questions about each
of those values and a more nuanced understanding of the complexity
of human beings. Is independence in fact the primary value? It is for
Western cultures, even more so for the United States, as evidenced by
the ways it mistrusts the "socialism" of other Western countries, but
none of us are truly independent. We are dependent on others for our
very lives and live in an increasingly interdependent world. Related to
independence, the value of "self-determination" needs the same kind
of nuanced critique. Do we espouse self-determination as a value for
everyone when, again, it can lead to the illusion that we make choices
independent of our dependence and interdependence? In many other
cultures, those two values of independence and self-determination are
more balanced with, or subservient to, values of family, connections,
and community.

The "Why am I?" question underlying productivity calls for a
similar critique of "productivity" as the purpose of human life. It is
a terrific goal to espouse as we find ways for people with intellectual
and developmental disabilities to use their gifts and thereby contribute to community life. But are their lives, or our own, solely valued
because we are "productive citizens"? That is very close to saying that

the primary values are utilitarian. Does the value of human life come from its productivity or from the very fact of its creation? If only from productivity, a spiritual critique would say that ignores the value derived from connections and relationships as well as other dimensions that bring meaning. We are all more than producers and consumers, despite what the gods of capitalism would have us believe.

The "Whose am I?" question under inclusion not only challenges our assumptions about independence and self-determination but also raises the question of where inclusion leads. The current social model of defining and understanding disability cites participation as one of the core dimensions of disability because of the barriers to participation in typical human life. Those can be corrected by initiatives in rights, accessibility, and inclusion but may still not lead to the depths of relationships characterized by a sense of being valued, wanted, and belonging—recognizing people of all kinds as full members of all kinds of human communities.

FROM PRECAUTIONS TO NEW POSSIBILITIES FOR PROFESSIONAL AND PERSONAL LEARNING

Exploring spirituality in disability, and disability in spirituality, can thus lead to crucial and powerful issues and feelings for the people on that journey as well as to questions that invite and force the critique and examination of popular values and beliefs about both disability and spirituality. We might talk about the latter as the process of "puncturing our illusions," a process that can be very good for us by bringing us closer to truth, but it may not feel that way at the time.[3] The most important illusion that needs puncturing is the assumption that these are separate worlds rather than, to borrow the title of a book about community building with people with disabilities, "members of each other."[4]

Multiple paths can serve as resources for that journey. First and foremost, of course, is the assistance of insights of people with intellectual and developmental disabilities and their families. A desire to get to know people well, in many dimensions of their lives, through careful listening and respect, is often repaid many times over by the willingness of people to share their lives with you in ways that lead to both personal and professional learning and growth. Personal and professional honesty both call for we who are professionals and friends to be able to acknowledge the gifts received in those relationships, especially in a world where so many people with disabilities and their families have to relate to services and supports in prescribed, controlled ways that make them into "receivers" only.

Second, getting to know the ways that disability is addressed in the context of varied cultural and religious traditions is another way to look at the assumptions we bring from our own cultural and faith traditions. Understanding the motivation and reasons that compel people from many backgrounds to support the lives of people with disabilities parallels that exploration. Both help us to understand our own motivations for care and support. What is it that enables people with disabilities, their families, their friends, and close caregivers to stand in the face of so many kinds of barriers to support and participation? What have they learned? What sustains them? Just asking the questions is a way to new learning and growth for those willing to listen, whatever role or background from which they (we) may come.

Third, one of the most exciting developments in the past few decades has been the rise of disability studies, a broad term that generally means the exploration of disability from academic disciplines other than those like medicine, psychology, and allied health disciplines, who have dominated the discourse in scientific models of disability. Disciplines involved in disability studies include many of the humanities: English, history, art, philosophy, education, anthropology, and theology. Those disciplines use their own frameworks of knowledge to address and understand disability while at the same time utilizing disability to critique theories and assumptions within those disciplines that overlooked the experience of disability or failed to see events or trends through the perspectives of people with disabilities. The benefits include new ways of both understanding and describing the lived experience of disability while also connecting issues within the worlds of disability to work being done that did not originate, at least explicitly, in trying to understand disability in medical or scientific terms. For example, there are extensive discussions in philosophy about the understandings of the stranger, the other, and personal identity.[5] There are any number of times that I and others have read books or materials coming out of research and work that is not about disability only to find, "This is not explicitly about disability, but it is all about disability."[6] Restoring disability into the discourse about spirituality and vice versa is not the only field in which that can and should happen.

BRINGING DISABILITY TO THE THEOLOGICAL TABLES, AND VICE VERSA

In the past two decades, the expanding field of theology (with its multiple disciplines) and disability has been fueled at both practical and academic levels by the spiritual, ethical, philosophical, and theological questions and revelations within the lived experience of disability as well as by initiatives, often led by people with disabilities and their families, to participate more fully in the life of faith communities. I am most familiar with that expansion in modern Christian, Jewish, and Muslim traditions, but it also includes other faiths and other historical periods.[7] This expansion has included (1) taking new looks at the ways disability is treated in sacred texts such as the Torah, Bible, and Talmud as well as (2) bringing what might be called a disability "hermeneutic" to the exploration of sacred texts—looking at traditional and contemporary ways of interpreting scripture and doing theology, whether explicitly related to disability or not, through the lens of disability.[8]

The focus of my work with faith communities and service providers in the arena of intellectual and developmental disability has primarily been practical: (1) seeking to motivate and guide congregations as they work on becoming more inclusive; (2) advising people with disabilities, family members, and others who are leading those initiatives; and (3) motivating and guiding advocacy and service organizations to include and address spirituality and collaborate more closely with faith communities. That experience has been the foundation for this book.

However, as more and more people of faith come to understand the implications of inclusive ministries and congregational supports, new understandings of scripture and tradition have arisen as people connect what feel like new experiences with ancient themes and images from their own scriptural and religious traditions. People begin to discover ways that age-old stories and traditions come alive by being the people of God together, with whatever level of ability or disability. Seven biblical themes have emerged for me in ways that reflect the movements of spirit and thinking underlying much of what is happening in inclusive faith supports. All seven are examples of seeing faith as "hoping backward and remembering forward."[9]

Hospitality to the Stranger

Congregations have begun to move beyond "special ministries to special people" to recovering the ancient call for hospitality to the stranger as a foundation for accessible, inclusive, and welcoming communities of faith. In a so-called normal world, people with disabilities are often the protypical "stranger," even beyond the diversity of strangers characterized by race, creed, and nationality. Hospitality to the stranger is being recovered as one of the core values of Jewish, Islamic, and Christian traditions, all of whom came out of the deserts of the Middle East, where hospitality was a matter of life and death. In the biblical imperative to welcome the stranger, the call to hospitality was not, in the last analysis, only about responsibility of the host to welcome and include. The host is in fact the one who may be receiving the gift, as one might imagine, through news from other places, different perspectives and traditions, and shared common experiences such as breaking bread together. In several biblical stories, the strangers turn out to be messengers from God, or, in the case of the Emmaus Road story in the New Testament, the messenger turns out to be Jesus himself.

Thus, the call to faith communities is to welcome people with disabilities and their families in ways that recognize the mutuality of the relationship because they are also children of God, created in God's image, and thus not a stranger at all, at least to God. The question is a very clear example of, "How do we welcome any stranger in our congregations and communities?" Elizabeth Hastings, a disability advocate and government official in Australia, reversed the question by saying that people with disabilities should not have to justify inclusion. They already are included by virtue of God's creation. Faith communities should have to justify exclusion.[10]

Re-membering the Body, Redemption, and Reconciliation

When people who have been excluded are now included, faith communities are "re-membering them," helping them become members again. For example, a young teenager at a synagogue in New Jersey gave a Youth Day sermon the same day that several adults with multiple disabilities from a nearby developmental center were celebrating their bar and bat mitzvahs. His task was to speak from the readings for the day, the very dry parts of Numbers that recite the census of the various tribes of Israel. Then he made a wonderful connection with what the synagogue was doing that day through the bar and bat mitzvahs. The Jewish community was counting them in again as "one of us." Jason Kingsley and Mitchell Levitz, two young adults with Down syndrome, made the same point with the title of their book, *Count Us In: Growing Up with Down Syndrome.*[11]

When a child or adult joins a faith community through various coming of age or transition rituals (e.g., baptism, confirmation, first Eucharist, bar and bat mitzvahs), they become members. When a child or adult with a disability does so after not having had the opportunity to do so at the typical age for those ceremonies, or after having been denied participation, then he or she is being re-membered. When people with disabilities are invited to join as full members, not just attend, they are being re-membered as part of the body of the people of faith.

There are powerful stories in the New Testament illustrating that call for one person, such as the shepherd going in search of the one while leaving the ninety and nine behind. It is a move from a person being "apart from" to being sought out to come back in and be "a part of."[12] In Paul's famous image of "one body, many parts" in 1 Corinthians 12, he writes:

> Even so the body is not made up of one part but of many. Now if the foot should say, "Because I am not a hand, I do not belong to the body," it would not for that reason stop being part of the body. And if the ear should say, "Because I am not an eye, I do not belong to the body," it would not for that reason stop being part of the body. If the whole body were an eye, where would the sense of hearing be? If the whole body were an ear, where would the sense of smell be? But in fact God has placed the parts in the body, every one of them, just as he wanted them to be. If they were all one part, where would the body be? As it is, there are many parts, but one body. The eye cannot say to the hand, "I don't need you!" And the head cannot say to the feet, "I don't need you!" On the contrary, those parts of the body that seem to be weaker are indispensable, and the parts that we think are less honorable we treat with special honor. And

the parts that are unpresentable are treated with special modesty, while our presentable parts need no special treatment. But God has put the body together, giving greater honor to the parts that lacked it, so that there should be no division in the body, but that its parts should have equal concern for each other. If one part suffers, every part suffers with it; if one part is honored, every part rejoices with it. (vv. 14-26 NIV)

In theological terms, when a person or people are saved from isolation, from being oppressed or enchained by stigma or environment, or from being seen as a person with no gifts or rights (outcast) to being a contributor, the theological word for that kind of re-membering is *redemption*. If it is about moving past wounding experiences of either spiritual neglect or abuse that a person or family might have had in the past with their clergy or congregation through forgiveness and reconnection in a genuine sense of belonging, then the biblical name for that kind of re-membering is *reconciliation*.

Restoring the Sanctuary

Inclusive and accessible congregations often focus on architectural accommodations to their buildings with special attention to the sacred spaces for worship, the sanctuaries. But "sanctuary" first implies and means a safe place, a place where one can be who one is, and come, as the old hymn says, "Just as I Am" with one's needs, weaknesses, and vulnerabilities as well as one's gifts, strengths, and abilities. When everyone feels welcome, it enhances that sense of sanctuary for all. A father of a young man with Down syndrome once told me about his son and the role he plays in their church and the religious life of their family. He noted, "Our sanctuary would not be the same without him."

For many children and adults with disabilities and their families, congregational sanctuaries have not been their safe places. A place is not safe if you cannot get into it, but, more importantly, it is not safe if the stigma, attitudes, prejudices, or fears about you tag along from the "world out there" into the religious sanctuary. When those stigmas or fears are given divine power or a disability is interpreted as a lack of faith, then the sanctuary is dangerous. In the books of the Torah and biblical tradition, claiming sanctuary was a freedom available in seven towns to those who believed that they were being unjustly accused. As congregations learn to help their worship space become safe as well as welcoming and accessible, perhaps the role of a sanctuary becomes even more significant for everyone.

A young man with Down syndrome sought to be baptized in his congregation. The pastor misunderstood his desire and thwarted it with a statement that "he doesn't need to be baptized, he is already there," meaning he is not responsible and would not understand. He and his mom did not give up, and, after some reeducation, another pastor on staff held a baptismal ceremony for him, but a private one with only family and friends. When he came out of the baptism immersion, someone noted the ring around the baptismal pool, whereupon the young man stated, "That's my sin." He got baptized, but the whole congregation (and this one was Baptist) lost out on being part of a sacred moment that would have brought renewed meaning to everyone's understanding of baptism.

As congregations make their sanctuaries accessible and welcoming, who comes back? Sometimes it is the older people or others that have been called "shut-ins" but may have been shut out by barriers of attitude and architecture. Rabbi Dan Grossman, of Temple Adath Israel in Lawrenceville, New Jersey, tells the story of how their new building, built to be as accessible as possible, enabled a member of more than ninety years to come back to services at least once a month. She could not get into the old building. When she died, the family was able to have the funeral at the new sanctuary. As he got to know her story, it turned out that woman and her husband had kept the synagogue alive during the Depression by paying the mortgage. As Jewish custom says, "May her memory be blessed." It was indeed, by virtue of her being re-membered.

Recovering the Gifts and Life as Gift

When the sanctuary is there, a person or family knows it and feels it. It is like the words of my seminarian classmate Tom Hunter's song: "It is awesome to be surrounded by people who are not sorry, by people who are not sorry, for what you cannot do."[13] Moving beyond pity is the first step. Remembering that everyone has gifts by virtue of his or her creation as a child of God, and thus being part of the people of God, is second.

When people begin to look at children and adults based on the gifts and strengths they bring, not just on their needs, then a congregation is beginning to practice what is the best of person-centered planning, and what asset-based community development theory calls "capacity vision."[14] It is the shared interests, abilities, skills, and strengths that connect us.

The transition to a new era is thus supported by an increased focus on gifts and interests. The pathways for connections and relationships are not built on the paradigm of disability/ability but on shared values, visions, interests, and gifts. One of the simple yet profound ways that some Catholic families have told me they have been included is to be able as a family to "bring down the gifts"—carry the bread and wine to the altar for the Eucharist. When we see gifts in everyone, whatever the size (think of the biblical story of the widow's mite[15]), then there is no gift that a congregation really does not need, or should not be able to find a place to use, if the faith community puts its creative imagination to work.

Reversing the Call: Everyone Has a Purpose

The importance of capacity vision and its celebration of gifts is that the real question for people of faith is not how so-called typical faith communities are called to welcome and include people with disabilities, but how all of us, people with disabilities included, are invited to respond to our understanding of God's call in our own lives as an individual and as a member of a people of faith. How does each person respond to the obligations of mitzvah, the call to discipleship, the practice of the five laws, or however "call" is understood in the religious tradition of which he or she is a part?

A woman named Cathy MacDonald was my first teacher on this, many years ago, at one of the first-ever conferences on inclusive faith communities that I helped organize. As she told her story about being sent to a large old state institution because of her cerebral palsy, her move out through group homes, and then to her own apartment, she ended with the challenge to all the audience: "You know, it is really important for you to be nice to handicapped people, but it is more important for you to let them be nice to you."

In the Christian tradition, a common phrase is, "It is more blessed to give than to receive." If most people are honest, it is also easier. People of faith are taught to be givers, to be helpers, contributors, stewards, committee members, followers, and disciples. It is harder for everyone to admit wants, or reveal needs, places where one would like to receive. Those all imply dependence. When children or adults with disabilities are implicitly labeled as the "designated receivers," the ones who only need, without gifts to give, then congregations fail to allow everyone the dignity, right, and responsibility to give to others out of their own sense of call. How are people with disabilities also called to roles of service?

Think of the loss, to everyone involved, if the following had not happened: A young man with Down syndrome was invited and trained to be a church usher in his Catholic parish. Who came to mass on one of his first Sundays of service? A man and woman, new grandparents, coming to the church for the first time in a long time, coming just after the birth of their grandson with Down syndrome, coming to seek sanctuary, solace, and understanding for the questions that were reverberating in their lives and souls. Think of what it meant to them to be greeted by this young usher at that mass, and then to have a long conversation with him after the mass about his life.

Faith beyond Reason: Recovering the Wholeness of Our Own Bodies

As congregations practice inclusion with people with many forms for sensory and motor impairments or disabilities, then what happens? Congregations learn new forms of communication and connection that help everyone to move beyond the spoken, heard, and read word, thereby helping everyone recover our senses of feeling, hearing, moving, tasting, smelling, and seeing.

As people with intellectual disabilities are included, worship sometimes has to become more spontaneous, with places for simplicity and spontaneity. Who enjoys that? Usually everyone. One does not have to look too far to find a story of a clergyperson whose rhetorical question in a sermon was spontaneously answered by someone with an intellectual disability who wanted to respond. Often it is an answer or question that others in the congregation wish they had said or one that reveals a new twist to what is being said.

When a congregation uses a sign language interpreter, it can seem like a form of liturgical dance that "typical" people enjoy watching just as much. A simple movement version of the Lord's Prayer that I used for years in services with people with intellectual disabilities is even more profound for those who have said the words for decades and now learn it in a new way. It helps revive other religious traditions of praying with one's whole body. With all the new technologies and assistive communication devices, there are so many ways for people to communicate through the heard, spoken, or seen word. As congregations learn to include people with visual impairments, people often are challenged to recover their use of touch, and the simple power of a guiding hand or elbow.

Amos Yong, a theologian from the Pentecostal tradition and the sibling of a man with an intellectual disability, uses the story of Pentecost in the book of Acts to talk about these gifts of new forms of communication that call us into relationship with anyone, no matter what kind of language they use. In the Pentecost story, the disciples and others were in an upper room in Jerusalem when the Holy Spirit descended upon them, an experience described as a mighty wind and tongues of fire. They began to speak in different tongues and went out into the city, where the Spirit compelled and enabled each one to go and speak to others in the city who had come from every part of the Mediterranean world—as diverse a group as could be imagined. How was it, those pilgrims wondered, were the disciples able to speak to them "in their own tongue"?[16]

Rekindling the Spirit

Recovering a creative use of color, taste, touch, sights, smells, sounds, symbols, and actions that speak beyond words can help communal worship and life to become more alive. When a sanctuary is truly safe, then all feelings are welcome, and even the scars and stigma of emotional and psychological illness can be addressed and soothed. The growth that occurs can include the community's confidence that together they can indeed embrace and sustain people with many forms of disability, both visible and invisible.

Congregations who have been welcoming and inclusive often come to the point of saying, in different ways in different traditions, "We are not doing so much for them, but rather, they are doing a whole lot for us. We are growing, not just in numbers, but also in liveliness and in our sense of spirit and community." People with intellectual and developmental disabilities often bring and share a sense of joyfulness in their participation with others in communal acts of worship and in other parts of congregational life. That is a gift that can be infectious, as is a more open sharing of both gifts and needs.

The rekindling of the spirit and spirituality through the lens of disability also comes from the ways we are pulled into the fundamental spiritual and theological questions about human life. Those theological questions include "What does it mean to be human?" "Who is God in light of disability?" and "What does it mean to be God's people?" From the perspective of the spiritual themes explored in this book, our identity is fundamentally shaped by the gift of life as a child of God, created in the image of God, and called into relationship with God, others, and the other parts of God's creation. Our lives are given meaning by loving God and loving our neighbors as ourselves. Each person is unique but also deeply connected with God, others, and the created world. Our call is to respond to this gift in a life of faithful stewardship in care of this world and one another with the gifts we have been given. Our call is to welcome and to love because we have first been welcomed and loved. That work is shaped with the vision of "repairing the breaches" (*tikkum olam*) that have come into the world through our illusions of knowing all (omniscience), misusing power in the mistreatment of others as well as the created world (omnipotence), assuming achievement is all our own doing (pride and control), and seeking various forms of immortality that deny our own limitations and vulnerabilities.

Dealing with those questions and issues is part of the journey of recovering wholeness. Our understanding of human life and the spirituality of our lives can thus be profoundly impacted by the embrace of spirituality in disability and our recognition of God's embrace of everyone.

SPIRITUALITY IN DISABILITY:
RE-MEMBERING WHOLENESS

The task, challenge, and intriguing journey of exploring the meaning of both disability and spirituality ends up leading both journeys into the world of the other. If that is the case, then talking about spirituality *and* disability may seem to indicate that one is talking about two separate entities, just as talking about people with and without disabilities would seem to presuppose two distinct kinds of human beings. Those are both false premises. Drawing distinctions may be helpful in terms of highlighting and understanding dimensions of the human experience, but they are all parts of the same human experience.

To say that slightly differently, the core issues around the many varieties and experiences of disability are ultimately core issues about what it means to be human, that is, they are about all of us. In the same way, spirituality may be expressed and experienced in different ways and times in our human experience. In exploring spirituality through our understanding about what it means to have a disability, we come to the core human (and sacred) dimensions of spirituality. Those core questions are thus not about "them" but about all of us.

There are any number of implications that follow, but let me end with three.

First, the "worlds" of disability and spirituality have so much to offer one another by broadening and deepening our understandings of each world. Each illuminates limitations in the usual theoretical frameworks and literature of the other. Each would be strengthened by more exploration of the other.

Second, the possible result of this merger in theory and practice can be lives that feel more whole by everyone involved and communities that are more whole because everyone has the chance to participate and belong. Thus, individual and community life has the chance to flourish in ways that draw upon understandings of individual and communal identity that are more honest and holistic, and thereby more truthful.

Third, and finally, we may be led to some answers but, more importantly, to a greater sense of curiosity, appreciation, and wonder about what it means to be human in all our forms and diversities. That does mean an embrace of experiences that have been very painful for many, even ourselves. As the journeys merge, there is the very real possibility and, one might say, responsibility to keep both our minds and bodies open to surprise, joy, and incredible tenacity of the human spirit. As W. H. Auden frames the spiritual journey in his long poem *For the Time Being*:

> He is the way,
> Seek him in the land of unlikeness
> And you will find strange beasts and unique adventures.
>
> He is the truth,
> Seek him in the kingdom of anxiety
> And you will come to a city that has expected your return for years.
>
> He is the Life,
> Seek him in the world of the flesh
> And at your marriage, all its occasions shall dance for joy.[17]

Notes

INTRODUCTION

1   The Baylor University Press series Studies in Religion, Theology, and Disability is one important example of this growth.

2   Louis Heifetz, "Integrating Religious and Secular Perspectives in the Design and Delivery of Disability Services," *Mental Retardation* 25, no. 3 (1987): 127–31.

1: NAMING AND DEFINING DISABILITY

1   A spiritual perspective would be "called." Thomas Merton once commented on a landscape photograph that had a crane's hook dangling in the middle, with the crane out of sight. He noted that "the picture was the only known photograph of God" ever taken. Available at Google Images by running a search for "Thomas Merton and the Picture of God" (accessed December 22, 2014).

2   Gen 2:19-20.

3   Loren Graham, "The Power of Names in Culture and Mathematics," *Proceedings of the American Philosophical Society* 157, no. 2 (2013): 229–34.

4   Fiona Campbell, *Contours of Ableism: Production of Disability and Abledness* (London: Palgrave Macmillan, 2009). Also see Sandra Levi, "Ableism," in *Encyclopedia of Disability*, ed. Gary Albrecht (Thousand Oaks, Calif.: Sage, 2006).

5   Kathy Snow, "Disability Is Natural," https://www.disabilityisnatural.com.

6   Lorna Wing, Judith Gould, and Christopher Gillberg, "Autism Spectrum Disorders in the *DSM-V*: Better or Worse Than the *DSM-IV*?" *Research in Developmental Disabilities* 32, no. 2 (2011): 768–73.

7   See Christopher Goodey, *A History of Intelligence and "Intellectual Disability": The Shaping of Psychology in Early Modern Europe* (Burlington, Vt.: Ashgate,

2011); and Michael Wehmeyer, *The Story of Intellectual Disability: An Evolution of Meaning, Understanding, and Public Perception* (Baltimore: Brookes, 2013).

8   Karrie Shogren, "Positive Psychology and Disability: A Historical Analysis," in *The Oxford Handbook of Positive Psychology and Disability*, ed. Michael Wehmeyer (New York: Oxford University Press, 2013), 19–33.

9   Amy Julia Becker's book about her daughter with Down syndrome, *A Good and Perfect Gift: Faith, Expectations, and a Little Girl Named Penny* (Bloomington, Minn.: Bethany Press, 2011); and her presentation at the 2012 Summer Institute on Theology and Disability (http://faithanddisability.org/2012-summer-institute/).

10 David Braddock and Susan Parish, "An Institutional History of Disability," in *Handbook of Disability Studies*, ed. Gary Albrecht, K. Seelman, and M. Bury (New York: Sage, 2001), 11–68.

11 Lynn Rose, "History of Disability: Ancient West," in *Encyclopedia of Disability*, ed. Gary Albrecht et al. (New York: Sage, 2006), 2:852–55.

12 Cf. John 9.

13 Geoffrey Hudson, "History of Disability: Early Modern West," in *Encyclopedia of Disability*, ed. Gary Albrecht et al. (New York: Sage, 2006), 2:855–58.

14 Hudson, "History of Disability," 2:855–58.

15 Philip Ferguson, "The Development of Systems of Supports: Intellectual Disability in Middle Modern Times (1800–1899)," in *The Story of Intellectual Disability: An Evolution of Meaning, Understanding, and Public Perception*, ed. Michael Wehmeyer (Baltimore: Brookes, 2013), 79–115.

16 Robert Bogdan, Martin Elks, and James Knoll, *Picturing Disability: Beggar, Freak, Citizen, and Other Photographic Rhetoric* (Syracuse, N.Y.: Syracuse University Press, 2012).

17 Wolf Wolfensberger, *The Principle of Normalization in Human Services* (Toronto: National Institute on Mental Retardation, 1972).

18 Joseph Shapiro, *No Pity: People with Disabilities Forging a New Civil Rights Movement* (New York: Three Rivers, 1994).

19 See both Robert Schalock, "Introduction to the Intellectual Disability Construct," in *The Story of Intellectual Disability: An Evolution of Meaning, Understanding, and Public Perception*, ed. Michael Wehmeyer (Baltimore: Brookes, 2013), 2–17; and David Braddock and Susan Parish, "An Institutional History of Disability," in *Handbook of Disability Studies*, edited by Gary Albrecht, K. Seelman, and M. Bury (New York: Sage, 2001), 11–68.

20 Harvey Switzky and Stephen Greenspan, eds., *What Is Mental Retardation: Ideas for an Evolving Disability in the 21st Century* (Washington, D.C.: American Association on Mental Retardation, 2006).

21 This chapter is decidedly focused on understandings of disability from Western perspectives. Many definitions and understandings of disability are now accepted on worldwide levels in health, human services, and policy circles, but cultural understandings of disability vary widely. There are also rich historical discussions about disability in Middle Eastern, Eastern, and other cultural

histories. See M. Miles, "Religion and Spirituality," in *International Encyclopedia of Rehabilitation*, ed. J. H. Stone and M. Blouin.

22 Robert Schalock and Ruth Luckasson, *Clinical Judgment*, 2nd ed. (Washington, D.C.: American Association on Intellectual and Developmental Disabilities, 2014).

23 World Health Organization, *International Classification of Impairments, Disabilities and Handicaps: A Manual of Classification Relating to the Consequences of Disease*, published in accordance with resolution WHA 29.35 of the Twenty-Ninth World Health Assembly, May 1976, repr. with foreword (Geneva: World Health Organization, 1993).

24 Neil Messer, *Flourishing: Health, Disease, and Bioethics in a Theological Perspective* (Grand Rapids: Eerdmans, 2014).

25 *What Is Disability?* Handicap International, accessed June 17, 2016.

26 Carmelo Masala and Donatella Petretto, "Models of Disability," in *International Encyclopedia of Rehabilitation*, ed. J. H. Stone and M. Blouin (2010).

27 Wil Buntinx, "Understanding Disability: A Strengths-Based Approach," in *The Oxford Handbook of Positive Psychology and Disability*, ed. Michael Wehmeyer (New York: Oxford University Press, 2013), 7–18. Buntinx is referencing *Mental Retardation: Definition, Classification, and Systems of Support*, ed. R. Luckasson, S. Brothwick-Duffy, E. A. Polloway, S. Reiss, R. L. Schalock, and M. E. Snell. 9th ed. Washington, DC: American Association on Mental Retardation, 1992.

28 This definition is one used by the AAIDD and the ARC in joint position statements, based on the resources mentioned in the quotation. For example, see the position statement on "Addressing the Causes and Effects of Intellectual and Developmental Disabilities," http://aaidd.org/news-policy/policy/position-statements/addressing-the-causes-and-effects-of-intellectual-and-developmental-disabilities#.WUAUiMbMwdV.

29 Robert Schalock et al., *Intellectual Disability: Definition, Classification, and Systems of Support*, 11th ed. (Washington, D.C.: American Association on Intellectual and Developmental Disabilities, 2010).

30 Buntinx, "Understanding Disability," 10.

31 Buntinx, "Understanding Disability," 11.

2: DISABILITY

1 Messer, *Flourishing*. In this book Neil Messer seeks to bring a theological interpretation to the debates in the worlds of philosophy, health, and ethics about the meaning of "health." One of the fascinating parts of the book is the author's premise that theology has significant contributions to make to those debates. The book includes a significant chapter on ways that the relatively recent work in theology and disability brings rich resources to the wider discussion about understandings of health.

2 For examples, see the work of David Larson, Harold Koenig, Christina Puchalski, and many others. Explore the work of the Templeton Foundation.

And look for spirituality interest groups, divisions, or projects in many classic disciplines in health and human services.

3   Those experiences will be described more fully in upcoming chapters on individuals with disabilities and families.

4   Timothy Shriver, *Fully Alive: Discovering What Matters Most* (New York: Sarah Crichton Books, 2014).

5   For example, see Harlan Hahn, "Civil Rights FOR Disabled Americans: The Foundation of a Political Agenda," Independent Living Institute, Sweden, 1987, www.independentliving.org/docs4/hahn.html. Ginny Thornburgh, one of the leaders in inclusive congregational supports, frequently used the phrase "attitudes before architecture" in her presentations. It is a theme that runs throughout her seminal book *That All May Worship*, http://www.aapd .com/wp-content/uploads/2016/03/That-All-May-Worship.pdf. One version of the phrase, "Your Attitude Just Might Be My Biggest Barrier," was put on a T-shirt by the disability advocacy and awareness company, the Nth Degree: http://www.thenthdegree.com/advocacy.asp.

6   See Christine Rosen, *Preaching Eugenics: Religious Leaders and the American Eugenics Movement* (London: Oxford University Press, 2004).

7   As of the time of the writing of this book, the CRPD has ironically not been ratified by the United States, even though most of it is modeled after the ADA. The CRPD has become a scapegoat in the political wars on Capitol Hill as well as the target for spurious attacks that it threatens U.S. sovereignty and the right to homeschooling.

8   At its origin in the 1970s, ADAPT originally stood for American Disabled for Accessible Public Transit or Transportation. After the ADA passed in 1990, the acronym changed to mean American Disabled for Attendant Programs Today. Eventually it just became ADAPT. For more on its history, go to http://www.adalegacy.com; and for its current work, http://www.adapt.org. ADAPT has sometimes been tagged as the most "radical" disability rights group, but it is the one that has been willing to stage sit-ins in government buildings, did a famous crawl up the Capitol building steps in D.C., and more. I once participated and assisted at an ADAPT march in Atlanta, helping some people negotiate the hills of downtown. I was with an older, white-haired, kind woman from Salt Lake City. She told me that she and colleagues had fought for years for accessible public transportation in Salt Lake City and got nowhere. Then "we chained ourselves to some buses and got change in twenty minutes."

9   John Plumadore and Susan Muehiherr, "The Golden Rule Across the World's Religions," ScoutingLife.ca, November/December 2009, accessed June 17, 2017, http://www.scouts.ca/sites/default/files/sl-Golden-Rule-Across-Religion .pdf.

10 Julia Watts Belser, *Guide to Jewish Values and Disability Rights* (New York: Jewish Funders, 2016).

11 Jonathan Sacks, *The Great Partnership: Science, Religion, and the Search for Meaning* (New York: Schocken Books, 2012).

12 Hans Reinders, *The Future of the Disabled in Liberal Society* (South Bend, Ind.: University of Notre Dame Press, 1990).

13 Buntinx, "Understanding Disability," 7–18. Wil Buntinx cites a speech by Michael Bach, vice president of the Canadian Association of Community Living, at the 2012 International Association for the Scientific Study of Intellectual Disability conference in Halifax. In Bach's view, the scientific task is to determine:

> Not if people with intellectual disabilities have a will and preference, but how to determine it even when its contours are occluded by our usual ways of seeing and knowing; not if people with even the most complex disabilities can live in the community, but how that is to be made possible . . . *Not if people with intellectual disabilities benefit from being supported to exercise self-determination and making their own choices . . . but how to enable others to respect and act on upon the legal power they possess.* It is only with such knowledge, founded on a law, science and ethics of inclusion, that we might nurture a new relationship between the state, society, and people with intellectual disabilities. ("Understanding Disability," 13 [emphasis added])

14 Hans Reinders, *Receiving the Gift of Friendship: Profound Disability, Theological Anthropology, and Ethics* (Grand Rapids: Eerdmans, 2008).

15 Hans Reinders, "Understanding Humanity and Disability: Building an Ecological Perspective," *Studies in Christian Ethics* 26, no. 1 (2013): 37–49. Elizabeth Hastings, a disability advocate, government officer, and church leader in Australia, made the same point years before in a speech to the Uniting Church of Australia entitled "A Thousand Tongues to Sing: Difference and Belonging," (unpublished address given September 24, 1995, to the Synod of New South Wales, Uniting Church in Australia).

16 Buntinx, "Understanding Disability," 11.

17 To name just a few leading researchers and writers in QOL, especially as applied to people with intellectual and developmental disabilities: Robert Schalock in the United States, David Felce and Roy Emerson in the United Kingdom, Wil Buntinx and Hans Reinders in the Netherlands, and Michael Verdugo in Spain. The Beach Center on Families and Disability, led by Rud and Ann Turnbull, has been the key leader in understanding QOL and its relationship to families.

18 Messer, *Flourishing*, 84.

19 Buntinx, "Understanding Disability," 12. I have taken the liberty of changing the order of the columns for the sake of this discussion.

20 Masala and Petretto, "Models of Disability."

21 Quality of Life Research Unit, University of Toronto, *The Quality of Life Model*, accessed October 19, 2014, http://sites.utoronto.ca/qol/qol_model.htm.

22 Coincidentally, *Believing, Belonging, and Becoming* is the title of a short video produced by the Wisconsin Council on Developmental Disabilities that shows

four vignettes of congregational inclusion for children and adults with intellectual and developmental disabilities. See http://faithanddisability.org/videos/.

23   The National Core Indicators Project in the United States inquires about the frequency of "going to church." As the data bank at the National Core Indicators Project grows, some informal research has found very interesting correlations between the number of times someone goes to church, employment, number of friends, and feelings of loneliness; see http://www.nationalcoreindicators .org/indicators/.

24   For an example, see Eleanor Liu, Erik Carter, Thomas Boehm, Naomi Annandale, and Courtney Evans Taylor, "In Their Own Words: The Place of Faith in the Lives of Young People with Autism and Intellectual Disability," *Intellectual and Developmental Disabilities* 52, no. 5 (2014): 368–404. The article is excellent, and their list of references is an excellent guide to a number of research studies in the past ten to twenty years. A listing of research articles can be found at the website of the Collaborative on Faith and Disability, http:// faithanddisability.org/resources/scholarship/.

25   Schalock and Luckasson, *Clinical Judgment*.

26   See discussion in the next chapter of "thin" and "thick" based on writings and conversations with John Swinton.

27   Michael Smull, Helen Sanderson, et al., *Essential Lifestyle Planning for Everyone* (Annapolis, Md.: Learning Community, 2009).

28   For example, some faith-based agencies are very deliberate about exploring spiritual interests, needs, and gifts as part of their planning processes with individuals they support.

29   William Gaventa, "Defining and Assessing Spirituality and Spiritual Supports: Moving from Benediction to Invocation," in *What Is Mental Retardation: Ideas for an Evolving Disability in the 21st Century*, ed. Harvey Switzky and Steven Greenspan (Washington, D.C.: American Association on Intellectual and Developmental Disabilities, 2006), 151–66.

3: SPIRITUALITY

1   Sacks, *Great Partnership*.

2   It is not clear how much research the writers of this definition have done because many people in different faith traditions would not call God a "superhuman controlling power." Judaism, for example, is founded on the belief in a God who gave man and woman free will, and a God who freed God's people.

3   Sacks, *Great Partnership*.

4   Parker Palmer, "Merging Two Worlds" (keynote speech given at the Merging Two Worlds conference, Rochester, N.Y., 1986).

5   William Gaventa, "Forgiveness, Gratitude And Spirituality," in *The Oxford Handbook of Positive Psychology and Disability*, ed. Michael Wehmeyer (New York: Oxford University Press, 2013), 226–38.

6　John Swinton and Stephen Pattison, "Moving beyond Clarity: Towards a Thin, Vague, and Useful Understanding of Spirituality in Nursing Care," *Nursing Philosophy* 11 (2010): 226–37.

7　Swinton and Pattison, "Moving beyond Clarity," 228–29. Thus, while they describe spirituality as a "thin and vague" but still useful concept, in other research and writing, Swinton notes that an in-depth understanding of spirituality involves a very "thick" definition that has eluded consensus. To quote from an e-mail he wrote to me:

> I borrowed the term from the anthropologist Clifford Geertz (Clifford Geertz, "Thick Description: Toward an Interpretive Theory of Culture," in *The Interpretation of Cultures: Selected Essays* [New York: Basic Books, 1973], 3–30). The task of the anthropologist Geertz insists, is to explore culture through the process of providing rich and thick descriptions of what is going on. A thick description tries to capture the complex dynamics of any given situation—its symbols, its perspectives, the meanings that are hidden to outsiders, the boundaries of that which is plausible and that which is not—and to present them in a way that helps the reader fully to understand the situation, experience or context. A thin description on the other hand is a simple, factual account without any interpretation and without any attempt to get to grips with the complexities of situations and human beings within situations. The problem with thin descriptions is not simply that they are inadequate, but that they are actually misleading. Bald facts without context or interpretation are only facts in a minimal sense. It is only really when we get into the thickness of a situation or experience that we discover what it truly is. My problem with spirituality and the so-called scientific investigations into religion and health is that they are far too thin and instrumental. What I think we need is thick descriptions that reveal something of the richness and depth of human experience and of that aspect of experience we choose to call spirituality (John Swinton, e-mail to Bill Gaventa, January 6, 2015).

8　Swinton, e-mail to Bill Gaventa, January 6, 2015. Also see Geertz, "Thick Description."

9　See n. 7.

10　Robert Chambers, *Whose Reality Counts? Putting the First Last* (London: Intermediate Technology, 1997).

11　George Fitchett, "The 7×7 Model For Spiritual Assessment," *Vision* 6, no. 3 (1996): 10–11.

12　American Association of Medical Colleges, *Contemporary Issues in Medicine: Communication in Medicine*, 1999, accessed December 10, 2014, https://members.aamc.org/.

13　George Washington Institute for Spirituality and Health, accessed December 10, 2014, http://smhs.gwu.edu/gwish/.

14　Those visits drew all kinds of reactions, from sheer delight by people who rarely received a card, much less a birthday celebration, to looks by staff of

"What does he think he is doing?" when I would tape the card on the railing of a bed or crib in which a person spent most of his or her days and nights. The most powerful experience was going to one such unit and asking, which one was Charlie? The staff pointed him out, sitting in a wheelchair by a window. I knelt in front of him, assuming he could not talk like the others on that unit. I said simply, "Charlie, I am Bill. I am the chaplain [*folding my hands like a prayer*]. It is your birthday. And I have a birthday card for you." Charlie was one of those elders who had a hundred wrinkles in his face. Like his mouth, they slowly started to move upward in a smile. He started to reach his hands toward the card, then suddenly withdrew it, and the wrinkles came back. Then he spoke, which almost knocked me over in surprise, "But I don't have anything to pay you for it." It was, for me, a primal lesson about the grace of love, acceptance, and celebration, and an indictment of an institution and world in which a core belief is that acceptance has to be earned.

15 Smull, Sanderson, et al., *Essential Lifestyle Planning for Everyone*.

16 See Petra Kuppers, "Crip Time," *Tikkun* 29, no. 4 (2014): 29–30; and online lectures by John Swinton, *Becoming Friends of Time: Disability, Timefulness and Gentle Discipleship* (Waco, Tex.: Baylor University Press, 2016).

17 Sacks, *Great Partnership*, 144–62.

18 Rainer Maria Rilke, *Letters to a Young Poet* (London: Dover, 2002).

19 Shriver, *Fully Alive*, 201.

20 Hans Reinders, *Disability, Providence, and Ethics: Bridging Gaps, Transforming Lives* (Waco, Tex.: Baylor University Press, 2014).

21 Arthur Frank, *At the Will of the Body* (New York: Houghton Mifflin, 1992).

22 Frank, *At the Will of the Body*.

23 Arthur Frank, *The Wounded Storyteller: Body, Illness, And Ethics* (Chicago: University of Chicago Press, 1995).

24 Tom Shakespeare, "A Point of View: Happiness and Disability," *BBC News Magazine*, May 31, 2014.

25 Rachel Cohen Rottenberg, "On Normalcy and Identity Politics," Disability and Representation: Changing the Cultural Conversation (blog), March 24, 2014; citing Lennard Davis, *Enforcing Normalcy: Disability, Deafness and the Body* (London: Verso, 1995), 26.

26 Naomi H. Annandale and Eric W. Carter, "Disability and Theological Education: A North American Study," *Theological Education* 48, no. 2 (2014): 83–102 (95).

4: SPIRITUALITY IN THE LIVES OF INDIVIDUALS WITH DISABILITIES

1 William Gaventa, "A Rosh Hashanah Birthday," *Jewish Digest* 27, no. 1 (1981): 41–44. Also, published in *American Baptist Magazine*, 179, no. 4 (1981): 14–16. Reprinted in recent years in a Jewish journal, two other collections of stories, and newsletter in the United Kingdom.

2 Like most tables, this one is meant to clarify and organize, but not to imply linear or separate areas. That criticism was leveled at the first WHO definition

of disability, leading to a more complex and dynamic model in 2002. Similarly, the areas in this table are all dynamically related to one another.

3 Wilfredo Gomez, "When Strangers Read My Body: Blurred Boundaries and the Search for Something Spiritual," *Tikkun* 29, no. 4 (2014): 41–42, 68–69.

4 Stella Young, "I Am Not Your Inspiration, Thank You Very Much," TED Talk, April 2014.

5 Wolf Wolfensberger, "Social Role Valorization: A Proposed New Term for the Principle of Normalization," *Mental Retardation* 21, no. 6 (1983): 234–39.

6 Jack Nelson, "When Stereotypes Tell the Story," *National Center on Disability and Journalism News* 3, no. 1 (2003): 1.

7 Liu et al., "In Their Own Words," 388–404.

8 Karin Melberg-Schwier, *Flourish: People with Disabilities Living Life with Passion* (Saskatoon, Calif.: Copestone, 2012).

9 That journey will be explored more fully in discussions on spiritual development, self-determination, and employment in chap. 6.

10 Judith Snow, "It's about Grace" (keynote presentation given at the 2014 Summer Institute on Theology and Disability, Dallas, Tex.).

11 Gomez, "When Strangers Read My Body."

12 Snow, "It's about Grace."

13 Snow, "It's about Grace."

14 Angela Amado, *Friends: Connecting People with Disabilities and Community Members* (Minneapolis: University of Minnesota, Institute on Community Integration, Research and Training Center on Community Living, 2013).

15 Erik Carter and Bill Gaventa, eds. "Spirituality: From Rights to Relationships," special issue, *TASH Connections* 38, no. 1 (2012).

16 Robert Raines, *Living the Questions* (Nashville: Word Books, 1976).

5: SPIRITUAL DEVELOPMENT AND FORMATION

1 Charles Davis, "Youth with Disabilities Talk about Their Spirituality and Their Transition to Independence" (unpublished article about a panel at the Treat Me as a Member, Not Mission conference, Portland, Ore., May 15, 2014).

2 Jean Vanier, *Tears of Silence: A Meditation* (Toronto: House of Anasi Press, 2014). That lack of early experiences of loving and bonding, explored most thoroughly by psychologists like Wilfred Bion, John Bowlby and Mary Ainsworth, and others in attachment theory, often has drastic impact on the personal development of identity and social skill.

3 Units like Disney and adult units in these institutions still looked like warehouses, catalogued most famously by the pictorial essay by Burton Blatt and Fred Kaplan, *Christmas in Purgatory: A Photographic Essay on Mental Retardation* (Syracuse, N.Y.: Human Policy, 1974).

4 James Fowler, *Stages of Faith: The Psychology of Human Development and the Quest for Meaning* (New York: HarperCollins, 1981).

5 John Westerhoff, *Will Our Children Have Faith?* (New York: Seabury Press, 1976).

6   I first used this work by John Westerhoff in a chapter published in the 1980s: William Gaventa, "Religious Ministries and Services with Adults with Developmental Disabilities," in *The Right to Grow Up: An Introduction to Adults with Developmental Disabilities*, ed. Jean Summers (Baltimore: Brookes, 1986), 191–226.

7   Westerhoff, *Will Our Children Have Faith?*, 91.

8   Jeff McNair and Erik Carter, "Knowledge, Faith Development, and Religious Education That Includes All," *Journal of Religion, Disability and Health* 14 (2010): 186–203.

9   Reinders, *Receiving the Gift of Friendship*.

10 Cristina Gangemi, Matteo Tobanelli, Giada Vincenzi, and John Swinton, *Everybody Has a Story: Enabling Communities to Meet People with Intellectual Disabilities and Respond Effectively to Their Expressed Spiritual and Religious Needs and Hopes; A Participatory Action Research Approach*, University of Aberdeen, Kairos Forum, from an e-mail from Cristina Gangemi to Bill Gaventa.

11 John Swinton, *A Space to Listen: Meeting the Spiritual Needs of People with Learning Disabilities* (London: Mental Health Foundation, 2001). This and other resources from the Space to Listen project are accessible at http://www.learningdisabilities.org.uk/publications/ (accessed April 15, 2015).

12 Henri Nouwen, *Adam: God's Beloved* (Maryknoll, N.Y.: Orbis Books, 1998).

13 Christopher de Vinck, *The Power of the Powerless: A Brother's Legacy of Love* (New York: Crossroad, 2002).

14 Kathleen Bolduc, *Autism and Alleluias* (Valley Forge, Pa.: Judson, 2010).

15 *Praying with Lior*, directed by Ilana Trachtman (Philadelphia: Ruby Pictures, 2007), accessed June 20, 2017, www.prayingwithlior.com.

16 See the PRAISE Project and related resources: Office of Ministries with Persons with Disabilities, Roman Catholic Archdiocese of Newark, accessed April 15, 2015, http://rcan.org/offices-and-ministries/ministry-disabilities.

17 William Gaventa and Roger Peters, "Spirituality and Self-Actualization: Recognizing Spiritual Needs and Strengths of Individuals with Cognitive Limitations," in *The Forgotten Generation: The Status and Challenges of Adults with Mild Cognitive Limitations*, ed. Alexander Tymchuk, Charlie Lakin, and Ruth Luckasson (Baltimore: Brookes, 2001), 299–320.

18 Davis, "Youth with Disabilities Talk about Their Spirituality and Their Transition to Independence."

19 Liu et al., "In Their Own Words," 388–404.

20 Another source for faith stories by young adults with intellectual and developmental disabilities is a themed issue of the TASH *Connections* newsletter on spirituality edited by Erik Carter and Bill Gaventa and entitled "Spirituality: From Rights to Relationships." The issue includes stories by Jacob Artsen (Jewish), Myron Otto (Christian), and Hazma Jaka (Muslim).

21 For examples, see Jean Vanier, *From Brokenness to Community* (Mahwah, N.J.: Paulist, 1992); Jean Vanier, *Community and Growth* (Mahwah, N.J.: Paulist,

1989); Nouwen, *Adam*; Henri Nouwen, *The Road to Daybreak: A Spiritual Journey* (New York: Doubleday, 1997).

22 Reinders, *Receiving the Gift of Friendship*.

23 Gangemi et al., *Everybody Has a Story*. Also see John Swinton, Harriet Mowat, and Susannah Baines, "Whose Story Am I? Re-describing Profound Intellectual Disability in the Kingdom of God," *Journal of Religion, Disability and Health* 15 (2011): 5–19.

24 *Oxford English Dictionary*, accessed June 7, 2017, https://en.oxforddictionaries .com/definition/educate.

25 See the writings of Parker Palmer, including *Leading from Within: Poetry That Sustains the Courage to Lead* (San Francisco: Jossey-Bass, 2007); *The Active Life: A Spirituality of Work, Creativity, and Caregiving* (San Francisco: Jossey-Bass, 1999); *To Know as We Are Known: A Spirituality of Education* (San Francisco: Harper & Row, 1983); and *The Courage to Teach: Recovering the Inner Landscape of a Teacher's Life* (San Francisco: Jossey-Bass, 1997). Related resources can be found at www.couragerenewal.org.

26 See a comparative chart in the Wikipedia article on Robert Kegan at http://en .wikipedia.org/wiki/Robert_Kegan.

6: SPIRITUALITY AND THE TRANSITION TO ADULTHOOD

1 Missouri Family to Family, *Charting the Life Course: A Guide for Individuals, Families, and Professionals* (Kansas City: Institute for Human Development, University of Missouri, Kansas City, 2012). This tool and the website http:// mofamilytofamily.org/?catid=296 post questions to help families plan for subsequent stages of life in relationship to major categories of life: daily life, housing, services/supports/financing, safety/security, health and wellness, social/ recreational, and family support. Spirituality is included in the category of social/recreational.

2 Reinders, *Disability, Providence, and Ethics*.

3 See books and videos on the PATH Process at http://www.inclusion.com/ inclusionpress.html; and the Learning Community for Person Centered Practices, http://tlcpcp.com; and other forms of transition planning.

4 Dean Preheim-Bartel and A. Neufeldt, *Supportive Care in the Congregation: Providing a Congregational Network of Care for Persons with Significant Disabilities* (Harrisburg, Pa.: Herald Press, 2011); and Dean Preheim-Bartel and Christine Guth, *Circles of Love: Stories of Congregations Caring for People with Disabilities and Their Families* (Harrisonburg, Va.: Menno Media, 2015).

5 The Group Action Planning model developed by Rud and Ann Turnbull is another model. See Ann P. Tumbull and H. Rutherford Turnbull, "Group Action Planning as a Strategy for Providing Comprehensive Family Support," in *Positive Behavioral Support: Including People with Difficult Behavior in the Community*, ed. L. K. Koegel, R. L. Koegel, and G. Dunlap (Baltimore: Brookes, 1996), 99–114. Also see the resources for circles of support and

person-centered planning at Inclusion Press, http://www.inclusion.com/inclusionpress.html.

6 That was not true, of course, for a major period in the history of the United States when slaves were legally deemed "less than a person" and when they, along with women, did not have the right to vote.

7 Atul Gawande, *Being Mortal: Medicine and What Matters in the End* (New York: Metropolitan Books, 2014).

8 Gawande, *Being Mortal*, 139–40.

9 Gawande, *Being Mortal*, 140.

10 Thomas Nerney and Donald Shumway, *Beyond Managed Care: Self-Determination for People with Disabilities* (Concord: University of New Hampshire, 1996).

11 Smull, Sanderson, et al., *Essential Lifestyle Planning for Everyone*; and the Learning Community for Person Centered Practices, http://tlcpcp.com/.

12 Sandor Gurbai, "Promoting Inclusion of Adults with Disabilities under Guardianship by Strengthening Solidarity based on Theology and Human Rights," *Journal of Disability and Religion* 18 (2014): 227–41.

13 Gurbai, "Promoting Inclusion of Adults with Disabilities," 233.

14 Gurbai, "Promoting Inclusion of Adults with Disabilities," 236.

15 The most graphic and succinct way I have heard that wish expressed is by one or more people who have said, "Don't use my disability to work out your crap."

16 Frederick Buechner, *Wishful Thinking: A Theological ABC* (New York: Harper & Row, 1973).

17 Much of the remaining part of this discussion on spirituality and employment is drawn from a paper, of which I am the primary author, that forms the vision of a grant-funded project, "Putting Faith to Work": Bill Gaventa, Wesley Allen, Harold Kleinert, and Erik W. Carter, "Putting Faith to Work: The Call and Opportunity for Faith Communities to Transform the Lives of People with Disabilities and their Communities" (Nashville: Vanderbilt Kennedy Center, 2014).

18 Lev 19:9, 23:22; Deut 24:19-21; Ruth 2:2-23.

19 Jer 31: 8-9.

20 Matt 25:14-30.

21 1 Cor 12.

22 National Interfaith Committee for Worker Justice, *The Quran and Worker Justice*, accessed June 14, 2017, www.wpusa.org/Interfaith-Council/Resources_quran.pdf.

23 See Crossroads Career, www.CrossroadsCareer.org; and Jobs for Life, http://www.jobsforlife.org, both accessed June 14, 2017.

24 Putting Faith to Work Project, funded by the Kessler Foundation, accessed June 14, 2017, http://faithanddisability.org/projects/putting-faith-to-work/.

25 "Jesus Walked This Lonesome Valley," https://www.songandpraise.org/jesus-walked-this-lonesome-valley-hymn-lyrics.htm.

7: SPIRITUALITY, AGING, AND END OF LIFE

1   A third is sexuality.

2   Parts of this chapter are adapted and taken from two chapters I have authored in edited collections: William Gaventa, "Spirituality Issues and Strategies: Crisis and Opportunity," in *End of Life Care for Children and Adults with Intellectual and Developmental Disabilities*, ed. Sandra Friedman and David Helm (Washington, D.C.: American Association on Intellectual and Developmental Disabilities, 2010), 245–60; and William Gaventa, "Spirituality and Faith: Beyond Beliefs to Practice," in *Supporting People with Intellectual Disabilities Experiencing Loss and Bereavement: Theory and Compassionate Practice*, ed. Sue Read (London: Jessica Kingsley, 2014), 71–82.

3   Granger Westberg, *Good Grief: A Constructive Approach to the Problem of Loss*, 35th anniversary ed. (Minneapolis: Fortress, 1997).

4   Ken Doka, "Struggling with Grief and Loss," in *End of Life Care for Children and Adults with Intellectual and Developmental Disabilities*, ed. Sandra Friedman and David Helm (Washington, D.C.: American Association on Intellectual and Developmental Disabilities, 2010), 261–71.

5   Leigh Ann Kingsbury, "Person Centered Planning and Communication of End-of-Life Wishes with People Who Have Developmental Disabilities," *Journal of Religion, Disability, and Health* 9, no. 2 (2005): 81–90. Leigh Ann Kingsbury, *People Planning: Communicating Healthcare and End of Life Wishes* (Washington, D.C.: American Association on Intellectual and Developmental Disabilities, 2010).

6   Or the newer planning instrument, Physicians Orders for Life Sustaining Treatment (POLST).

7   Examples include Charlene Luchterhand and Nancy Murphy, *Helping Adults with Mental Retardation Grieve a Death Loss* (Philadelphia: Taylor & Francis, 1998); Sheila Hollins and Noel Blackman, *When Somebody Dies* (London: Books Beyond Words, 2003); Marc Markell, *Helping People with Mental Retardation Mourn: Practical Rituals for Caregivers* (Fort Collins, Colo.: Companion, 2005); Linda Van Dyke, *Lessons in Grief and Death: Supporting People with Developmental Disabilities in the Healing Process* (Joliet, Ill.: High Tide Press, 2003); and Sue Read, ed., *Supporting People with Intellectual Disabilities Experiencing Loss and Bereavement: Theory and Compassionate Practice* (London: Jessica Kingsley, 2014).

8   Park Ridge Center, *The Challenges of Aging: Retrieving Spiritual Traditions* (Chicago, Ill.: Park Ridge Center for the Study of Health, Faith, and Ethics, 1999).

9   Ira Wohl was the director of two documentary films about his cousin, Philly, *Best Boy* (Los Angeles: Only Child Motion Pictures, 1979); and *Best Man: "Best Boy" and All of Us, Twenty Years Later* (Los Angeles: Only Child Motion Pictures, 1997), which documented Philly's journey out of Letchworth Developmental Center in New York State in the 1970s back into Brooklyn.

10 See multiple Books Beyond Words titles at http://www.booksbeyondwords.co.uk.

11 Used with permission and first used in Gaventa, "Spirituality and Faith," 71–82.

12 Examples include Markell, *Helping People with Developmental Disabilities Mourn*; Van Dyke, *Lessons in Grief and Death;* and Harvey Sterns, Elizabeth Kennedy, and Chad Sed, *Person-Centered Planning for Late Life: A Curriculum for Adults with Mental Retardation* (Chicago: University of Illinois, Rehabilitation Research and Training Center on Developmental Disabilities and Health, 2000).

13 California Coalition for Compassionate Care, *Thinking Ahead: My Life at the End* (Sacramento: California Coalition for Compassionate Care, 2007). Both the workbook and DVD are available in three languages (English, Spanish, and Chinese) free of charge on their website: http://coalitionccc.org/tools-resources/people-with-developmental-disabilities/.

14 Jeff Kauffman, *Guidebook on Helping Persons with Mental Retardation Mourn* (Amityville, N.Y.: Baywood, 2005).

15 Kauffman, *Guidebook on Helping Persons with Mental Retardation Mourn*, 10.

8: SPIRITUALITY AND FAMILIES

1 Erik Carter, Thomas Boehm, Naomi Annandale, and Courtney Taylor, "Supporting Congregational Inclusion for Children and Youth with Disabilities and Their Families," *Exceptional Children* 82, no. 3 (2016): 372–89. See also Courtney Taylor, Erik Carter, Naomi Annandale, Thomas Boehm, and Aimee Logeman, *Welcoming People with Developmental Disabilities and Their Families: A Practical Guide for Congregations* (Nashville: Vanderbilt Kennedy Center, 2014).

2 See a series of archived webinars coordinated by the Collaborative on Faith and Disability exploring integration of spirituality in service agencies and creative responses by congregations, entitled *Honoring Spiritual Needs and Gifts: From Inertia to Collaborative Action by Providers and Congregations*, webinar series, 2015, archived at http://faithanddisability.org/webinar/.

3 Jason Whitt, "A Place for Camille," *Christian Century*, January 12, 2015, 24–25, 27.

4 Rud Turnbull, e-mail correspondence, July 16, 2014.

5 Rolf Forsberg, *Mother Tiger, Mother Tiger*, directed by Rolf Forsberg (Los Angeles: Franciscan Communications, 1974).

6 Elizabeth Kubler Ross, *On Death and Dying* (New York: Simon & Schuster, 1969).

7 Note the similarity to Arthur Frank's three narratives of illness in *Wounded Storyteller*, discussed in chap. 4.

8 Patrick O'Malley, "Getting Grief Right," *New York Times*, January 10, 2015.

9 A "non-anxious presence" is a phrase attributed to several people, including Henri Nouwen. A more reliable attribution is to Ed Friedman, a world-famous rabbi, psychologist, and therapist. See David Cox, The Edwin Friedman Model of Family Systems Thinking: Lessons for Organizational Leaders. Arkansas State University, 2006, http://www.vredestichters.nl/page6/files/artikel%20Edwin%20Friedman.pdf.

10 Saul Olshansky, "Chronic Sorrow: A Response to Having a Mentally Defective Child," *Social Casework* 43 (1962): 190–93.

11 Jean Ann Summers, Shirley K. Behr, and Ann P. Turnbull, "Positive Adaptation and Coping Strengths of Families Who Have Children with Disabilities," in *Support for Caregiving Families: Enabling Positive Adaptation to Disability*, ed. G. H. Singer and L. K. Irvin (Baltimore: Brookes, 1989), 27–40.

12 The name changed to the Association for Retarded Citizens and is now simply known as The Arc.

13 Harold Kushner, *When Bad Things Happen to Good People* (New York: Schocken Books, 1981).

14 Archibald MacLeish, *J.B.* (New York: Houghton Mifflin & Harcourt, 1958).

15 David Patterson, *Helping Your Handicapped Child* (Minneapolis: Augsburg, 1970), 41.

16 Sacks, *Great Partnership*.

17 Reinders, *Disability, Providence, and Ethics*.

18 Reinders, *Disability, Providence, and Ethics*.

19 Parent to Parent website: http://www.p2pusa.org. Most states have chapters, and there are many other national networks organized around specific disabilities.

20 Carol Levine, "The Top Ten Things Caregivers Don't Want to Hear . . . and a Few Things They Do," United Hospital Fund of New York City, 2006.

21 Emily Perl Kingsley, "Welcome to Holland," National Down Syndrome Society (1987).

22 Kathleen Bolduc, *The Spiritual Art of Raising a Child with Special Needs* (Valley Forge, Pa.: Judson, 2014). She writes from her Christian tradition, but there are also books and websites by parents and families from Jewish and Muslim traditions as well. Other authors include Amy Julia Becker, Martha Beck, Ian Brown, Rud Turnbull, and Emily Colson. Based on her experience as parent and pastor, Lorna Bradley has a new book to help clergy and congregations develop family support groups: *Special Needs Parenting: From Coping to Thriving* (Edina, Minn.: Huff, 2015).

23 One of the worst stories of "spiritual abuse" I have heard was from a father of a young man who has cerebral palsy. They had a friend or acquaintance who was convinced the son would be healed by his twenty-first birthday. That friend called the father shortly before midnight of that birthday, needed to see him, and said that he was convinced that the father or mother had done something terribly wrong and just needed to confess that before the birthday so that the healing could take place.

24 Whitt, "Place for Camille," 24–25, 27.

25 Alice Walsh, Mary Beth Walsh, and William Gaventa, *Autism and Faith: A Journey into Community* (New Brunswick, N.J.: Elizabeth M. Boggs Center, 2008).

26 Karin Melburg-Schwier and David Hingsburger, *Sexuality: Your Sons and Daughters with Developmental Disabilities* (Baltimore: Brookes, 2000).

27   Preheim-Bartel and Neufeldt, *Supportive Care in the Congregation*. Al Etman-
     ski, *A Good Life for You and Your Relative with a Disability* (Vancouver: Planned
     Lifetime Advocacy Network, 2004).

28   William Gaventa, "The Challenge and Power of Location and Role: Pastoral
     Counseling in the Lives of Children with Disabilities and Their Families,"
     Sacred Spaces (American Association of Pastoral Counselors) 6 (2014): 53–86.

29   E-mail correspondence, September 4, 2015.

30   Michelle Reynolds, *Charting a Life Course: A Framework and Strategies for Sup-
     porting Individuals with Developmental Disabilities and Their Families* (Boggs
     Center Developmental Disabilities Lecture Series, New Brunswick, N.J.,
     November 2, 2012). For information on the Life Course Tools and Commu-
     nity of Practice, go to http://mofamilytofamily.org/projects/lifecourse-tools/.

31   Missouri Family to Family, *Charting the Life Course*.

32   Individual education planning sessions, mandated in public education, involve
     teachers, other professionals as appropriate, family, and administration.

33   Duane Ruth-Heffelbower, *After We're Gone: Providing a Congregational Net-
     work of Care for Persons with Significant Disabilities; A Christian Perspective on
     Estate and Life Planning for Families That Include a Dependent Member with a
     Disability* (Harrisonburg, Va.: Menno Media, 2011).

34   See chap. 2.

35   Rud Turnbull, *The Exceptional Life of Jay Turnbull: Dignity and Disability in
     America, 1967–2009* (Amherst, Mass.: White Poppy Press, 2011).

36   Rud Turnbull and Ann Turnbull, "Group Action Planning as a Strategy for
     Providing Comprehensive Family Support" (Lawrence, Kans.: Beach Center),
     accessed September 3, 2015, https://kuscholarworks.ku.edu/handle/1808/6243.

37   Tom Hunter, "It's Awesome," on a cassette tape entitled *Connections*. Pro-
     duced in collaboration with the Beach Center on Families and Disability.
     Available from http://tomhunter.com/#Songs%20for%20grownups. Tom also
     wrote a number of other children's songs to help them understand people with
     disabilities, including "Seeing with my Ears" and "How Can I Learn to Talk
     to You If You Are So Different Than Me."

9: RESPITE CARE

 1   In professional literature, this kind of respite care is sometimes referred to as
     "secondary respite," a service or support that is not necessarily focused on respite
     care but provides that break as one component of it. For example, most families
     with children receive "secondary respite" when their children are in school. See
     Christine Salisbury and J. Intagliata, eds., *Respite Care: Support for Persons with
     Developmental Disabilities and Their Families* (Baltimore: Brookes, 1986).

 2   National Information Center for Children and Youth with Handicaps,
     "Respite Care: A Gift of Time," *NICHCY News Digest*, November 12, 1989.

 3   NICHCY, *Respite Care*, 1 (emphasis added).

 4   Salisbury and Intagliata, *Respite Care*, 201–2.

5 Shaun Heasley, "Disability Caregiving May Lead to Memory Decline in Moms," *Disability Scoop*, April 10, 2015.

6 National Alliance for Caregiving, http://www.caregiving.org.

7 NICHCY, *Respite Care*, 2 (emphasis added).

8 Shel Silverstein, *The Giving Tree* (New York: Harper & Row, 1964).

9 Bernard of Clairvaux, *The Four Loves*, modernized and abridged by Stephen Tompkins, ed. and prepared for the web by Dan Graves, Christian History Institute.

10 Levine, "Top Ten Things Caregivers Don't Want to Hear."

11 Erik Carter, "The Other Six Days" (plenary presentation at the 2014 Summer Institute on Theology and Disability, Highland Park United Methodist Church, Dallas, Tex.)

12 See the description of faith given by Paul Lehmann, p. 267.

10: INTEGRATING SPIRITUALITY IN PROFESSIONAL SERVICES AND ROLES

1 *Oxford English Dictionaries*, s.v. "professional," accessed November 24, 2016, https://en.oxforddictionaries.com/definition/professional.

2 Dictionary.com, s.v. "profession," accessed January 20, 2015, http://dictionary.reference.com/browse/profession.

3 "Origin of the Word 'Professional,'" Google Answers, accessed January 20, 2015, http://answers.google.com/answers/threadview/id/383208.html.

4 Council on Quality and Leadership, "Spirituality," accessed June 14, 2017, https://www.c-q-l.org/resource-library/publications/cql-publications-for-free/quality-in-practice-guides/spirituality.

5 See a PBS *Newshour* report about an African American family with a young adult son with autism. "Children of Color with Autism Face Disparities of Care and Isolation," *Newshour*, February 7, 2017. The report includes one story of being rejected by a church but ends with shots of the young man enthusiastically participating in another congregation that accepted him completely.

6 Joint Commission, *Advancing Effective Communication, Cultural Competence, and Patient- and Family-Centered Care: A Roadmap for Hospitals* (Oakbrook Terrace, Ill.: Joint Commission, 2010).

7 Michael Smull and Susan Burke Harrison, *Supporting People with Severe Reputations in the Community* (Alexandria, Va.: National Association of State Directors of Developmental Disabilities Services, 1992).

8 Gordon Hilsman, "Spiritual Pathways: One Response to the Current Standards Challenge," *Vision* (Newsletter of the National Association of Catholic Chaplains), June 1997, 8–9.

9 Christina Puchalski, "The FICA Spiritual History Tool," George Washington Institute for Spirituality and Health.

10 George Fitchett, *Assessing Spiritual Needs: A Guide for Caregivers* (Minneapolis: Augsburg/Fortress, 1993).

11   Judith Laundau-Stanton, Colleen Clements, Alex Tartaglia, Jackie Nudd, and Elisabeth Espaillat-Pina, "Spiritual, Cultural, and Community Systems," in *AIDS, Health and Mental Health: A Primary Sourcebook*, ed. Judith Landau-Stanton and Colleen D. Clements (New York: Bruner/Mazel, 1993), 267–98.

12   Office for People with Developmental Disabilities, "Faith Based Educational and Training Materials," accessed December 10, 2014, http://www.opwdd.ny.gov/opwdd_community_connections/faith_based_initiatives/training_material.

13   Council on Quality and Leadership, "Spirituality."

14   John Swinton and Hazel Morgan, *No Box to Tick* (London: Foundation for People with Learning Disabilities, 2004). There are multiple resources from this project, most of which can be found and downloaded from the foundation's website by typing in "Spirituality" to their search function.

15   Denise Poston and Ann Turnbull, "Role of Spirituality and Religion in Family Quality of Life for Families of Children with Disabilities," *Education and Training in Developmental Disabilities* 39, no. 2 (2004): 95–108.

16   James Thompson, "Presidential Address 2013—Race to Catch the Future," *Journal of Intellectual and Developmental Disabilities* 51, no. 6 (2014): 516 (emphasis added).

17   Daniel Hall, "Practicing Medicine Faithfully" (lecture and unpublished manuscript, Baylor University, Waco, Tex., October 10, 2014).

18   Physician Atul Gawande advocates strongly for just such an approach in *Being Mortal*.

19   Henri Nouwen, acceptance speech for the Congress on Ministries in Specialized Settings Award, 1994, accessed April 10, 2017, https://www.youtube.com/watch?v=50_jBm6r8MQ.

20   Palmer, *Courage to Teach*.

21   Mark Jones, Paul Lewis, and Kelly Reffitt, *Toward Human Flourishing: Character, Practical Wisdom and Professional Formation* (Macon, Ga.: Mercer University Press, 2013).

22   Bill Gaventa, "A Professional Self-Assessment" (unpublished; available on request).

11: SPIRITUALITY, CARE, AND COMMITMENT

1   Shapiro, *No Pity*.

2   That is an ongoing task. It was exemplified in 2015 by a coalition that led activities centering on the twenty-fifth anniversary of the Americans with Disabilities Act. See the ADA Legacy Project, http://www.adalegacy.com.

3   In my career the name has changed from the American Association on Mental Deficiency to AAMR (above) to its current name, the American Association on Intellectual and Developmental Disabilities.

4   This chapter draws on an article of mine in a journal issue focusing on direct care: "Re-kindling Commitment: Reflections from a Pastoral Educator Enmeshed in Direct Support Professional Workforce Development and

Person Centered Supports," *Journal of Intellectual Disability Research* 52, no. 7 (2008): 598–607.

5   David Schwartz, *Who Cares? Rediscovering Community* (Denver: Westview, 1996). In Illich's theory "paradoxical counter-productivity" is evident when prisons end up creating more criminals, schools make people dumber, hospitals make people sick, etc.

6   Steve Taylor, "The Paradox of Regulations: A Commentary," *Mental Retardation* 30 (1992): 185–90.

7   Sheryl Larson and Amy Hewitt, *Staff Recruitment, Retention, and Training Strategies for Community Human Services Organizations* (Baltimore: Brookes, 2005).

8   As an example, almost a decade ago the New Jersey state government passed a new law called Danielle's Law (New Jersey Office of the Public Advocate, 2007), whose impetus came from an avoidable death of a young woman in a group home, leading to a political movement by frustrated parents and friends who wanted the political system to prevent anything like that from happening again. It is not unlike several similar laws with names attached to them, which end up trying to correct instances of poor judgment with a series of regulations and procedures that simply call for compliance, with financial and disciplinary consequences if they are not followed.

9   David Maister, *True Professionalism: The Courage to Care about Your People, Your Clients, and Your Career* (New York: Touchstone, 1997); and Steven Holburn, "Rhetoric and Realities in Today's ICF/MR: Control Out of Control," *Mental Retardation* 30 (1992): 133–41.

10 William Ebenstein, "Organizational Change and the Emerging Partnership between Direct Support Workers and People with Disabilities," in *Opportunities for Excellence: Supporting the Frontline Workforce*, ed. Thomas Jasculski and W. Ebenstein (Washington, D.C.: President's Committee on Mental Retardation, Administration for Children and Families, U.S. Department of Health and Human Services, 1996), 107. Christopher Hatton, Eric Emerson, M. Rivers, H. Mason, R. Swarbrick, and L. Mason, "Factors Associated with Intended Staff Turnover and Job Search Behaviour in Services for People with Intellectual Disability," *Journal of Intellectual Disability Research* 45 (2016): 258–70; and Amy Hewitt, Sheryl Larson, Charles Lakin, John Sauer, Susan O'Nell, and Lorrie Sedlezky, "Role and Essential Competencies of the Frontline Supervisors of Direct Support Professionals in Community Services," *Mental Retardation* 42 (2004): 122–35.

11 Barbara Frank and Steve Dawson, *Issue Brief: Health Care Workforce Issues in Massachusetts*, with assistance from Andy Van Kleunen, Mary Ann Wilner, and Dorie Seavey (Boston Massachusetts Health Policy Forum, 2000).

12 Theresa Demar, presentation as part of workshop panel "Developing Effective Recruitment and Retention Strategies," Alliance for Full Participation, Washington, D.C., September 2005.

13 Kathy Walsh, associate director, Arc of Bergen County, survey response.

14 Dr. Bill Thomas, "The Green House Movement," *Newshour*, January 23, 2008.

15 My biggest problem with the word "consumer" assumes one only consumes and never gives, a label that feeds right into a public stereotype that disability is a hole into which public investment gets poured while reaping few outcomes or rewards.

16 A summary of some of the findings can be found in Armenio Rego and Miguel Pina e Cunha, "Workplace Spirituality and Organizational Commitment: An Empirical Study," *Journal of Organizational Change Management* 21, no. 1 (2008): 53–75. There is a journal focused on this area, *The Journal of Management, Spirituality, and Religion*.

17 Rego and Pina e Cunha, "Workplace Spirituality and Organizational Commitment," 71. They go on to note, seemingly without awareness of the irony, that an understanding of a firm as a "community of spirit" rather than as exclusively focused on economic and financial criteria, leads to more creative and committed employees, which then results in "higher organization competitiveness."

18 Palmer, *Courage to Teach*.

19 Parker Palmer, "A New Professional: The Aims of Education Revisited," *Change: The Magazine of Higher Learning* 39, no. 6 (2007): 6–13.

20 Wolf Wolfensberger, "The Prophetic Voice and Presence of Mentally Retarded People in the World Today," in *The Theological Voice of Wolf Wolfensberger*, ed. William Gaventa and David Coulter (Binghamton, N.Y.: Haworth, 2001), 11–48.

21 John Swinton, *Spirituality in Mental Health Care: Rediscovering a "Forgotten" Dimension* (London: Jessica Kingsley, 2001).

22 Reinders, *Future of the Disabled in Liberal Society*.

23 Examples include John O'Brien and Beth Mount, *Make a Difference: A Guidebook for Person-Centered Direct Support* (Toronto: Inclusion Press, 2001); and CDs recorded by Peter Leidy about direct care work, http://peterleidy.com (accessed June 15, 2017).

24 Nate Hajdu, "My Friend Charlie" (delivered at the Interfaith Disability presummit, Washington, D.C., September 22, 2005), used with permission.

25 John O'Brien, with staff from Creative Living Services, *"It's How You Look at Your Work That Makes the Difference": Direct Support Workers Consider the Meaning of Their Jobs* (Lithonia, Ga.: Responsive Systems Associates, 2004).

26 William Gaventa, "A Place for All of Me and All of Us: Rekindling the Spirit in Services and Supports," *Mental Retardation* 43, no. 1 (2005): 48–54.

27 Parker Palmer's model is "circles of trust" (Center for Courage & Renewal, http://www.couragerenewal.org/approach/). Others include shared written stories or "case studies," models that come out of many modes of professional training, including clinical pastoral education. Helen Sanderson Associates, "Four Plus One Questions" from ELP is another (http://www.helensanderson associates.co.uk/person-centred-practice/person-centred-thinking-tools/4 -plus-1-questions/). It does not include, and could add, a question or two about what kinds of questions or reflections an experience raised within a caregiver's own feelings, life, or values. But the focus should be on the story and

the relationship rather than a clinical analysis of the person being served or supported.

28 Ebenstein, "Organizational Change and the Emerging Partnership between Direct Support Workers and People with Disabilities," 107.

29 Bruce Anderson, *Our Door Is Open: Creating Welcoming Cultures in Helping Organizations* (Vashon, Wash.: Community Activators, 2010).

30 Bruce Anderson, *Hope at Work: Creating Positive, Resilient Organizations* (Vashon, Wash.: Community Activators, 2010).

12: GIFT AND CALL

1 This chapter is adapted by permission of Paul H. Brookes Publishing Co. Inc., from one I wrote for one of the early books on friendships and people with intellectual and developmental disabilities: Gaventa, "Gift and Call," in *Friendships and Community Connections between People with and without Developmental Disabilitie*s, ed. Angela Amado (Baltimore: Brookes, 1993), 41–66.

2 C. S. Lewis, *The Four Loves* (London: Fontana Books, 1960).

3 Hans Reinders explores the paradox of how a liberal society and its systems may proclaim the rights and dignity of all persons with intellectual and developmental disabilities but, by its own values of freedom, choice, and reason, struggle to believe that people would choose to be friends with people with intellectual and developmental disabilities who cannot embody those values in usual ways. His book *Receiving the Gift of Friendship* is a must read for people interested in the spirituality and theology of friendships and disability.

4 Zana Lutfiyya, *Reflections on Relationships between People with Disabilities and Typical People* (Syracuse, N.Y.: Syracuse University, Center on Human Policy, 1988).

5 Robert N. Bellah, Richard Madsen, William Sullivan, Ann Swidler, and Stephen M. Tipton, *Habits of the Heart: Individualism and Commitment in American Life* (New York: Harper & Row, 1985).

6 Lewis, *Four Loves*.

7 Larry Ken Graham, "Friendship," in *The Dictionary of Pastoral Care and Counseling*, ed. Rodney Hunter (Nashville: Abingdon, 1990).

8 Paul Waddell, *Friendship and the Moral Life* (Notre Dame, Ind.: University of Notre Dame Press, 1989).

9 Graham, "Friendship."

10 Bellah et al., *Habits of the Heart*, 115.

11 Gordon Meilander, *Friendship: A Study in Theological Ethics* (Notre Dame, Ind.: University of Notre Dame Press, 1979).

12 Bellah et al., *Habits of the Heart*, 118–35.

13 Lewis, *Four Loves*, 61.

14 This is one of the core dimensions of a Christian theology of friendship as explored in Hans Reinders' book *Receiving the Gift of Friendship*. He is using stories of the lives of people with profound intellectual and developmental disabilities to argue that only through friendship, freely given to others without expectation of response or reward, can we understand the motivation that

compels and draws many to deep relationships with people with profound disabilities. In classic, liberal terms, friendship is reciprocity, but how is there reciprocity if one cannot know that another responds? Nor is God's friendship and love of us, he argues, dependent on our reason and will (capacity to respond) but is a free gift, which calls us simply to learn how to receive.

15 Nor can I adequately turn to deep understandings of connection, relationship, and friendship that exist in other religious and cultural traditions, e.g., the African understanding of Ubuntu or Native American spirituality.

16 Deut 6:5; Lev 19:18; Matt 22:37-40; Luke 10:27.

17 John Landgraf, "Love and Friendship," *Minister's Magazine* 10, no. 1 (1989): 3–9 (3).

18 1 John 4:11, 20.

19 For examples: Job complains bitterly to friends that they have vanished, scorned him, failed him, or, like God, pursued him. In times of trouble, writes a psalmist, "My friends and companions stand aloof from my plague, and my kinsmen stand afar off" (Ps 38:11 RSV). Friends can be too quickly tied to wealth (Prov 19:6-7), and the wrong friends (such as friendship with an "angry man") can lead you astray (Prov 22:24). They can too quickly deceive (Jer 38:22). But, as the writer of Proverbs says, "There are friends who pretend to be friends, but there is a friend who sticks closer than a brother" (18:24 RSV). Thus is a faithful friend a sure shelter. "Your friend, and your father's friend, do not forsake, and do not go to your brother's house in the day of your calamity. Better is a neighbor who is near than a brother who is far away" (Prov 27:10). Jesus' disciples, whom he has called friends rather than servants, desert him when the going gets tough (Mark 14:66-72; Luke 24:52-64; John 18:15-27).

20 For examples: "Didst thou not, O God, drive the inhabitants out, and give it forever to the descendants of Abraham thy friend" (2 Chr 20:6 RSV). "Israel, Jacob, the offspring of Abraham my friend, you whom I took from ends of the earth, saying, 'You are my servant, I have chosen you and will not cast you off. Fear not, for I am with you, be not dismayed, I am your God. I will strengthen you, I will uphold you'" (Isa 41:8-10 RSV; cited also in the New Testament, in Jas 2:23 RSV, "Abraham, called the friend of God"). Thus the Lord used to speak to Moses, face to face, as a man speaks to his friend (Exod 33:11):

> "This is my commandment, that you love one another as I have loved you. Greater love has no man than this, that a man lay down his life for his friends. You are my friends if you do what I command you. No longer do I call you servants, for the servant does not know what his master is doing; but I have called you friends, for all that I have heard from my Father I have made known to you. You did not choose me, but I chose you and appointed you so that you should be go and bear fruit and that your fruit should abide; so whatever you ask the Father in my name, he may give it to you. This I command you, to love one another" (John 15:12-17 RSV).

21 See https://www.haaretz.com/news/speeches-by-jimmy-carter-menachem -begin-anwar-sadat-at-the-white-house-after-the-signing-of-the-camp -david-accords-1.45205.

22 Meilander, *Friendship*; Alistair Campbell, *Professionalism and Pastoral Care* (Philadelphia: Fortress, 1985).

23 Amado, *Friends*.

24 Bellah et al., *Habits of the Heart*.

25 Robert Perske, *Circle of Friends* (Nashville: Abingdon, 1988); John O'Brien and Connie Lyle O'Brien, "Members of Each Other: Perspectives on Social Supports for People with Severe Disabilities," in *Natural Supports in School, at Work, and in the Community for People with Severe Disabilities*, ed. J. Nesbit (Baltimore: Brooks Publishing, 1992), 17–64; and Amado, *Friendships and Community Connections between People with and without Developmental Disabilities*.

26 John McKnight, *Regenerating Community: The Recovery of a Space for Citizens* (Evanston, Ill.: Northwestern University Center for Urban Affairs and Policy Research, 1993). Mary O'Connell, *The Gift of Hospitality: Opening the Doors to Community Life to People with Disabilities* (Evanston, Ill.: Northwestern University Center for Urban Affairs and Policy Research, 1988). In addition, see any of the writings of Jean Vanier, including *Community and Growth*.

27 Palmer, *To Know as We Are Known*.

28 Bellah et al, *Habits of the Heart*.

29 Alistair Campbell, *Professional Care: Its Meaning and Practice* (Philadelphia: Fortress, 1984).

30 Reinders, *Receiving the Gift of Friendship*.

31 O'Brien and O'Brien, "Members of Each Other."

32 The apostle Paul, talking about growth in a community of faith (1 Cor 3:6-7).

33 Palmer, *To Know as We Are Known*.

34 Landgraf, "Love and Friendship."

35 See the discussion in the earlier chapter on community building but also see the strategies recommended in Amado's online *Friends*. Her exploration of ways to help people with challenging behaviors in the development of relationships is particularly intriguing.

36 Davy Falkner, "Special Needs, Euphemisms, and Disability," SpringerOpen Blog, January 17, 2017.

37 Vanier, *Community and Growth*; and Wolf Wolfensberger, "Common Assets of Mentally Retarded People That Are Commonly Not Acknowledged," *Mental Retardation* 26, no. 2 (1988): 63–70.

13: RELATIONSHIPS ARE NOT EASY

1 Here, I am thinking of patron saints whose fame first arose because they reached out to people with one form of illness or another, such as St. Dymphna, whose stories led to the establishment of the remarkable town of Geel, in

which people and pilgrims with mental illness were cared for in the homes of that community.

"The ability to cure sick and tortured souls was increasingly brought about by the intercession of saints and martyrs, whose relics were believed to have miraculous power to heal the sick, reanimate the halt and the lame, and restore sight to the blind. The tombs of saints like St. Margaret of Antioch and St. Dymphna of Geel, who had both been beheaded, were popular choices for those seeking relief from mental distress, as was the shrine of St. Thomas à Becket, whose murder in Canterbury Cathedral is here shown in a mid-thirteenth-century codex. The saint's blood was thought to cure insanity, blindness, leprosy, and deafness, not to mention a host of other ailments." (Andrew Scull, "Madness and Meaning: Depictions of Insanity through History," *Paris Review*, April 22, 2015).

Or certainly the example of Jesus, who "came near," "sat with," "touched," "ate with," "stopped for," "talked with," and cared for many of those ostracized by their illness and behavior, assumed to be caused by sin. I am not referring to the many who have claimed to be (and promoted themselves as) "faith healers." There are far too many stories by people with disabilities of one kind or another for whom their experience with "faith healers" has been a form of public abuse and shaming by a supposed lack of faith or sin, thus magnifying the blame already existent.

2   Deborah Schadler and Catherine Heller, "Labels Are for Soup Cans" (PowerPoint presentation, Peaceful Living Conference, Souderton, Penn., September 16, 2014).

3   Smull and Harrison, *Supporting People with Severe Reputations in the Community*.

4   Chimamanda Adichie, "The Danger of a Single Story," TED Talk, July 2009.

5   I am writing this during the days of the riots in Baltimore following the death of another person in police custody. One of the posts about these events cites an *Atlantic* monthly article by Ta-Naehisi Coates, "Nonviolence as Compliance," April 27, 2015.

6   David Pitonyak, *10 Things You Can Do to Support a Person with Difficult Behavior*, November 20, 1993.

7   Sharon Lohrmann and Fredda Brown, *Working Together: A Guide to Positive Behavior Support for Families and Professionals* (Baltimore: TASH, 2005).

8   This section is heavily based on the first two chapters of Wayne Sailor, Glen Dunlap, George Sugai, and Rob Horner, eds., *A Handbook of Positive Behavior Supports* (New York: Springer, 2009). Much of this history also occurs during my own professional career in which I clearly remember some of the ways the evolution of these theories was lived out in practice.

9   George Singer and Mian Wang, "The Intellectual Roots of Positive Behavior Support and Their Implications for Its Development," in *A Handbook of Positive Behavior Supports*, ed. Wayne Sailor, Glen Dunlap, George Sugai, and Rob Horner (New York: Springer, 2009), 22.

10 Singer and Wang, "Intellectual Roots of Positive Behavior Support and Their Implications for Its Development," 21.

11 Because of their assumed lack of reason and their lack of capacity for choice and will.

12 Singer and Wang, "Intellectual Roots of Positive Behavior Support and Their Implications for Its Development," 28.

13 Glen Dunlap, Donald Kincaid, and Donald Jackson, "Positive Behavior Support: Foundations, Systems, and Quality of Life," in *The Oxford Handbook of Positive Psychology and Disability*, ed. Michael Wehmeyer (New York: Oxford University Press, 2013), 303–16; and the New Jersey Positive Behavior Supports in Schools Project, http://www.njpbs.org.

14 Singer and Wang, "Intellectual Roots of Positive Behavior Support and Their Implications for Its Development," 37–38.

15 See "Judge Rotenberg Center Survivor's Letter," January 15, 2013; and Amy Burkholder, "Controversy over Shocking People with Autism, Behavioral Disorders," *CBS News*, August 5, 2014. Both accessed September 7, 2015.

16 Pitonyak, *10 Things You Can Do to Support a Person with Difficult Behavior*.

17 *Positive Behavior Support Guidelines*, rev. ed. (Jefferson City: Missouri Division of Mental Retardation and Developmental Disabilities, 2008), 61.

18 Barbara Newman, *Accessible Gospel, Inclusive Worship* (Wyoming, Mich.: CLC Network, 2014). This is the most recent publication of an impressive group of publications and other resources available from the CLC Network, including *Autism and Your Church, Helping Kids Include Kids with Disabilities*, and more. For a listing, go to www.clcnetwork.org.

19 PRAISE Program and related resources, Archdiocese of Newark, http://rcan.org/offices-and-ministries/ministry-disabilities/catechetics.

20 Emily Colson and Charles Colson, *Dancing with Max: A Mother and Son Who Broke Free* (Grand Rapids: Zondervan, 2010).

21 Singer and Wang, "Intellectual Roots of Positive Behavior Support and Their Implications for Its Development," 24.

14: SPIRITUALITY, DIVERSITY, AND COMMUNITY

1 This chapter is based extensively on two of my previous publications: William Gaventa, "Creating and Energizing Caring Communities," in *Caregiving and Loss: Family Needs, Professional Responses*, ed. Ken Doka (Washington, D.C.: Hospice Foundation of America, 2001), 57–77; and William Gaventa, "Lessons in Community Building from Including the 'Other': Caring for One An-Other," *Journal of Religion, Disability, and Health* 16, no. 4 (2012): 231–47.

2 Lynne Seagle, "Hope House," TED Talk (2014).

3 John O'Brien and Connie Lyle O'Brien, *Members of Each Other: Building Community in Company with People with Developmental Disabilities* (Toronto: Inclusion Press, 1997).

4 Palmer, *To Know as We are Known*, 124.

5   Jane Harlan, Jennie Todd, and Peggy Holtz, *A Guide to Building Community Membership for Older Adults with Disabilities* (Bloomington, Ind.: Indiana Institute on Disability and Community, 1998).

6   Gary Bauslaugh, *Robert Latimer, a Story of Justice and Mercy* (Toronto: James Lorimer, 2010).

7   Parker J. Palmer, *Healing the Heart of Democracy: The Courage to Create a Politics Worthy of the Human Spirit* (San Francisco: Jossey-Bass, 2011). Also see the Center for Courage and Renewal, founded on the principles of this book, http://www.couragerenewal.org/democracy/.

8   William C. Gaventa, "Re-Imaging the Role of Clinical Training for Hospital Chaplaincy and Pastoral Care: Moving beyond the Institutional Walls to the Community," *Journal of Religion in Disability and Rehabilitation* 2, no. 4 (1996): 27–41.

9   Schwartz, *Who Cares?*

10 John McKnight, "Regenerating Community," *Social Policy*, Winter 1987, 54–58.

11 For examples, see http://www.inclusion.com/path.html for resources, such as John O'Brien and Jack Pearpoint, *Person-Centered Planning with MAPS and PATH: A Workbook for Facilitators* (Toronto: Inclusion Press, 2003). Mary Falvey, Marcia Forest, Jack Pearpoint, and Richard Rosenberg, *All My Life's a Circle: Using the Tools—Circles, MAPS and PATH*, new expanded ed. (Toronto: Inclusion Press, 1997).

12 John Kretzmann and John McKnight, *Building Communities from the Inside Out: A Path Toward Finding and Mobilizing a Community's Assets* (Evanston, Ill.: ACTA, Northwestern University, 1993).

13 Bill Moyers. "On Our Own Terms: Moyers on Dying in America." 4 part, 6 hour series, 2000.

13 Gaventa, "Lessons in Community Building from Including the 'Other,'" 231–47.

14 Schwartz, *Who Cares?*

15 Jack Pearpoint, *From Behind the Piano: Building Judith Snow's Unique Circle of Friends* (Toronto: Inclusion Press, 1990).

16 Palmer, *Active Life.*

17 Antoine de Saint-Exupery, *The Little Prince* (New York: Reynall & Hitchcock, 1943).

18 Cf. Bill Gaventa, "Communities of Celebration that Reawaken Desire," *Journal of Disability and Religion* 19 (2015): 97–105.

19 The Asset Based Community Development Institute, and its publications, through ACTA Publications, 4848 North Clark St., Chicago, Illinois 60540, (800) 397–2282. The key book is Kretzmann and McKnight, *Building Communities from the Inside Out.*

20 Nancy Eiesland, "Liberation, Inclusion, and Justice: A Faith Response to Persons with Disabilities," *Impact* 14, no. 3 (2001–2002): 2–3, 35.

21 John McKnight, *The Careless Society: Community and Its Counterfeits* (New York: Basic Books, 1995).

22 John Howard Griffin and Thomas Merton, *A Hidden Wholeness: The Visual World of Thomas Merton* (New York: Houghton Mifflin, 1979).

23 Bill Gaventa, "The Journey toward Cultural Competence," New Jersey Statewide Network for Cultural Competence conference, October 19, 2012.

24 Lesslie Newbigin, "Not Whole without the Handicapped," in *Partners in Life: The Handicapped and the Church*, ed. Geiko Muller-Fahrenholz (Geneva: World Council of Churches Publications, 1979), 17–25.

CONCLUSION: RESTORING WHOLENESS

1 I am grateful to Parker Palmer for my first hearing of the use of the words "re-membering" and "dis-membering" in his 1986 keynote at the Merging Two Worlds conference in Rochester, N.Y.

2 Atul Gawande, "Oliver Sacks: Postscript," *New Yorker Magazine*, September 7, 2015.

3 Palmer, "Merging Two Worlds."

4 O'Brien and O'Brien, *Members of Each Other*.

5 Richard Kearney and Kascha Semonovitch, eds., *Phenomenologies of the Stranger: Between Hostility and Hospitality* (New York: Fordham University Press, 2011).

6 Two other books that are not about disability per se but deal with issues that are very real in the world of disability have been cited in previous chapters: Chambers, *Whose Reality Counts?*; and Miroslav Volf, *Exclusion and Embrace: A Theological Exploration of Identity, Otherness, and Reconciliation* (Nashville: Abingdon, 1996).

7 See the work of M. Miles, for example, a two-issue collection of some of his papers, "Disability in Asian Cultures and Beliefs: History and Service Development—Some Collected Papers," *Journal of Religion, Disability and Health* 6, nos. 2–3 (2002). One of the gifts of his research has been to illumine the long history of discourse related to disability in traditions such as Buddhism, Hinduism, and Islam, a corrective to the far too quick Western assumption that there do not seem to be as many contemporary writers and thinkers in this area as there are in Judeo-Christian circles. Miles has other annotated historical resource collections online; e.g., Disability and Deafness, in the context of Religion, Spirituality, Belief and Morality, in Middle Eastern, South Asian and East Asian Histories and Cultures: Annotated Bibliography. https://www.independentliving.org/docs7/miles200707.html.

8 I will not try to include a comprehensive listing of this literature because it would be out of date by the time this manuscript is published. I invite readers to explore the website of the national Collaborative on Faith and Disabilities, www.faithanddisability.org, which also houses the audio- and videotapes from the Summer Institute on Theology and Disability. A second research strategy is simply to put your preferred words related to theology, ministry, disability, spirituality, religious education, Bible, Judaism, Islam, etc., in a Google, Amazon, or Barnes and Noble search.

9   William Gaventa, "Signs of the Times: Theological Themes in the Changing Forms of Ministries and Spiritual Supports with People with Disabilities," *Disability Studies Quarterly* 26, no. 4 (2006).

10   Hastings, "Thousand Tongues to Sing.

11   Jason Kingsley and Michael Levitz, *Count Us In: Growing Up with Down Syndrome* (New York: Harcourt, 1994).

12   Matt 18:12-14 and Luke 15:3-7 NIV.

13   Tom Hunter, "It's Awesome." The album was developed in partnership with the Beach Center for people with disabilities and their families in Lawrence, Kansas, after Tom spent some time with them listening to family stories.

14   Kretzmann and McKnight, *Building Communities from the Inside Out.*

15   Mark 12:41-44 and Luke 21:1-4.

16   Amos Yong, *Theology and Down Syndrome: Reimagining Disability in Late Modernity* (Waco, Tex.: Baylor University Press, 2007).

17   W. H. Auden, *For the Time Being* (Princeton, N.J.: Princeton University Press, 1944).

Bibliography

Adichie, Chimamanda. "The Danger of a Single Story." TED Talk. July 2009. Accessed March 15, 2015. http://www.ted.com/talks/chimamanda _adichie_the_danger_of_a_single_story/transcript?language=en.

Amado, Angela. *Friends: Connecting People with Disabilities and Community Members*. Minneapolis: University of Minnesota, Institute on Community Integration, Research and Training Center on Community Living, 2013. Accessed September 2, 2015. http://rtc.umn.edu/ docs/Friends_Connecting_people_with_disabilities_and_community _members.pdf.

———, ed. *Friendships and Community Connections between People with and without Developmental Disabilities*. Baltimore: Brookes, 1993.

American Association of Medical Colleges. *Contemporary Issues in Medicine: Communication in Medicine*. 1999. Accessed December 10, 2014. https:// www.aamc.org/initiatives/msop/.

Anderson, Bruce. *Hope at Work: Creating Positive, Resilient Organizations*. Vashon, Wash.: Community Activators, 2008. CD. Accessed June 17, 2017. http://www.communityactivators.com/home/hope-at-work/.

———. *Our Door Is Open: Creating Welcoming Cultures in Helping Organizations*. Vashon, Wash.: Community Activators, 2010. CD. Accessed June 17, 2017. http://www.communityactivators.com/home/our-door/.

Annandale, Naomi H., and Eric W. Carter. "Disability and Theological Education: A North American Study." *Theological Education* 48, no. 2 (2014): 83–102.

315

Auden, W. H. *For the Time Being*. Princeton, N.J.: Princeton University Press, 1944.

Bauslaugh, Gary. *Robert Latimer, a Story of Justice and Mercy*. Toronto: James Lorimer, 2010.

Becker, Amy Julia. *A Good and Perfect Gift: Faith, Expectations, and a Little Girl Named Penny*. Bloomington, Minn.: Bethany Press, 2011.

Bellah, Robert, Richard Madsen, William Sullivan, Ann Swidler, and Stephen M. Tipton. *Habits of the Heart: Individualism and Commitment in American Life*. New York: Harper & Row, 1985.

Belser, Julia Watts. *Guide to Jewish Values and Disability Rights*. New York: Jewish Funders, 2016.

Bernard of Clairvaux. *The Four Loves*. Modernized and abridged by Stephen Tompkins, edited and prepared for the web by Dan Graves. *Christian History Institute*. Accessed June 15, 2017. https://www.christianhistory institute.org/study/module/bernard/.

Best Boy. Directed by Ira Wohl. Los Angeles: Only Child Motion Pictures, 1979.

Best Man: "Best Boy" and All of Us, Twenty Years Later. Directed by Ira Wohl. Los Angeles: Only Child Motion Pictures, 1997.

Blatt, Burton, and Fred Kaplan. *Christmas in Purgatory: A Photographic Essay on Mental Retardation*. Syracuse, N.Y.: Human Policy, 1974.

Bogdan, Robert, Martin Elks, and James Knoll. *Picturing Disability: Beggar, Freak, Citizen, and Other Photographic Rhetoric*. Syracuse, N.Y.: Syracuse University Press, 2012.

Bolduc, Kathleen. *Autism and Alleluias*. Valley Forge, Pa.: Judson, 2010.

———. *The Spiritual Art of Raising a Child with Special Needs*. Valley Forge, Pa.: Judson, 2014.

Braddock, David, and Susan Parish. "An Institutional History of Disability." In *Handbook of Disability Studies*, edited by Gary Albrecht, K. Seelman, and M. Bury, 11–68. New York: Sage, 2001.

Bradley, Lorna. *Special Needs Parenting: From Coping to Thriving*. Edina, Minn.: Huff, 2015.

Buechner, Frederick. *Wishful Thinking: A Theological ABC*. New York: Harper & Row, 1973.

Buntinx, Wil. "Understanding Disability: A Strengths-Based Approach." In *The Oxford Handbook of Positive Psychology and Disability*, edited by Michael Wehmeyer, 7–18. New York: Oxford University Press, 2013.

Burkholder, Amy. "Controversy Over Shocking People with Autism, Behavioral Disorders." *CBS News*, August 5, 2014. Accessed September 7, 2015. http://www.cbsnews.com/news/controversy-over -shocking-people-with-autism-behavioral-disorders/.

California Coalition for Compassionate Care. *Thinking Ahead: My Life at the End*. Sacramento: California Coalition for Compassionate Care, 2007. Accessed June 15, 2017. http://coalitionccc.org/tools-resources/people-with-developmental-disabilities/.

Campbell, Alistair. *Professional Care: Its Meaning and Practice*. Philadelphia: Fortress, 1984.

———. *Professionalism and Pastoral Care*. Philadelphia: Fortress, 1985.

Campbell, Fiona. *Contours of Ableism: Production of Disability and Abledness*. London: Palgrave Macmillan, 2009.

Carter, Erik. "The Other Six Days." Plenary presentation at the 2014 Summer Institute on Theology and Disability, Highland Park United Methodist Church, Dallas, Tex. Accessed June 16, 2017. http://faithanddisability .org/2014-summer-institute/.

Carter, Erik, and William Gaventa, eds. "Spirituality: From Rights to Relationships." Special issue, *Connections* 38, no. 1 (2012).

Carter, Erik, Thomas Boehm, Naomi Annandale, and Courtney Taylor. "Supporting Congregational Inclusion for Children and Youth with Disabilities and Their Families." *Exceptional Children* 82, no. 3 (2016): 372–89.

Chambers, Robert. *Whose Reality Counts? Putting the First Last*. London: Intermediate Technology, 1997.

"Children of Color with Autism Face Disparities of Care and Isolation." *Newshour*, February 7, 2017. Accessed February 10, 2017. http://www.pbs .org/newshour/bb/children-color-autism-face-disparities-care-isolation/.

Coates, Ta-Nehisi. "Nonviolence as Compliance." *Atlantic*, April 27, 2015.

Collaborative on Faith and Disability. *Honoring Spiritual Needs and Gifts: From Inertia to Collaborative Action by Providers and Congregations*. Webinar series, 2015. Archived at http://faithanddisability .org/webinar/.

Colson, Emily, and Charles Colson. *Dancing with Max: A Mother and Son Who Broke Free*. Grand Rapids: Zondervan, 2010.

Council on Quality and Leadership. "Spirituality." Accessed June 17, 2017. https:// www.c-q-l.org/resource-library/publications/cql-publications-for-free/ quality-in-practice-guides/spirituality.

Davis, Charles. "Youth with Disabilities Talk about Their Spirituality and Their Transition to Independence." Unpublished article about a panel at the Treat Me as a Member, Not a Mission conference, Portland, Ore., May 15, 2014.

Davis, Lennard. *Enforcing Normalcy: Disability, Deafness and the Body*. London: Verso, 1995.

Demar, Theresa. Presentation as part of workshop panel "Developing Effective Recruitment and Retention Strategies." Alliance for Full Participation, Washington, D.C., September 2005.

de Vinck, Christopher. *The Power of the Powerless: A Brother's Legacy of Love.* New York: Crossroad, 2002.

Doka, Ken. "Struggling with Grief and Loss." In *End of Life Care for Children and Adults with Intellectual and Developmental Disabilities*, edited by Sandra Friedman and David Helm, 261–71. Washington, D.C.: American Association on Intellectual and Developmental Disabilities, 2010.

Dunlap, Glen, Donald Kincaid, and Donald Jackson. "Positive Behavior Support: Foundations, Systems, and Quality of Life." In *The Oxford Handbook of Positive Psychology and Disability*, edited by Michael Wehmeyer, 303–16. New York: Oxford University Press, 2013.

Ebenstein, William. "Organizational Change and the Emerging Partnership between Direct Support Workers and People with Disabilities." In *Opportunities for Excellence: Supporting the Frontline Workforce*, edited by Thomas Jasculski and W. Ebenstein, 107. Washington, D.C.: President's Committee on Mental Retardation, Administration for Children and Families, U.S. Department of Health and Human Services, 1996.

Eiesland, Nancy. "Liberation, Inclusion, and Justice: A Faith Response to Persons with Disabilities." *Impact* 14, no. 3 (2001–2002): 2–3, 35. Accessed June 13, 2017. https://ici.umn.edu/products/impact/143/.

Etmanski, Al. *A Good Life for You and Your Relative with a Disability.* Vancouver: Planned Lifetime Advocacy Network, 2004.

Falkner, Davy. "Special Needs, Euphemisms, and Disability." SpringerOpen Blog, January 17, 2017. Accessed February 21, 2017. http://blogs.springer open.com/springeropen/2017/01/17/special-needs-euphemisms -disability/.

Falvey, Mary, Marcia Forest, Jack Pearpoint, and Richard Rosenberg. *All My Life's a Circle: Using the Tools—Circles, MAPS and PATH.* New expanded ed. Toronto: Inclusion Press, 1997.

Ferguson, Philip. "The Development of Systems of Supports: Intellectual Disability in Middle Modern Times (1800–1899)." In *The Story of Intellectual Disability: An Evolution of Meaning, Understanding, and Public Perception*, edited by Michael Wehmeyer, 79–115. Baltimore: Brookes, 2013.

Fitchett, George. "The 7×7 Model for Spiritual Assessment." *Vision* 6, no. 3 (1996): 10–11.

Forsberg, Rolf. *Mother Tiger, Mother Tiger.* Directed by Rolf Forsberg. Los Angeles: Franciscan Communications, 1974.

Fowler, James. *Stages of Faith: The Psychology of Human Development and the Quest for Meaning.* New York: HarperCollins, 1981.

Frank, Arthur. *At the Will of the Body.* New York: Houghton Mifflin, 1992.

———. *The Wounded Storyteller: Body, Illness, and Ethics.* Chicago: University of Chicago Press, 1995.

Frank, Barbara, and Steve Dawson. *Issue Brief: Health Care Workforce Issues in Massachusetts.* With assistance from Andy Van Kleunen, Mary Ann Wilner, and Dorie Seavey. Boston: Massachusetts Health Policy Forum, 2000. Accessed June 15, 2017. https://phinational.org/sites/default/files/clearinghouse/frank00-MAworkforce.pdf.

Gangemi, Cristina, Matteo Tobanelli, Giada Vincenzi, and John Swinton. *Everybody Has a Story: Enabling Communities to Meet People with Intellectual Disabilities and Respond Effectively to Their Expressed Spiritual and Religious Needs and Hopes; A Participatory Action Research Approach.* University of Aberdeen: Kairos Forum. Accessed March 5, 2015.

Gaventa, William. "The Challenge and Power of Location and Role: Pastoral Counseling in the Lives of Children with Disabilities and Their Families." *Sacred Spaces* (American Association of Pastoral Counselors) 6 (2014): 53–86. Accessed June 16, 2017. https://c.ymcdn.com/sites/aapc.site-ym.com/resource/resmgr/files/SacredSpaces/Vol._6.SacredSpaces.2014.Chi.pdf.

———. "Creating and Energizing Caring Communities." In *Caregiving and Loss: Family Needs, Professional Responses*, edited by Ken Doka, 57–77. Washington, D.C.: Hospice Foundation of America, 2001.

———. "Defining and Assessing Spirituality and Spiritual Supports: Moving from Benediction to Invocation." In *What Is Mental Retardation: Ideas for an Evolving Disability in the 21st Century*, edited by Harvey Switzky and Steven Greenspan, 151–66. Washington, D.C.: American Association on Intellectual and Developmental Disabilities, 2006.

———. "Forgiveness, Gratitude and Spirituality." In *The Oxford Handbook of Positive Psychology and Disability*, edited by Michael Wehmeyer, 226–38. New York: Oxford University Press, 2013.

———. "Gift and Call." In *Friendships and Community Connections between People with and without Developmental Disabilities.* Edited by Angela Amado, 41–66. Baltimore: Brookes, 1993.

———. "The Journey toward Cultural Competence." New Jersey State-wide Network for Cultural Competence conference, October 19, 2012. http://www.nj.gov/njsncc/documents/conf/journey_toward_cultural_competence.pdf.

————. "Lessons in Community Building from Including the 'Other': Caring for One An-Other." *Journal of Religion, Disability, and Health* 16, no. 4 (2012): 231–47.

————. "A Place for All of Me and All of Us: Rekindling the Spirit in Services and Supports." *Mental Retardation* 43, no. 1 (2005): 48–54.

————. "Re-imaging the Role of Clinical Training for Hospital Chaplaincy and Pastoral Care: Moving beyond the Institutional Walls to the Community." *Journal of Religion in Disability and Rehabilitation* 2, no. 4 (1996): 27–41.

————. "Re-kindling Commitment: Reflections from a Pastoral Educator Enmeshed in Direct Support Professional Workforce Development and Person Centered Supports." *Journal of Intellectual Disability Research* 52, no. 7 (2008): 598–607.

————. "Religious Ministries and Services with Adults with Developmental Disabilities." In *The Right to Grow Up: An Introduction to Adults with Developmental Disabilities*, edited by Jean Summers, 191–226. Baltimore: Brookes, 1986.

————. "A Rosh Hashanah Birthday." *American Baptist Magazine* 179, no. 4 (1981): 14–16.

————. "Signs of the Times: Theological Themes in the Changing Forms of Ministries and Spiritual Supports with People with Disabilities." *Disability Studies Quarterly* 26, no. 4 (2006). Accessed June 16, 2017. http://dsq-sds.org/article/view/815/990.

————. "Spirituality and Faith: Beyond Beliefs to Practice." In *Supporting People with Intellectual Disabilities Experiencing Loss and Bereavement: Theory and Compassionate Practice*, edited by Sue Read, 71–82. London: Jessica Kingsley, 2014.

————. "Spirituality Issues and Strategies: Crisis and Opportunity." In *End of Life Care for Children and Adults with Intellectual and Developmental Disabilities*, edited by Sandra Friedman and David Helm, 245–60. Washington, D.C.: American Association on Intellectual and Developmental Disabilities, 2010.

Gaventa, William, and Roger Peters. "Spirituality and Self-Actualization: Recognizing Spiritual Needs and Strengths of Individuals with Cognitive Limitations." In *The Forgotten Generation: The Status and Challenges of Adults with Mild Cognitive Limitations*, edited by Alexander Tymchuk, Charlie Lakin, and Ruth Luckasson, 299–320. Baltimore: Brookes, 2001.

Gaventa, William, Wesley Allen, Harold Kleinert, and Erik W. Carter. *Putting Faith to Work: The Call and Opportunity for Faith Communities to Transform the Lives of People with Disabilities and Their Communities.*

Nashville: Vanderbilt Kennedy Center, 2014. Accessed June 17, 2017. http://faithanddisability.org/wp-content/uploads/2015/12/Putting-Faith-to-Work-White-Paper-07-14-2014.pdf.

Gawande, Atul. *Being Mortal: Medicine and What Matters in the End.* New York: Metropolitan Books, 2014.

————. "Oliver Sacks: Postscript." *New Yorker Magazine*, September 7, 2015. Accessed June 17, 2017. http://www.newyorker.com/magazine/2015/09/14/oliver-sacks.

Geertz, Clifford. "Thick Description: Toward an Interpretive Theory of Culture." Pages 3–30 in *The Interpretation of Cultures: Selected Essays.* New York: Basic Books, 1973.

Gomez, Wilfredo. "When Strangers Read My Body: Blurred Boundaries and the Search for Something Spiritual." *Tikkun* 29, no. 4 (2014): 41–42, 68–69.

Goodey, Christopher. *A History of Intelligence and "Intellectual Disability": The Shaping of Psychology in Early Modern Europe.* Burlington, Vt.: Ashgate, 2011.

Graham, Larry Ken. "Friendship." In *The Dictionary of Pastoral Care and Counseling*, edited by Rodney Hunter. Nashville: Abingdon, 1990.

Graham, Loren. "The Power of Names in Culture and Mathematics." *Proceedings of the American Philosophical Society* 157, no. 2 (2013): 229–34.

Griffin, John Howard, and Thomas Merton. *A Hidden Wholeness: The Visual World of Thomas Merton.* New York: Houghton Mifflin, 1979.

Gurbai, Sandor. "Promoting Inclusion of Adults with Disabilities under Guardianship by Strengthening Solidarity based on Theology and Human Rights." *Journal of Disability and Religion* 18 (2014): 227–41.

Hahn, Harlan. "Civil Rights FOR Disabled Americans: The Foundation of a Political Agenda." Independent Living Institute, Sweden, 1987. www.independentliving.org/docs4/hahn.html.

Hajdu, Nate. "My Friend Charlie." Delivered at the Interfaith Disability presummit, Washington, D.C., September 22, 2005.

Hall, Daniel. "Practicing Medicine Faithfully." Lecture and unpublished manuscript, Baylor University, Waco, Tex., October 10, 2014.

Harlan, Jane, Jennie Todd, and Peggy Holtz. *A Guide to Building Community Membership for Older Adults with Disabilities.* Bloomington, Ind.: Indiana Institute on Disability and Community, 1998.

Hastings, Elizabeth. "A Thousand Tongues to Sing: Difference and Belonging." Unpublished address given to the Synod of New South Wales, Uniting Church in Australia, September 24, 1995.

Hatton, Christopher, Eric Emerson, M. Rivers, H. Mason, R. Swarbrick, and L. Mason. "Factors Associated with Intended Staff Turnover and

Job Search Behaviour in Services for People with Intellectual Disability." *Journal of Intellectual Disability Research* 45 (2016): 258–70.

Heasley, Shaun. "Disability Caregiving May Lead to Memory Decline in Moms." Disability Scoop, April 10, 2015. Accessed April 10, 2015. http://www.disabilityscoop.com/emailers/ds150410.html.

Heifetz, Louis. "Integrating Religious and Secular Perspectives in the Design and Delivery of Disability Services." *Mental Retardation* 25, no. 3 (1987): 127–31.

Hewitt, Amy, Sheryl Larson, Charles Lakin, John Sauer, Susan O'Nell, and Lorrie Sedlezky. "Role and Essential Competencies of the Frontline Supervisors of Direct Support Professionals in Community Services." *Mental Retardation* 42 (2004): 122–35.

Hilsman, Gordon. "Spiritual Pathways: One Response to the Current Standards Challenge." *Vision* (Newsletter of the National Association of Catholic Chaplains), June 1997, 8–9.

Holburn, Steven. "Rhetoric and Realities in Today's ICF/MR: Control Out of Control." *Mental Retardation* 30 (1992): 133–41.

Hollins, Sheila, and Noel Blackman. *When Somebody Dies.* London: Books Beyond Words, 2003.

Hudson, Geoffrey. "History of Disability: Early Modern West." In *Encyclopedia of Disability*, edited by Gary Albrecht et al., 2:55–58. New York: Sage, 2006.

Joint Commission. *Advancing Effective Communication, Cultural Competence, and Patient- and Family-Centered Care: A Roadmap for Hospitals.* Oakbrook Terrace, Ill.: Joint Commission, 2010. Accessed June 17, 2017. http://www.jointcommission.org/assets/1/6/ARoadmapfor Hospitalsfinalversion727.pdf.

Jones, Mark, Paul Lewis, and Kelly Reffitt. *Toward Human Flourishing: Character, Practical Wisdom and Professional Formation.* Macon, Ga.: Mercer University Press, 2013.

"Judge Rotenberg Center Survivor's Letter." January 15, 2013. Accessed September 7, 2015. http://www.autistichoya.com/2013/01/judge -rotenberg-center-survivors-letter.html.

Kauffman, Jeff. *Guidebook on Helping Persons with Mental Retardation Mourn.* Amityville, N.Y.: Baywood, 2005.

Kearney, Richard, and Kascha Semonovitch, eds. *Phenomenologies of the Stranger: Between Hostility and Hospitality.* New York: Fordham University Press, 2011.

Kingsbury, Leigh Ann. *People Planning: Communicating Healthcare and End of Life Wishes.* Washington, D.C.: American Association on Intellectual and Developmental Disabilities, 2010.

———. "Person Centered Planning and Communication of End-of-Life Wishes with People Who Have Developmental Disabilities." *Journal of Religion, Disability, and Health* 9, no 2 (2005): 81–90.

Kingsley, Emily Perl. "Welcome to Holland." National Down Syndrome Society. 1987. Accessed June 17, 2017. http://www.ndss.org/Resources/ New-Expectant-Parents/A-Parents-Perspective/.

Kingsley, Jason, and Michael Levitz. *Count Us In: Growing Up with Down Syndrome.* New York: Harcourt, 1994.

Kretzmann, John, and John McKnight. *Building Communities from the Inside Out: A Path toward Finding and Mobilizing a Community's Assets.* Evanston, Ill.: ACTA, Northwestern University, 1993.

Kubler Ross, Elizabeth. *On Death and Dying.* New York: Simon & Schuster, 1969.

Kuppers, Petra. "Crip Time." *Tikkun* 29, no. 4 (2014): 29–30.

Kushner, Harold. *When Bad Things Happen to Good People.* New York: Schocken Books, 1981.

Landgraf, John. "Love and Friendship." *Minister's Magazine* 10, no. 1 (1989): 3–9.

Larson, Sheryl, and Amy Hewitt. *Staff Recruitment, Retention, and Training Strategies for Community Human Services Organizations.* Baltimore: Brookes, 2005.

Laundau-Stanton, Judith, Colleen Clements, Alex Tartaglia, Jackie Nudd, and Elisabeth Espaillat-Pina. "Spiritual, Cultural, and Community Systems." In *AIDS, Health and Mental Health: A Primary Sourcebook*, edited by Judith Landau-Stanton and Colleen D. Clements, 267–98. New York: Bruner/Mazel, 1993.

Learning Community for Person Centered Practices. Accessed June 16, 2017. http://tlcpcp.com.

Levi, Sandra. "Ableism." In *Encyclopedia of Disability*, edited by Gary Albrecht, 1–4. Thousand Oaks, Calif.: Sage, 2006.

Levine, Carol. "The Top Ten Things Caregivers Don't Want to Hear . . . and a Few Things They Do." United Hospital Fund of New York City, 2006. Accessed January 13, 2015. http://www.uhfnyc.org/publications/417469.

Lewis, C. S. *The Four Loves.* London: Fontana Books, 1960.

Liu, Eleanor, Erik Carter, Thomas Boehm, Naomi Annandale, and Courtney Evans Taylor. "In Their Own Words: The Place of Faith in the Lives of

Young People with Autism and Intellectual Disability." *Intellectual and Developmental Disabilities* 52, no. 5 (2014): 368–404.

Lohrmann, Sharon, and Fredda Brown. *Working Together: A Guide to Positive Behavior Support for Families and Professionals.* Baltimore: TASH, 2005.

Luchterhand, Charlene, and Nancy Murphy. *Helping Adults with Mental Retardation Grieve a Death Loss.* Philadelphia: Taylor & Francis, 1998.

Lutfiyya, Zana. *Reflections on Relationships between People with Disabilities and Typical People.* Syracuse, N.Y.: Syracuse University, Center on Human Policy, 1988.

MacLeish, Archibald. *J.B.* New York: Houghton Mifflin & Harcourt, 1958.

Maister, David. *True Professionalism: The Courage to Care about Your People, Your Clients, and Your Career.* New York: Touchstone, 1997.

Markell, Marc. *Helping People with Mental Retardation Mourn: Practical Rituals for Caregivers.* Fort Collins, Colo.: Companion, 2005.

Masala, Carmelo, and Donatella Petretto. "Models of Disability." In *International Encyclopedia of Rehabilitation*, edited by J. H. Stone and M. Blouin, 2010. Accessed November 20, 2014. http://cirrie.buffalo.edu/encyclopedia/en/article/135/.

McKnight, John. *The Careless Society: Community and Its Counterfeits.* New York: Basic Books. 1995.

———. "Regenerating Community." *Social Policy*, Winter 1987, 54–58. Accessed September 4, 2015. http://mn.gov/mnddc/parallels2/pdf/80s/87/87-RC-JLM.pdf.

———. *Regenerating Community: The Recovery of a Space for Citizens.* Evanston, Ill.: Northwestern University Center for Urban Affairs and Policy Research, 1993. Accessed June 17, 2017. https://resources.depaul.edu/abcd-institute/publications/publications-by-topic/Documents/regenerating.pdf.

McNair, Jeff, and Erik Carter. "Knowledge, Faith Development, and Religious Education That Includes All." *Journal of Religion, Disability and Health* 14 (2010): 186–203.

Meilander, Gordon. *Friendship: A Study in Theological Ethics.* Notre Dame, Ind.: University of Notre Dame Press, 1979.

Melberg-Schwier, Karin. *Flourish: People with Disabilities Living Life with Passion.* Saskatoon, Calif.: Copestone, 2012.

Melberg-Schwier, Karin, and David Hingsburger. *Sexuality: Your Sons and Daughters with Developmental Disabilities.* Baltimore: Brookes, 2000.

Messer, Neil. *Flourishing: Health, Disease, and Bioethics in a Theological Perspective.* Grand Rapids: Eerdmans, 2014.

Miles, M. "Disability in Asian Cultures and Beliefs: History and Service Development—Some Collected Papers." *Journal of Religion, Disability and Health* 6, nos. 2–3 (2002).

———. "Religion and Spirituality." In *International Encyclopedia of Rehabilitation*, edited by J. H. Stone and M. Blouin. Accessed November 20, 2014. http://cirrie.buffalo.edu/encyclopedia/en/article/1/.

Missouri Family to Family. *Charting the Life Course: A Guide for Individuals, Families and Professionals.* Kansas City: Institute for Human Development, University of Missouri, Kansas City, 2012. http://www.lifecoursetools .com/charting-the-life-course-guide/. Accessed March 22, 2015.

National Information Center for Children and Youth with Handicaps. "Respite Care: A Gift of Time." *NICHCY News Digest,* November 12, 1989.

Nelson, Jack. "When Stereotypes Tell the Story." *National Center on Disability and Journalism News* 3, no. 1 (2003).

Nerney, Thomas, and Donald Shumway. *Beyond Managed Care: Self-Determination for People with Disabilities.* Concord: University of New Hampshire, 1996.

Newbigin, Lesslie. "Not Whole without the Handicapped." In *Partners in Life: The Handicapped and the Church,* edited by Geiko Muller-Fahrenholz, 17–25. Geneva: World Council of Churches Publications, 1979.

Newman, Barbara. *Accessible Gospel, Inclusive Worship.* Wyoming, Mich.: CLC Network, 2014.

Nouwen, Henri. *Adam: God's Beloved.* Maryknoll, N.Y.: Orbis Books, 1998.

———. *The Road to Daybreak: A Spiritual Journey.* New York: Doubleday, 1997.

O'Brien, John, and Beth Mount. *Make a Difference: A Guidebook for Person-Centered Direct Support.* Toronto: Inclusion Press, 2001.

O'Brien, John, and Connie Lyle O'Brien. *Members of Each Other: Building Community in Company with People with Developmental Disabilities.* Toronto: Inclusion Press, 1997.

———. "Members of Each Other: Perspectives on Social Supports for People with Severe Disabilities." In *Natural Supports in School, at Work, and in the Community for People with Severe Disabilities,* edited by J. Nesbit, 17–64. Baltimore: Brooks Publishing, 1992.

O'Brien, John, and Jack Pearpoint. *Person-Centered Planning with MAPS and PATH: A Workbook for Facilitators.* Toronto: Inclusion Press, 2003.

O'Brien, John, with staff from Creative Living Services. *"It's How You Look at Your Work That Makes the Difference": Direct Support Workers Consider the Meaning of Their Jobs.* Lithonia, Ga.: Responsive Systems Associates,

2004. Accessed June 15, 2017. http://www.inclusion.com/downloads/ obrienarchive/Direct%20Support/DS%20meaning.pdf.

O'Connell, Mary. *The Gift of Hospitality: Opening the Doors to Community Life to People with Disabilities.* Evanston, Ill., Northwestern University Center for Urban Affairs and Policy Research, 1988. Accessed June 16, 2017. https://resources.depaul.edu/abcd-institute/publications/ publications-by-topic/Documents/regenerating.pdf.

Office for People with Developmental Disabilities. "Faith Based Educational and Training Materials." Acessed December 10, 2014. http://www .opwdd.ny.gov/opwdd_community_connections/faith_based _initiatives/training_material.

Olshansky, Saul. "Chronic Sorrow: A Response to Having a Mentally Defective Child." *Social Casework* 43 (1962): 190–93.

O'Malley, Patrick. "Getting Grief Right." *New York Times*, January 10, 2015. Accessed January 13, 2015. http://opinionator.blogs.nytimes .com/2015/01/10/getting-grief-right/?smid=fb-share&_r=0.

Palmer, Parker. *The Active Life: A Spirituality of Work, Creativity, and Caregiving.* San Francisco: Jossey-Bass, 1999.

———. *The Courage to Teach: Recovering the Inner Landscape of a Teacher's Life.* San Francisco: Jossey-Bass, 1997.

———. *Healing the Heart of Democracy: The Courage to Create a Politics Worthy of the Human Spirit.* San Francisco: Jossey-Bass, 2011.

———. *Leading from Within: Poetry That Sustains the Courage to Lead.* San Francisco: Jossey-Bass, 2007.

———. "Merging Two Worlds." Keynote speech given at the Merging Two Worlds conference, Rochester, N.Y., 1986. http://faithand disability.org.

———. "A New Professional: The Aims of Education Revisited." *Change: The Magazine of Higher Learning* 39, no. 6 (2007): 6–13. Accessed September 8, 2015. http://www.tandfonline.com/doi/abs/10.3200/CHNG.39.6.6-13.

———. *To Know as We Are Known: A Spirituality of Education.* San Francisco: Harper & Row, 1983.

Park Ridge Center. *The Challenges of Aging: Retrieving Spiritual Traditions.* Chicago, Ill.: Park Ridge Center for the Study of Health, Faith, and Ethics, 1999.

PATH. Accessed June 17, 2017. http://www.inclusion.com/path.html.

Patterson, David. *Helping Your Handicapped Child.* Minneapolis: Augsburg, 1970.

Perske, Robert. *Circle of Friends.* Nashville: Abingdon, 1988.

Pearpoint, Jack. *From Behind the Piano: Building Judith Snow's Unique Circle of Friends.* Toronto: Inclusion Press. 1990

Pitonyak, David. *10 Things You Can Do to Support a Person with Difficult Behavior.* November 20, 1993. Accessed April 28, 2015. http://www .worksupport.com/documents/10things4.pdf.

Positive Behavior Support Guidelines, rev. ed. Jefferson City: Missouri Division of Mental Retardation and Developmental Disabilities, 2008. Accessed September 7, 2015. http://www.nasddds.org/uploads/documents/MO _Pos_Behav_Support_guide08.pdf.

Poston, Denise, and Ann Turnbull. "Role of Spirituality and Religion in Family Quality of Life for Families of Children with Disabilities." *Education and Training in Developmental Disabilities* 39, no. 2 (2004): 95–108.

Preheim-Bartel, Dean, and Christine Guth. *Circles of Love: Stories of Congregations Caring for People with Disabilities and Their Families.* Harrisonburg, Va.: Menno Media, 2015.

Preheim-Bartel, Dean, and A. Neufeldt. *Supportive Care in the Congregation: Providing a Congregational Network of Care for Persons with Significant Disabilities.* Harrisburg, Pa.: Herald Press, 2011.

Puchalski, Christina. "The FICA Spiritual History Tool." George Washington Institute for Spirituality and Health. Accessed December 10, 2014. http:// smhs.gwu.edu/gwish/clinical/fica/spiritual-history-tool.

Quality of Life Research Unit, University of Toronto. *The Quality of Life Model.* Accessed October 19, 2014. http://sites.utoronto.ca/qol/qol_model.htm.

Raines, Robert. *Living the Questions.* Nashville: Word Books, 1976.

Read, Sue, ed. *Supporting People with Intellectual Disabilities Experiencing Loss and Bereavement: Theory and Compassionate Practice.* London: Jessica Kingsley, 2014.

Rego, Armenio, and Miguel Pina e Cunha. "Workplace Spirituality and Organizational Commitment: An Empirical Study." *Journal of Organizational Change Management* 21 no. 1 (2008): 53–75.

Reinders, Hans. *Disability, Providence and Ethics: Bridging Gaps, Transforming Lives.* Waco, Tex.: Baylor University Press, 2014.

———. *The Future of the Disabled in Liberal Society.* South Bend, Ind.: University of Notre Dame Press, 1990.

———. *Receiving the Gift of Friendship: Profound Disability, Theological Anthropology, and Ethics.* Grand Rapids: Eerdmans, 2008.

———. "Understanding Humanity and Disability: Building an Ecological Perspective." *Studies in Christian Ethics* 26, no. 1 (2013): 37–49.

Reynolds, Michelle. *Charting a Life Course: A Framework and Strategies for Supporting Individuals with Developmental Disabilities and Their*

Families. Boggs Center Developmental Disabilities Lecture Series, New Brunswick, New Jersey, November 2, 2012. http://rwjms.rutgers.edu/boggscenter/documents/Reynoldspacket11-2-12.pdf.

Rilke, Rainer Maria. *Letters to a Young Poet*. London: Dover, 2002.

Rose, Lynn. "History of Disability: Ancient West." In *Encyclopedia of Disability*, edited by Gary Albrecht et al., 2:852–55. New York: Sage, 2006.

Rosen, Christine. *Preaching Eugenics: Religious Leaders and the American Eugenics Movement*. London: Oxford University Press, 2004.

Rottenberg, Rachel Cohen. "On Normalcy and Identity Politics." Accessed June 17, 2017. http://www.disabilityandrepresentation.com.

Ruth-Heffelbower, Duane. *After We're Gone: Providing a Congregational Network of Care for Persons with Significant Disabilities; A Christian Perspective on Estate and Life Planning for Families That Include a Dependent Member with a Disability*. Harrisonburg, Va.: Menno Media, 2011.

Sacks, Jonathan. *The Great Partnership: Science, Religion, and the Search for Meaning*. New York: Schocken Books, 2012.

Sailor, Wayne, Glen Dunlap, George Sugai, and Rob Horner, eds. *A Handbook of Positive Behavior Supports*. New York: Springer, 2009.

Saint-Exupery, Antoine de. *The Little Prince*. New York: Reynall & Hitchcock, 1943.

Salisbury, Christine, and J. Intagliata, eds. *Respite Care: Support for Persons with Developmental Disabilities and Their Families*. Baltimore: Brookes, 1986.

Schalock, Robert. "Introduction to the Intellectual Disability Construct." In *The Story of Intellectual Disability: An Evolution of Meaning, Understanding, and Public Perception*, edited by Michael Wehmeyer, 2–17. Baltimore: Brookes, 2013.

Schalock, Robert, and Ruth Luckasson. *Clinical Judgment*. 2nd ed. Washington, D.C.: American Association on Intellectual and Developmental Disabilities, 2014.

Schalock, Robert, et al. *Intellectual Disability: Definition, Classification, and Systems of Support*. 11th ed. Washington, D.C.: American Association on Intellectual and Developmental Disabilities, 2010.

Schwartz, David. *Who Cares? Rediscovering Community*. Denver: Westview, 1996.

Scull, Andrew. "Madness and Meaning: Depictions of Insanity through History." *Paris Review*, April 22, 2015. Accessed June 17, 2017. http://www.theparisreview.org/blog/2015/04/22/madness-and-meaning/.

Seagle, Lynne. "Hope Talk." TED Talk. 2014. Accessed June 17, 2017. https://livestream.com/tedx/HRVA/videos/68626574.

Shakespeare, Tom. "A Point of View: Happiness and Disability." *BBC News Magazine*, May 31, 2014. Accessed June 17, 2017. http://www.bbc.com/news/magazine-27554754.

Shapiro, Joseph. *No Pity: People with Disabilities Forging a New Civil Rights Movement*. New York: Three Rivers, 1994.

Shogren, Karrie. "Positive Psychology and Disability: A Historical Analysis." In *The Oxford Handbook of Positive Psychology and Disability*, edited by Michael Wehmeyer, 19–33. New York: Oxford University Press, 2013.

Shriver, Timothy. *Fully Alive: Discovering What Matters Most*. New York: Sarah Crichton Books, 2014.

Silverstein. Shel. *The Giving Tree*. New York: Harper & Row, 1964.

Singer, George, and Mian Wang. "The Intellectual Roots of Positive Behavior Support and Their Implications for Its Development." In *A Handbook of Positive Behavior Supports*, edited by Wayne Sailor, Glen Dunlap, George Sugai, and Rob Horner, 17–46. New York: Springer, 2009.

Smull, Michael, and Susan Burke Harrison. *Supporting People with Severe Reputations in the Community*. Alexandria, Va.: National Association of State Directors of Developmental Disabilities Services, 1992.

Smull, Michael, Helen Sanderson, et al. *Essential Lifestyle Planning for Everyone*. Annapolis, Md.: Learning Community, 2009.

Snow, Judith. "It's about Grace." Keynote presentation given at the 2014 Summer Institute on Theology and Disability. Dallas, Texas. http://faithanddisability.org/2014-summer-institute/.

Sterns, Harvey, Elizabeth Kennedy, and Chad Sed. *Person-Centered Planning for Late Life: A Curriculum for Adults with Mental Retardation*. Chicago: University of Illinois, Rehabilitation Research and Training Center on Developmental Disabilities and Health, 2000.

Summers, Jean Ann, Shirley K. Behr, and Ann P. Turnbull. "Positive Adaptation and Coping Strengths of Families Who Have Children with Disabilities." In *Support for Caregiving Families: Enabling Positive Adaptation to Disability*, edited by G. H. Singer and L. K. Irvin, 27–40. Baltimore: Brookes, 1989.

Swinton, John. *Becoming Friends of Time: Disability, Timefulness and Gentle Discipleship*. Waco, Tex.: Baylor University Press, 2016.

———. *A Space to Listen: Meeting the Spiritual Needs of People with Learning Disabilities*. London: Mental Health Foundation, 2001.

———. *Spirituality in Mental Health Care: Rediscovering a "Forgotten" Dimension*. London: Jessica Kingsley, 2001.

Swinton, John, and Hazel Morgan. *No Box to Tick*. London: Foundation for People with Learning Disabilities, 2004. Accessed June 17, 2017.

https://www.mentalhealth.org.uk/learning-disabilities/publications/
no-box-tick.

Swinton, John, and Stephen Pattison. "Moving beyond Clarity: Towards a
Thin, Vague, and Useful Understanding of Spirituality in Nursing Care."
Nursing Philosophy 11 (2010): 226–37.

Swinton, John, Harriet Mowat, and Susannah Baines. "Whose Story Am I?
Re-describing Profound Intellectual Disability in the Kingdom of God."
Journal of Religion, Disability and Health 15 (2011): 5–19.

Switzky, Harvey, and Stephen Greenspan, eds. *What Is Mental Retardation:
Ideas for an Evolving Disability in the 21st Century.* Washington, D.C.:
American Association on Mental Retardation, 2006.

Taylor, Courtney, Erik Carter, Naomi Annandale, Thomas Boehm, and
Aimee Logeman. *Welcoming People with Developmental Disabilities and
Their Families: A Practical Guide for Congregations.* Nashville: Vanderbilt
Kennedy Center, 2014.

Taylor, Steve. "The Paradox of Regulations: A Commentary." *Mental Retardation* 30 (1992) 185–90.

Thomas, Bill. "The Green House Movement," *Newshour,* January 23,
2008, Accessed June 17, 2017. http://www.pbs.org/newshour/bb/
health-jan-june02-eden_2-27.

Thompson, James. "Presidential Address 2013—Race to Catch the Future."
Journal of Intellectual and Developmental Disabilities 51, no. 6 (2014): 516.

Thornburgh, Ginny. *That All May Worship.* Accessed June 17, 2017.
http://www.aapd.com/wp-content/uploads/2016/03/That-All-May
-Worship.pdf.

Trachtman, Ilana. *Praying with Lior.* Philadelphia: Ruby Pictures, 2007.
Accessed June 20, 2017. www.prayingwithlior.com.

Turnbull, Ann P., and H. Rutherford Turnbull. "Group Action Planning
as a Strategy for Providing Comprehensive Family Support." In *Positive Behavioral Support: Including People with Difficult Behavior in the
Community,* edited by L. K. Koegel, R. L. Koegel, and G. Dunlap, 99–114.
Baltimore: Brookes, 1996.

Turnbull, Rud. *The Exceptional Life of Jay Turnbull: Dignity and Disability in
America, 1967–2009.* Amherst, Mass.: White Poppy Press, 2011.

Van Dyke, Linda. *Lessons in Grief and Death: Supporting People with Developmental Disabilities in the Healing Process.* Joliet, Ill.: High Tide Press, 2003.

Vanier, Jean. *Community and Growth.* Mahwah, N.J.: Paulist, 1989.

———. *From Brokenness to Community.* Mahwah, N.J.: Paulist, 1992.

———. *Tears of Silence: A Meditation.* Toronto: House of Anasi Press, 2014.

Volf, Miroslav. *Exclusion & Embrace: A Theological Exploration of Identity, Otherness, and Reconciliation.* Nashville: Abingdon, 1996.

Waddell, Paul. *Friendship and the Moral Life.* Notre Dame, Ind.: University of Notre Dame Press, 1989.

Walsh, Alice, Mary Beth Walsh, and William Gaventa. *Autism and Faith: A Journey into Community.* New Brunswick, N.J.: Elizabeth M. Boggs Center, 2008. Accessed January 13, 2015. http://rwjms.umdnj.edu/boggscenter/products/documents/AutismandFaith.pdf.

Wehmeyer, Michael. *The Story of Intellectual Disability: An Evolution of Meaning, Understanding, and Public Perception.* Baltimore: Brookes, 2013.

Westberg, Granger. *Good Grief: A Constructive Approach to the Problem of Loss.* 35th anniversary ed. Minneapolis: Fortress, 1997.

Westerhoff, John. *Will Our Children Have Faith?* New York: Seabury Press, 1976.

What Is Disability? Handicap International. Accessed June 17, 2016. http://www.making-prsp-inclusive.org/it/6-disability/61-what-is-disability/613-the-who-definition.html.

Whitt, Jason. "A Place for Camille." *Christian Century*, January 12, 2015, 24–25, 27. Accessed January 20, 2015. http://www.christiancentury.org/article/2014-12/place-camille.

Wing, Lorna, Judith Gould, and Christopher Gillberg. "Autism Spectrum Disorders in the *DSM-V*: Better orWorse Than the *DSM-IV*?" *Research in Developmental Disabilities* 32, no. 2 (2011): 768–73.

Wisconsin Council on Developmental Disabilities. "Believing, Belonging, Becoming: Stories of Faith Inclusion" (video). Accessible at http://faithanddisability.org/videos/.

Wohl, Ira. *Best Boy.* Los Angeles: Only Child Motion Pictures, 1979.

———. *Best Man: "Best Boy" and All of Us, Twenty Years Later.* Los Angeles: Only Child Motion Pictures, 1997.

Wolfensberger, Wolf. "Common Assets of Mentally Retarded People That Are Commonly Not Acknowledged." *Mental Retardation* 26, no. 2 (1988): 63–70.

———. *The Principle of Normalization in Human Services.* Toronto: National Institute on Mental Retardation, 1972.

———. "The Prophetic Voice and Presence of Mentally Retarded People in the World Today." In *The Theological Voice of Wolf Wolfensberger*, edited by William Gaventa and David Coulter, 11–48. Binghamton, N.Y.: Haworth, 2001.

World Health Organization. *International Classification of Impairments, Disabilities and Handicaps: A Manual of Classification Relating to the*

Consequences of Disease. Published in accordance with resolution WHA 29.35 of the Twenty-Ninth World Health Assembly, May 1976. Repr. with foreword. Geneva: World Health Organization, 1993.

Yong, Amos. *Theology and Down Syndrome: Reimagining Disability in Late Modernity*. Waco, Tex.: Baylor University Press, 2007.

Young, Stella. "I Am Not Your Inspiration, Thank You Very Much." TED Talk. April 2014. Accessed January 6, 2015. http://www.ted .com/talks/stella_young_i_m_not_your_inspiration_thank_you_very _much?language=en.

Index

ALSO AVAILABLE IN THE SRTD SERIES

Crippled Grace: Disability, Virtue Ethics, and the Good Life
Shane Clifton

The Bible and Disability: A Commentary
Edited by Sarah J. Melcher, Mikeal C. Parsons, and Amos Yong

Pastoral Care and Intellectual Disability: A Person-Centered Approach
Anna Katherine Shurley

*Becoming Friends of Time: Disability, Timefullness, and Gentle
Discipleship*
John Swinton

Disability and World Religions: An Introduction
Edited by Darla Y. Schumm and Michael Stoltzfus

Madness: American Protestant Responses to Mental Illness
Heather H. Vacek

Disability, Providence, and Ethics: Bridging Gaps, Transforming Lives
Hans S. Reinders

Flannery O'Connor: Writing a Theology of Disabled Humanity
Timothy J. Basselin

*Theology and Down Syndrome: Reimagining Disability
in Late Modernity*
Amos Yong